THE TRUE STORY OF THE NUGAN HAND BANK SCANDAL

MERCHANTS OF MENACE

PETER BUTT

BLACKWATTLE PRESS
BP

Peter Butt is an Australian investigative filmmaker specialising in history, crime and espionage. His multi-award winning docudrama *Who Killed Dr Bogle & Mrs Chandler?* solved one of Australia's most iconic cold cases and remains the highest-rating documentary in ABC TV history. His book on the Bogle Chandler mystery was shortlisted for the Douglas Stewart Prize for Non Fiction in the 2014 NSW Premier's Literary Awards.

First published by Blackwattle Press 2015
This revised edition published in 2021.
Blackwattle Press
Sydney
www.merchantsofmenace.net

Copyright © 2015, 2021 in text: Peter Butt
Copyright © 2015, 2021 in photographs: Peter Butt and individual copyright holders.
Copyright © 2015, 2021 Blackwattle Press

All rights reserved. No part of this publication may be reproduced, stored in a retrieval system or transmitted, in any form or by any means, electronic, mechanical, photocopying, recording or otherwise, without the prior written permission of the publishers and copyright holders.

A catalogue record of this book is available at the National Library of Australia

ISBN: 978-0-9923252-8-2

Publisher: Peter Butt
Associate Publisher: Sarah Staveley
Editor: Scott Forbes
Cover and internal design: Luke Harris, WorkingType
Printer: Griffin Press

This project has been kindly assisted by the City of Sydney History Publication Sponsorship Program

CONTENTS

Introduction		v
List of characters		vii
Prologue	Wealthy, handsome guys	1
Chapter 1	Watch out for the crocodiles	9
Chapter 2	Jurisprudence is crap	21
Chapter 3	The Spaniard	24
Chapter 4	Take-off	27
Chapter 5	The man who fell to Earth	33
Chapter 6	The Contra	38
Chapter 7	Turkey farming	44
Chapter 8	The return	52
Chapter 9	What happened at the circus	56
Chapter 10	The hub of good and evil	67
Chapter 11	Paymaster	75
Chapter 12	Ricochet	78
Chapter 13	Infiltration	85
Chapter 14	The phantom	101
Chapter 15	The business of murder	113
Chapter 16	Killing the goose	124
Chapter 17	Coup d'état	128
Chapter 18	In the Lord's hands	133
Chapter 19	The fortune of war	136
Chapter 20	Bernie of Arabia	143
Chapter 21	The architect of fact	149

Chapter 22	The last supper	155
Chapter 23	Eternity	162
Chapter 24	The twilight zone	173
Chapter 25	The gap	182
Chapter 26	Where the buck stops	184
Chapter 27	Inquest	192
Chapter 28	The magician	202
Chapter 29	Resurrection	210
Chapter 30	Listed ASIO	215
Chapter 31	All the way to the White House	219
Chapter 32	The horns of Jericho	229
Chapter 33	Whitewash	233
Chapter 34	Under the gun	241
Chapter 35	The hunt for Michael Hand	251
Chapter 36	As crime goes by	262
Acknowledgements		271
Endnotes		273
Index		280

INTRODUCTION

Deep in conversation over dinner, I was barely aware that my host had left the table, until I noticed a metallic glint out of the corner of my right eye and a moment later the barrel of a silver pistol pressed flush against my nose. Another dinner guest chuckled, as the host removed the gun and handed it to me without a word said. It was a disquieting moment reminiscent of a scene from the movie *Chinatown*, in which a thug played by director Roman Polanski thrusts a flick knife up the nostril of a 'very nosey' private investigator, Jake Gittes, played by Jack Nicholson. As a documentary filmmaker, specialising in controversial Cold War cases, I am also very nosey by nature.

I was in Tulsa, Oklahoma, reinvestigating the notorious Nugan Hand merchant bank, which collapsed in 1980 following the mysterious death of its Australian founder, Frank Nugan. My pistol-thrusting host, Douglas A Sapper III, had served with Nugan's partner Michael Hand in Vietnam and later carried out sensitive and occasionally dangerous money-moving operations for the bank throughout Southeast Asia and southern Africa. One of those assignments had gone wrong and landed him in a Kathmandu prison. By the time of his release, Nugan was dead, Hand had disappeared and a dozen Australian and international police and corporate inquiries were probing the bank over sensational allegations involving drug traffickers, gunrunning and the CIA.

The abiding mysteries of Frank Nugan's death and Michael

Hand's escape drew me to this project. Many of the surviving Australian investigators who assisted me believed that Nugan's death at the young age of thirty-seven was not a simple suicide. Indeed, evidence found on his body suggested that there had to be more to it. They also believed that the CIA, or a former employee of the spy agency, had facilitated Hand's disappearance.

During my three-day stay in Tulsa, I recorded eleven hours of interviews with Doug Sapper. His startling insights into the leading personalities, the bank's CIA and drug-trafficking connections and the role of the FBI in the Nugan Hand story allowed my project to break free of its chrysalis and take flight.

As he bid me farewell at Tulsa Airport, Sapper implored me to find his old friend Michael Hand. I never did ask him what he had meant by his menacing pistol episode over dinner. I simply took it as a warning along the lines of, 'If you are intent on investigating Nugan Hand, then I am the kind of hard-arse you are going to be dealing with.'

LIST OF CHARACTERS

Alexander, Brian (1939–c. 1981) Law clerk with John Aston & Co, Sydney. Associated with criminals and with police engaged in drug enforcement. Disappeared in 1981, believed dead.

Allen, Gary* Sydney merchant banker.

Aston, John (1944–*) Sydney solicitor who represented Frank and Ken Nugan and Murray Riley and had alleged improper connections with the Mr Asia drug syndicate.

Bailey, Phil* Federal Bureau of Narcotics investigator.

Beazley, Donald E (1942–) Florida banker who took over presidency of Nugan Hand in 1979.

Black, General Edwin F (1915–85) Managed Nugan Hand's Hawaii office. Later worked with merchant bank Bishop Baldwin Rewald Dillingham and Wong, whose offices were a conduit for various CIA covert operations.

Clines, Thomas (1928–2013) CIA covert operations officer who turned to gunrunning. Helped Bernie Houghton leave Australia following the collapse of Nugan Hand. Later became a prominent figure in the Iran-Contra Affair.

Cocke Jr, Brigadier General Earle (1921–2000) Nugan Hand's Washington DC representative whose expertise lay in clandestine banking.

Colby, William (1920–96) Director of the CIA 1972–76; became a legal advisor to the Nugan Hand bank in 1979.

Collings, Clive (1937–*) Director of Nugan Hand in Hong Kong.

Countis, George 'Duke' (1915 -*) Restaurateur turned professional gambler and wheeler-dealer with connections to Australian and US underworld.

Dowd, John* Liberal Party member for Lane Cove in the NSW Legislative Assembly, 1975–91.

Arina (1925–) Bud King's Thai housekeeper.

Evans, Neil (1937–*) Established and managed Nugan Hand's Chiang Mai branch.

Fratianno, James 'The Weasel' (1913–93) US organised crime figure. Associate of Murray Riley and Duke Countis.

Hand, Helene (1936–) Michael Hand's Sydney-born wife. They married in 1968.

Hand, Michael (1941–) New York-born former Green Beret. Served in the Vietnam War and was awarded the second-highest US award for bravery. Went to work for the CIA in Laos under William Colby. Deputy CEO of the Nugan Hand group of companies.

Hill, Stephen* Money manager with the Nugan Hand group.

Holmgren, Dale (1935–) Former head of flight services for a CIA airline who ran the Nugan Hand Taiwan office.

Houghton, Bernie (1920–2000) Son of a Texas oil driller, he served in World War II, arrived in Sydney in 1967 then set up Kings Cross restaurants and nightclubs, including the Bourbon & Beefsteak. In 1978 he became the Middle Eastern representative for Nugan Hand bank. Suspected CIA operative.

Kelly, Keith (1933–2007) Former NSW detective.

King, Kermit 'Bud' (1936–1975) Californian-born former CIA pilot who in 1967 following service in Laos during the Vietnam War, turned up in Sydney with Michael Hand to sell real estate for the Ocean Shores development.

Krahe, Fred (1919–81) Notorious NSW detective who gained a reputation as a gangland enforcer.

Lowe, Andrew (1943–*) Convicted heroin trafficker. Introduced traffickers to Nugan Hand.

McDonald, Walt (1925–91) Former deputy director of the CIA's Economic Research Department. Became a Nugan Hand consultant in 1979, based in Maryland.

McDonnell, Detective Sergeant Bill* Investigated Frank Nugan's death.

Maloney, Michael* Bernie Houghton's lawyer who took charge of the bank's Sydney operations following Nugan's death.

Nicholson QC, Geoffrey (1949–2012) Senior investigator with the NSW Corporate Affairs Commission.

Nugan, Frank (1942–1980) Griffith-born to immigrant parents. Tax lawyer. Nugan Hand CEO.

Nugan, Ken (1940–86) Frank Nugan's older brother, who managed the Nugan Fruit Group based in Griffith, NSW.

Nugan, Lee (1944–) Born Charlotte Lee Sofge in Tennessee. Married Frank Nugan in 1970.

O'Brien, John* Court-appointed liquidator to the Nugan Hand bank.

Owen, John (1937–*) Former Royal Navy officer who managed Nugan Hand's Bangkok branch.

Owens, Paul* Lay preacher who befriended Frank Nugan.

Pauker, Dr Guy (1917–2002) Specialist on Southeast Asia for the Rand Corporation. Introduced to Nugan Hand by Earl Yates; has been described as a CIA operative.

Porter, Rick* NSW Corporate Affairs Commission investigator.

Pulger-Frame, Ron* Nugan Hand money mover.

Riley, Murray Stewart (1925–*) Former policeman turned drug trafficker who used Nugan Hand's money-laundering facility.

Sapper III, Douglas A (1940–2013) Born in Mount Vernon, Illinois. US Special Forces colleague of Michael Hand who became a Nugan Hand fixer.

Shaw, George (1930–*) Lebanese Australian who handled the bulk of Nugan Hand's drug clients.

Small, Clive* NSW Police detective with the Joint Task Force investigation into the Nugan Hand bank.

Spencer, James Oswald (1940–2011) Born James Spencer Oswald in Arizona. US Special Forces–trained CIA operative who assisted Michael Hand's departure from Australia.

Stocker, Paul (1924–2014) Born in Everett, Washington, became a lawyer and Washington state legislator. Later recruited Hand and King in Laos to move to Australia to sell Ocean Shores land.

Swan, Patricia* Frank Nugan's executive assistant.

Wainwright, Harry (1923–*) Louisiana-born lawyer. Served in US Air Force as a pilot in World War II, retired as a major. Represented West-Coast US Mafia figures. Migrated to Australia in 1968.

Walker, Frank (1942–2012) Attorney-General of NSW (Labor Government), 1976–83.

Wedderburn, Colin* Police prosecutor who assisted the coroner during the Nugan inquest.

Wilcox, Peter * British Secret Service agent.

Wilson, Edwin P (1928–2012) Former CIA and US Naval Intelligence officer turned arms trafficker. Convicted in 1983 of illegally selling explosives to Libya and spent two decades in prison. The US Department of Justice declared that the CIA had covered up evidence in the case.

Yates, Rear Admiral Earl 'Buddy' (1923–) Retired chief of US strategic planning for Asia and the Pacific. President of the Nugan Hand bank 1977–79.

**Details unknown or withheld

PROLOGUE

WEALTHY, HANDSOME GUYS

On 15 October 1979, a mysterious procession of late-model Mercedes Benz motored slowly through Sydney past the Opera House, up Macquarie Street, around Hyde Park and along William Street, taking in the atmosphere of the city. Anyone who caught sight of the ostentatious procession may have pondered the identity of the occupants. Perhaps they were foreign dignitaries, maybe celebrities. In fact, they were international representatives of a little-known merchant bank, Nugan Hand, which in a mere matter of months would make headline news across Australia and around the world.

The purring silver and gold chariots turned left into Darlinghurst Road and entered Kings Cross, the so-called 'glittering mile of dreams', which, curiously, measured a half mile at most. Below garish neon signs, strip-show spruikers were pacing bloodstained pavements, circling potential customers like swamp mosquitoes sniffing out a feast. In nearby bars, battalions of suburban warriors were fomenting war against bouncers or anyone else who might cross their path. After a bit of blood and chunder, they would likely stumble into the narrow alleyways where sweaty pimps offered up an assortment of their glazed-eye, scantily clad doxies. What had started in the 1900s with sly-groggers, fortune tellers and goodtime girls was now Australia's heartland of vice and crime, in which drugs and sex were the major currencies.

The fleet cruised by the famed flesh palaces, the Pink Pussy Cat and Les Girls nightclubs, and slowed reverentially at the next bend, opposite the Bourbon & Beefsteak Bar and Restaurant.

'This is where it all began,' they had been told over and over. 'At the Bourbon; that's where Mike and Frank first met!'

*

The tour terminated at the elegant Gazebo Hotel, the tallest building in Kings Cross, where the merchant bankers had already been gathered for a company talkfest for the past three days.

In an anteroom, Michael Hand gathered his thoughts. He was pushing thirty-eight and the mirror in front of him didn't lie. Since leaving the military, he'd worked hard to maintain his muscled physique at the gym. He'd even installed a treadmill in his Hong Kong office, but all the long business lunches, the international travel and the steroids had taken their toll and he'd gone to mush. Still, a Singapore tailor had crafted a suit that concealed his expanding girth and, when all was said and done, with his thick, dark brown hair and manicured nails, he still looked 'suave de boney', as his army buddy Douglas A Sapper III used to say.

Michael entered the conference room. The two dozen delegates took their seats as he walked over to the lectern and tapped the microphone. The large banner behind him, adorned with the flags of thirteen nations, suggested that Nugan Hand was a firm of great success and repute. Michael stood silently for a moment, as if conjuring up a prayer, just as he had at the start of previous sessions. But this time his piercing blue eyes gradually hinted mischievous intent.

In a rich Bronx drawl, he roared: 'Hey troops, I want to thank you all again for coming down to Sydney!'

The delegates whooped and whistled in delight until Michael held up his hand and silence returned.

'From what we've discussed over the past days, I'd have to say the firm is well placed for a record year. Of course, much of our success is due to Frank Nugan.'

Mike scanned the delegates. 'Where the hell is Frank?'

George Shaw, a round-faced Lebanese-Australian staffer, hurried over to the door. At the end of the dimly lit corridor, he could make out the figure of Frank Nugan, leaning against a wall, trying to light a Cuban cigar with a recalcitrant lighter.

'Come on Frank, Mike's started.'

To enthusiastic applause, Frank appeared at the door, smiling and waving his Cuban in the air like a big shot and looking a million dollars in his high-sheen, silver-grey suit. As he took a seat in the front row, Admiral 'Buddy' Yates, a genial, bald-headed American in his mid-sixties, leaned forward and gave him an encouraging pat on the back.

'In the beginning,' Michael continued, 'Frank Nugan was the one with the technical expertise and I was the salesman. Isn't that right Frank?'

'That's how it was, Mike. That's how it was, for sure.'

'Now, I'm the pen pusher and Frank has turned into Dale Carnegie!'[1]

The delegates laughed as Frank expelled a cloud of cigar smoke.

'Frank's made us a great deal of money out of tax avoidance and that has underpinned our expansion. As the brochure says, Nugan Hand is now a global enterprise with a billion-dollar turnover. Only the Good Lord knows where we'll be in another seven years. But if they have money in the Afterlife, Nugan Hand International will be there! God Bless!'

As a staffer corralled the delegates together for a group photograph, Frank piped in, 'I just want to remind everyone what I said yesterday. The dough is not ours, okay? We'll go to jail if one dollar is missing — right? We are wealthy, handsome guys who wouldn't look good in arrows ... okay?'[2]

The delegates smiled nervously as the camera flash froze the moment for posterity.

★

Despite the brash opulence and optimism on display at the conference, the Nugan Hand financial empire was a house of cards buckling under the weight of its own ambition and ineptitude. Most of its international executives were former career military officers or ex-CIA, including Michael Hand. Remarkably, only one senior executive had prior banking experience.

Just three months after the conference, it all came tumbling down when the police discovered Frank Nugan dead in his Mercedes Benz, with a bullet in his brain and a military rifle in his lap. The police declared that Nugan had taken his own life. But items found in the car linking the bank to dozens of drug traffickers and to William Colby, the former director of the CIA, suggested something sinister was at play.

The NSW attorney-general, Frank Walker, called in his Corporate Affairs Commission investigators. On arrival at Nugan Hand's Sydney office, they walked into a crime scene. Most of the bank's records had either been destroyed or hurriedly moved to secret locations across the city in the dark of night.

A dozen international and Australian investigations ensued. When stories appeared in newspapers linking the bank to drug traffickers and the CIA, Michael Hand disappeared. His lawyer suggested to reporters that he had been abducted and possibly murdered. Homicide police believed otherwise. In July 1980, they issued a warrant for Hand's arrest for attempting to pervert the course of justice. Fearing that he may have skipped the country, they asked Interpol to make inquiries in the United States. But Michael Hand had vanished into the ether and hasn't been seen since.

★

With its cast of shady characters, the Nugan Hand saga played out like a political thriller, whose plotline ultimately splintered into a number of seemingly unsolvable mysteries. One writer suggested that Frank Nugan's death opened 'a can of worms, a mass of confusing strands from which the complete story almost certainly will never emerge.'[3]

When the story broke in 1980, I was enthralled by the fact that this international scandal was happening in my hometown of Sydney. I devoured every twist and turn but found it difficult to differentiate fact from speculation or conspiracy theory. Frustration peaked when, seven years later, the Royal Commission of Inquiry into the Activities of the Nugan Hand Group handed down its findings. The commission dismissed allegations that the bank was involved in drugs, gunrunning and CIA operations based on 'a lack of evidence'.

Three decades on, I felt that enough time had passed to revisit the case dispassionately to see what I could uncover. Perhaps there was a documentary to be made. As a starting point, I accessed the available investigation reports and interviewed on camera the surviving investigators and crime-busting politicians involved in the notorious case. Finding Nugan Hand staff willing to talk proved nigh on impossible, however. I traced the whereabouts of half a dozen people who worked for the bank. Some denied that they were the person I was trying to reach. Others promised to get back to me but never did. One high-ranking Nugan Hand executive threatened legal action if I dared even to mention his name. Another wanted to be helpful but became fearful that someone would identify him as the source.

It took two years to trace the owner of a bankbook found in Nugan's car. It turned out to be Michael Hand's driver, who had moved to Hollywood to work as an actor. He wouldn't talk either. Such reactions suggested that there was still information out there that could place people in danger.

Indeed, many people had since died, some in suspicious circumstances. These included an American-born bit player in the story who had assisted police investigators in return for immunity from prosecution. His wife told me that he had passed away unexpectedly on a visit back to the United States. She intimated that his death was suspicious and may have had something to do with Nugan Hand.

I also investigated the death of a former CIA pilot, Bud King, who had arrived in Australia with Michael Hand in 1967 to sell real estate in northern New South Wales. He died in Sydney in 1975. I learned that King's family back in America had been given two different stories about his death. His autopsy report revealed that neither version was true and that he had died in suspicious circumstances that were never properly investigated.

Eighteen months into my research I tracked down Doug Sapper, Michael Hand's Special Forces buddy in Vietnam. Sapper provided astonishing insights into the three main characters in the story: Michael Hand, Frank Nugan and Texas-born Kings Cross bar owner Bernie Houghton, who ended up running the bank's lucrative Middle East branches.

Sapper also revealed the bank's connections to intelligence agencies and Asian underworld groups, which were unknown at the time of the earlier investigations. And, in a surprising admission, Sapper told me of an extraordinary incident when associates of Houghton had asked him to travel to Sydney to carry out a murder.

Clearly, Nugan Hand was not some aberrant finance company operating in a vacuum and merely interested in ripping off millions of dollars from its customers. In Australia, the bank's operations crossed paths with dozens of major criminal cases, including a political assassination and the murder of two drug informants. On the world stage, Nugan Hand set itself up in major drug-trafficking hubs and areas of Cold War tension. It was as if Nugan Hand had deliberately positioned itself at the unholy nexus where organised crime and clandestine operations merge.

While the Australian investigators had unearthed some extraordinary linkages, they had also found a number of official doors closed to them. By accessing, through Freedom of Information, thousands of pages of documents from the FBI, US Department of State, ASIO and other government bodies I discovered how the Nugan Hand bank story had hit a raw nerve in US-intelligence and law-enforcement circles and caused diplomatic headaches, which I traced all the way to the White House.

*

When I embarked on this project, I hoped to discover the origins of this unique international scandal. To achieve that end, I needed to understand why Nugan died and why Michael Hand had disappeared. I set about creating a timeline of the Nugan Hand story, complete with episodes uncovered by the original investigations, and then researched the holes and imponderables in the timeline. Throughout the story there were dozens of actions taken by Nugan or Hand that left investigators bewildered. These included Hand's surprise resignation from the bank eighteen months after it began and Frank Nugan's ultimatum to his staff three months before his death to rid the bank of its illegal operations. Thirty-five years later, those mysteries are no longer mysteries.

And as for the greatest mystery of all, Michael Hand's whereabouts? He hasn't been seen since he fled Sydney in 1980.

I had read enough of the various inquiry reports to know that he was cunning and capable of extreme menace. I knew that if I ever traced Hand, he would be uncooperative. That said, I made numerous attempts to find him without success. Clearly, he had changed his name, and possibly his face, to evade detection.

As I neared completion of the first draft of this book, I made one final attempt to uncover his whereabouts. In a matter of hours, amongst a labyrinth of false trails, a path unexpectedly revealed itself, leading to a small, isolated town half a world away, where the darkest episode from Hand's past merged with his unfulfilled dream for the future of the Nugan Hand empire.

Even a highly-skilled CIA officer trained in the art of disappearance must appreciate that one fateful day someone could still trace him and announce, 'Time's up.' For Michael Hand, one of the world's most elusive corporate fugitives, that day has arrived.

1

WATCH OUT FOR THE CROCODILES

Standing atop of a rickety 10-metre-high tower in early 1964, Douglas A Sapper III, a twenty-one-year-old tough nugget of a man from Mount Vernon, Illinois, felt like the King of the World. The State of Georgia sure looked green and inviting from up there. On a clear night, they said, you could see the lights of Atlanta, more than 160 kilometres to the north.

When his trainer yelled, 'Jump!' there was no time for regrets. On the way down, Sapper just prayed that the parachute harness on his back would maintain its intimate relationship with the cable. This was only jump school at Fort Benning; a war zone was going to offer up far more hazards, including the likelihood of enemy fire. But he had joined up for exactly that kind of challenge.

It was during parachute training that Sapper met New York-born Michael Hand. Five-ten, with steel blue-eyes and a crazy laugh, Michael was buffed and handsome — the image of the all American boy.

'We were in the same class and we bonded,' Sapper later recalled. 'We were like birds of a feather. We realised, without statements on either side, that we were going to be professional soldiers.'[11]

Michael had been born into war. By Sapper's calculation, Michael's mother would have gone into labour during the Japanese attack on

Pearl Harbor. The following day, 8 December 1941, as President Roosevelt announced the declaration of war, Michael made his entry into the world.

His father, Oscar, was a clerk with the Department of Finance. The family lived in an apartment on Walton Avenue in the Bronx, one of New York's five boroughs, which had been taken over during the Prohibition years by bootleggers and gangs and gone into serious decline by the 1950s. On leaving school, Michael enrolled in a one-year course at the New York State Ranger School. After only nine months there he moved to California, and for most of 1960 managed a sports school in Los Angeles. In May 1963, Michael enlisted in the army. Following basic training, he was selected for Special Forces training with the elite Green Berets.

Despite their youth, life had already delivered both recruits a first-hand appreciation of mortality. In Doug Sapper's graduation year, while driving his father's Cadillac, he ran into a thirteen-year-old local boy who was riding a bicycle. The impact of the crash catapulted the boy into the windshield of the car and his body remained on the car as it skidded and crashed into a power pole. The boy died at the scene.

The year Michael Hand graduated from De Witt-Clinton High, his mother, Sally, fell to her death from the family's apartment window. Michael rarely spoke of his mother and Sapper sensed that it was not a subject he should raise:

> Michael did not advertise his background, or that his mother had killed herself, or accidentally fell off a balcony. I know that Michael went to several different educational institutions and gravitated to join the army and never looked back. In fact, throughout military training the thing you noticed about Michael was that he was driven.[2]

1 Watch out for the crocodiles

Hand and Sapper were indoctrinated in the art of unconventional warfare at Fort Bragg in North Carolina:

> When you were selected for Special Forces training, you could pretty much look people in the eye and say, 'I'm one of the chosen few.' We weren't boy scouts. This wasn't a church camp. We were trained to go in and destroy things. Michael did not have an aversion to closing the distance with another human being and he was the kind of guy people wanted on their Special Forces team. Michael looked good in a uniform. He had that prize-winning smile and that twinkle in his eye. But he was also the kind of guy who looked for loyalty, bravery and commitment. One of the things that bonded us was a rash of spinal meningitis going through that training cycle. There had already been one soldier die from it. We were in the barracks one night when one of the trainees had convulsions and started foaming at the mouth and fell on the floor. Everybody thought it was meningitis and so I tried to help him and I told everybody to get out of the barracks and Michael stayed and we attended that kid until the ambulance came. I think at that point there was a bond there. We knew that no matter how deep the shit got, he and I would still be standing there. And that was the beginning of a long, long friendship.[3]

In February 1965, they arrived in Tay Ninh Province, Vietnam. That month, the United States began its campaign of sustained bombing raids of North Vietnam, dubbed Operation Rolling Thunder:

> In the background of everybody's mind was the knowledge that being in a Special Forces camp in Vietnam was hazardous. One of the worst fears was of the camp being over-run and so

you didn't want a bunch of guys who were really adept at opening a tuna fish can but didn't have their shit together to defend you. Michael was a radio operator, he was a good teammate and everybody knew that Michael Hand, when push came to shove, could be seriously dangerous.[4]

In early June 1965, Hand was dispatched to a camp at Dong Xoai, 100 kilometres northeast of Saigon. Manned by four hundred Montagnard troops and nineteen Special Forces and US Navy construction specialists called Seabees, the camp sat at the end of the Ho Chi Min trail — a choke point for the Vietnamese Communists trying to move into South Vietnam. In such a strategic location it was never a question of 'will we be attacked?', only a question of 'when?'

Just before midnight on 9 June 1965, explosions rocked the camp. Michael Hand recalled that night in an army radio broadcast:

When the initial mortar barrage started at quarter to twelve, there was so much screaming and confusion and death in the immediate vicinity; everybody tried to do the most sensible thing in dispersing themselves around our perimeter wall. Everybody had their individual weapons as well as the crew-type weapons. For the first two hours of the battle, heavy mortar, machine guns, small arms and Chinese rifles were used against us. The Americans in the compound, which included the Special Forces and the Seabee attachment, dispersed themselves along the wall and tried to give them a good volume of fire to hold down the North Vietnamese who were attacking us. Two hours in, the VC hit us with flamethrowers as well as an increased barrage of fire.[5]

As the intense onslaught of mortars and recoilless rifle rounds, grenades and flame-throwers hammered the camp, fifteen hundred Viet Cong guerrillas moved in and overwhelmed the defenders. Hurtling through a gauntlet of razor wire and enemy rounds, Hand and four of his comrades withdrew to the district chief's compound on the other side of the camp. So began one of the first major battles of the Vietnam War.

Doug Sapper was on reconnaissance mission elsewhere, but happened to be on radio watch when Dong Xoai was hit:

> The first mortar round took out one of their radios and the next mortar round went through the team-house roof and I don't remember all the people that it wounded or killed but the Viet Cong got inside the wire almost immediately and it was a very bloody, intense, right-up-close-and-personal battle. They killed or wounded many of the American defenders. Michael, along with the executive officer of the team, Lieutenant Williams, held that team together in defence. It was so intense it was like the defenders of the Alamo; they had to drop back, drop back, drop back. In the last hour or so of the battle, they ended up in the inside of an artillery pit and they were running out of ammunition. At that point, Mike had already been fighting for forty-eight hours.[6]

The last radio still operating at Dong Xoai sent out a desperate plea for support: 'I am using my last battery for the radio and there is no more ammunition; we are all wounded, some of the more serious are holding grenades with the safety pins already pulled. The VC are attacking in human waves. The last wave has been defeated, but we are expecting the next wave now.'[7]

Sapper scrambled aboard one of the three helicopters that departed on the rescue mission into Dong Xoai:

> I was with what they call an extraction team or a hatchet force, to go in and try to get fighters into the camp to reinforce these guys. We couldn't get near it. We got shot off the LZ [landing zone]. By this time, Michael was out of bullets and, realising that death was probably just minutes away, he had a psychotic break. All he had was his Ka-bar knife. He mutilated quite a few of them with that. One of the VC grabbed him and Michael stabbed him and ripped the knife up through his sternum and the guy hit the ground and Michael put his foot on the guy's leg and grabbed his head and literally lifted it up and separated his head from his body. That was a Kodak moment. Yes, he tore the guy's head completely off his body … I don't know if the Viet Cong or the North Vietnamese Army that attacked the camp that night knew his name, but I guarantee after that they remembered Michael because he killed a truckload of them. It was his finest hour.[8]

Mounting a second desperate rescue mission, US military helicopters successfully landed on the Dong Xoai soccer field. Hand had been hit twice by mortar shrapnel but, before evacuating, volunteered to go back and retrieve another wounded comrade. As the choppers departed, the area was hit by mortar fire and raked by large-calibre machine guns. Only six of the nineteen Americans survived. All were wounded.

> Just by the grace of God, Michael and several other people were able to escape. Michael came to Saigon to the Third Field Hospital. No major wounds, but just a thousand little wounds, basically small pieces of shrapnel that had embedded in his skin. I stayed at the hospital to take care of Michael while he was recovering. If you were to ask me did I think that transformed Michael, I think that would transform just about anybody. You

pull somebody's head off their body and blood is squirting up about a foot over their shoulders, now that would transform you. He was pretty screwed up. I mean, he thought he was going to die, and he was just going to take as many of these people with him as he possibly could. He just became a robot, just went nuts; that is one of the reasons he survived. There are stories that he killed twenty guys with his bare hands.[9]

During the battle Hand risked his life to retrieve four wounded men. He was awarded the Distinguished Service Cross (DSC), the military's second highest award for heroism. Following his discharge from hospital, he was reassigned to the John F Kennedy Center for Special Warfare at Fort Bragg, North Carolina, where he received special instruction from CIA paramilitary officers for another mission — something completely off the radar.*

Doug Sapper saw it as a natural development for someone like Hand, who was unshaken in his belief that his country was on the side of right in the Vietnam War: 'In Special Forces there wasn't anything we couldn't accomplish. You give us a mission; we'll get it done. And Michael was a product of that environment. So when Michael got out of the military, he went to work for the Central Intelligence Agency. It was the next step.'[10]

After three months of intensive training, the CIA loaded Mike onto a Continental Air Services transport bound for Laos on a top-secret mission dubbed 'Project 404'. Laos was a neutral country, but in 1965 intelligence reports warned Washington that Vietnamese communist forces were spilling over the border into Laos. By the time Mike Hand arrived, Laos was in the thick of the largest covert

---

* During the Vietnam War, Special Forces followed the protocols of the military, but in reality the CIA called the shots. The CIA funded their missions, helped build their camps and directed their missions.

military operation in the CIA's history. He was assigned to a group called 'Requirements Organization', training Hmong hill tribesmen in the dark arts of counterinsurgency to oppose the North Vietnamese–backed Pathet Lao communists.

According to Doug Sapper, being in Laos was like being in a war that didn't exist: 'I used to describe it as a place far, far away, populated by people that don't exist, where things never happened. And Michael got thrust into that. He taught the Hmong different things about communications, about weapons, demolitions, about ambushes and then sent them out on patrols.'[11]

In Laos, Mike Hand met CIA pilot Kermit Walker King, a willowy, forty-year-old with a hollow 'Gomer Pyle' grin and a gung-ho attitude, who went by the name 'Bud'. In a small, twin-engine, unarmed Piper Apache aircraft, King carried out night-time airdrops over the Ho Chi Minh Trail, directed Laotian strike planes to their targets and ferried men, weapons and provisions into mountainous, precarious locations.

King introduced Mike Hand to Paul Stocker, a big-shot American lawyer who'd served two terms in the Washington State Legislature in the 1950s. In a scenario befitting *Catch 22*, Stocker was travelling around Laos in the middle of a covert war selling blocks of coastal land in Australia to employees of Air America and the CIA. Stocker talked Bud and Mike into signing up to his real estate venture, not as buyers but as salesmen.

In late 1966, following his Laos service, Michael Hand returned to the United States. Wearing a crisp shirt, tie and tailored suit, he walked into the Australian consulate on New York's Fifth Avenue and was ushered into the office of an official named Waddell. Michael looked on as Waddell opened a large envelope and extracted a letter with a photograph of fingerprints attached.

'The New Jersey police say you're an upright citizen,' said Waddell, as he picked up Hand's visa application and scanned it.

Hand had stated that he had won a DSC and that after his service in Vietnam he'd worked for the US Government in 'communications'. With the stroke of a pen, and for the princely sum of a single dollar, the young American was given permanent residency in Australia. As Hand stood to leave, Waddell took one last scan of his application.

'You say here you are going to be looking for construction work in the Northern Territory?'

'Yes, Sir.'

'Tough country up there. Watch out for the crocodiles.' [12]

*

If Hand intended on settling in the Northern Territory, he got off at the wrong stop. In October 1967, he flew into Sydney and gravitated to King Cross, where the only evidence of reptilian life was the blue-tongued spruikers parading up and down outside the ubiquitous strip clubs.

Hand and King met with Paul Stocker at the newly opened Bourbon & Beefsteak Bar and Restaurant. Stocker handed them a bunch of glossy brochures and a sales script and told them to get to work. Coincidentally, or not, the first planeload of US servicemen on R&R from the Vietnam War had just arrived in Sydney. They were bussed to an R&R centre, where they were given a run-down of the city and told that Kings Cross was the ideal place to spend their week's leave. After partaking of the sexual services on offer around the Cross, the servicemen flocked to the 'Bourbon' for American home-style food and entertainment. Its forty-eight-year-old Texas-born proprietor, Bernie Houghton, was the perfect host. Bernie had run servicemen's bars in Saigon and Bangkok and seemed to have had foreknowledge of the US Government's choice of Sydney as its upcoming R&R hotspot for the US forces.

Detective Sergeant Clive Small probed Bernie Houghton's early years in Sydney:

> Houghton was one of the most mysterious characters that you would meet in Kings Cross in those days. He set up his business effectively in the months before approval was given for US military resources to come to Australia on R&R from the Vietnam War. You could be forgiven for suspecting that he knew something in advance and was taking advantage of it.[13]

With Bernie's blessing, Mike and Bud based themselves at the Bourbon & Beefsteak and started selling slices of paradise to young, impressionable GIs fresh from a war zone. The blocks on offer were part of a large coastal development in subtropical northern New South Wales, called 'Ocean Shores'. The scheme was bankrolled by a big American tycoon and boasted popular singer Pat Boone as its figurehead. The genius of working out of the Bourbon was that fresh groups of GIs and navy guys were arriving in Kings Cross every week. With every sale Mike and Bud earned a tidy 25 per cent commission.

In December 1968, Bud King returned to Laos and flew back two weeks later via Darwin in a Piper Apache aircraft he'd just purchased from Continental Air Service, a CIA airline. Bud figured that if any potential buyer proved a hard nut to crack, he would fly them up to Ocean Shores to seal the deal. A few weeks later, his Thai housekeeper, Arina, flew in from the Laotian capital, Vientiane, to help cater for buyers and dignitaries visiting Ocean Shores, including Pat Boone and Hollywood actor William Holden.

In 1970, Doug Sapper and an army buddy flew from Saigon to Sydney on R&R:

> We went down to Kings Cross — well of course everybody

talks about Kings Cross and we had heard about the Bourbon & Beefsteak, where all these GIs went, so we went down there. We saw the same GIs there every day on a five-day R&R. They didn't go on cruises of Sydney Harbour. They would spend almost all their time in that bar. Well, it was because they felt safe there. There was camaraderie there. There was an easy ear they could talk to — Bernie or one of his managers — and they could get things done. If someone said, 'Bernie, where can I get laid?' or 'Bernie, where can I get this?' he knew. So when they got back, it was 'How was Sydney?' 'I guess it's great man, that bar is really a hell of a place to be.' In that, you have to assume there was some illegal activity somewhere. Bars, alcohol, prostitution, some drugs, whatever — it all kind of fits in a package.[14]

At the Bourbon, Sapper learned to his astonishment that Michael Hand was living in Sydney. He called him up and went over to his home for dinner. The biggest surprise was that Mike had recently married a beautiful Australian woman — a former model, who worked for a flash Sydney jeweller.

> Helene was her name. She was older than he was by about five or so years. A phenomenal woman, I mean a very strong personality but very supportive and extremely loyal. He married her within just a little over a year of arriving in Australia. It didn't take him long to fall under her spell, I guess you'd say. In a quiet moment I said to Michael, 'How the hell did you end up here?' When he left Laos I just assumed that he had returned to New York. He said he was selling some kind of real estate investment. I just said, 'Now that's a shift in direction.'[15]

Curious about his army buddy's transformation from war hero to salesman, Sapper headed back to the Bourbon on his last night in Sydney:

There was Michael, perfectly tied tie, starched shirt, good-looking suit. He comes around the table and you could just tell this is Dale Carnegie — a sort of a super-salesman persona. He was getting all the right hook lines and getting all the right timing. He was magnetic. But he was a real estate salesman? I could tell that Michael was in survival mode, and he wasn't going to be satisfied with selling land down in this property development. He was looking for something that had a future.

2

JURISPRUDENCE IS CRAP

Intelligent. Boisterous. Stubborn. Aggressive. Creative. Self-opinionated. Capricious. At different times, Frank Nugan could reveal any of these traits.

In December 1942, Frank Nugan came into the world accompanied by his twin sister, Gwen. They grew up in the New South Wales town of Griffith, located 50 kilometres south of the halfway point between Melbourne and Sydney. Frank's parents, like other European migrants, were lured to the booming fruit and vegetable growing town in search of work. Within a few years they had taken up land of their own, had become growers and, with energy and foresight, incorporated the Nugan Fruit Group, which packed produce and transported it to market. After school and during the holidays, young Frank and his two older brothers were obliged to help their father pack fruit and vegetables.

By puberty, Frank possessed a stocky upper frame on top of a pair of spindly legs. His defining features were thick wavy hair, a widow's peak and a broad, slightly bulbous nose, which underwent reconstruction surgery when he was fourteen. He told a school friend it had something to do with his sinuses. The friend assumed it really had more to do with his considerable vanity.

At Griffith High, Frank was an A-grader with a flair for debating and composition. He was also a keen participator in tennis, rugby, swimming and cadets. Young Frank's expertise lay in channeling his latent energy into causing a stir. If his brother Ken was studying, Frank would turn up the volume of his radio and ignore every request to turn it down.[1] Provoking outrage allowed him to ponder human nature and determine how far he could push people.

In his final year of school, he famously boasted to his class, 'I'm going to university and straight to the top.' His gobsmacked teacher fired back, 'You're a little upstart, Nugan.'

According to a school friend, a nonentity was the one thing Frank Nugan was determined he would never be:

> He was always the best, the biggest, the fastest; that was Frank's attitude. He behaved as if he could do anything and do it better than anyone else. There was the time when Frank's father won a pony in a raffle. We took it out for a ride. I don't think Frank had ever ridden a horse but he set off at full gallop down a hill and fell off. There was skin and hair flying everywhere. We had to chase the blighter down and Frank got right back on and rode it home. In everything he did it was, 'I can do that!'[2]

By the time Frank sat for his leaving certificate, his family owned the largest packing and transport company in the state. His father, Alfred, was keen for his sons to acquire a university education. At Sydney University, Ken studied economics, while Frank pursued a law degree. But city living and higher education did little to smooth Frank's rough edges. His law professor recalled him taking to his feet in a lecture and proclaiming, 'Jurisprudence is crap'; a clear sign that reverence for the law was not one of his early ambitions.

In 1965, Frank moved to California to gain his master's at University of California, Berkeley, then to Toronto, Canada, with the intention of obtaining his doctorate. But he dropped out and took a position with the Canadian public service, giving him an income with which he could feed his penchant for fast cars, girls and gliding lessons.

Frank returned to Sydney in July 1968 after almost four years in North America. He registered himself as a solicitor and embarked on a merry-go-round of interviews with law firms, brandishing a bloated curriculum vitae in which he claimed he had played a substantial role in the framing of corporate and securities law for the Canadian Government. If prospective employers had decided to check his claims, they would have discovered that the Ontario Securities Commission had no record of Frank Nugan in that context.[3]

Frank finally secured a position with Freehill, Hollingdale and Page, one of Sydney's largest and oldest law firms. But within a year at Freehills he came to the conclusion that his migrant background was always going to be a barrier to advancement. So he handed in his resignation, rented an office and started his own legal practice. From that day on, he set about converting the sizable chip on his shoulder into a brickbat to shove up 'the proverbial' of the old-school legal fraternity.

Frank's measure of success was money. He went straight to the coalface and looked for the richest seams he could mine — property developers, doctors, dentists and wealthy businessmen — offering general legal services and his expertise in tax minimisation. When the work started coming in, he purchased a pinstripe suit and rented an Art-Deco apartment block in bohemian Macleay Street in Potts Point, a few hundred metres down the road from the exciting, neon-lit nightclub strip of Kings Cross, the city's lusty, beating heart of crime and prostitution.

3

THE SPANIARD

According to legend, one morning in late 1968, Frank Nugan ambled along Darlinghurst Road, Kings Cross, armed with a flash leather attaché case and a bunch of freshly printed business cards to hand out to business owners along the nightclub strip. Sidestepping a band of intoxicated American sailors, the go-getting, twenty-five-year-old entered the Bourbon & Beefsteak. He approached the bar and asked the short, plumpish man sorting the till with a hand missing two fingers if he could speak to Mr Maurice Houghton, the proprietor. The fellow straightened his tie, offered a hospitable smile and in a broad Texas twang said that he was the owner, who went by his middle name, Bernie.

Frank handed Bernie his card and said that he was a lawyer and that if he ever needed legal services he should contact him. At the end of the bar, a grey-headed, Greek-looking American in his late forties, glanced up from his racing form guide and quipped, 'A lawyer with a briefcase will rob you faster than a gun-toting thief.'

Frank fired back that he was no ordinary lawyer: he was a tax lawyer and could run rings around the slugs down at the tax department. Bernie introduced the earnest young shark to his meddlesome friend, Duke Countis, who managed the salubrious Caprice Restaurant at Rose Bay, overlooking Sydney Harbour.

3 The Spaniard

Frank boldly slid a business card down the bar to the Duke.

The Duke pondered the card.

'Tax lawyer? The IRS brought down a lot of my friends in San Francisco in the late 1950s. They lost their businesses and their families ended up on welfare. They had tax lawyers. A lot of good it did them.'

As Frank shrugged and picked up his attaché case to depart, Bernie winked to the Duke. 'Strange name, Nu-gan. Sounds Vietnamese to my delicate Texan ear.'

'Spanish,' Frank deftly countered, 'My parents are Spanish.'

Frank was proud of his Spanish background. Many of his schoolmates were children of Italian migrants with surnames like Gavioli, Salvestro, Sergi and Calabria. On interschool sports days, the Anglo boys from nearby Wagga or Yanco often jibed 'Mafia' to the Italians. Frank copped the insult, too. But he took it in his stride. He would simply lock eyes with the perpetrator and groan, 'Nah, you've got it wrong, we're the Spanish Mafia.'[1]

*

In reality, Frank didn't have a drop of Spanish blood in his veins. His father, Alfred Neugarten, had been born to Jewish parents in Brackwede, Germany.[2] Alfred moved to Spain, married in Madrid in 1930 and raised a son. When the Spanish Civil War broke out, he went off to fight with the International Brigade against the Fascists. In 1938, Alfred and his son caught a ship headed for Palestine*, where they met the recently divorced Anneliese Meinhardt. Born into a German Jewish family from Schweldt, Anneliese and her first husband had migrated to Palestine in 1933 to escape living under Nazi rule.

In late December 1938, Alfred and Anneliese married in Jerusalem.

---

* The fate of Alfred's first wife is unknown.

A few months later they applied to immigrate to Australia as Jewish refugees. They arrived in Melbourne only weeks before Britain and Australia declared war on Germany. Immigration records reveal that in December 1939 they changed their German-sounding name, Neugarten, to Nugan by deed poll.³

Frank's school friends knew nothing of his family origins, or that the Nazis had murdered his mother's parents. As a migrant boy growing up in xenophobic Australia, Frank had likely come to the conclusion that it was far wiser to declare himself 'Spanish Mafia' than 'German Jew.'

*

The Duke peered over his racing form. 'Not one of those goddamn Spanish communistas are you, Frank?'

Frank allegedly laughed and quipped, 'That's right, a goddamn communist millionaire.'

The Duke, a well-known follower of fashion, looked him up and down. 'That sports coat you're wearing says you ain't no millionaire.'

Frank sat back and blurted, 'One day I'm going to be the richest bloody man in this city.'

Bernie's internal barometer hit red. He was in two minds about Frank Nugan, with his ten-gallon mouth blowing a gale. The Duke, however, was curious about the brash Spaniard who didn't look Spanish but thought he could tap-dance on quicksand. As Frank collected up his attaché case, the Duke asked him for another business card. He said there was an enterprising American friend of his and Bernie's — a real-life war hero — he thought he should meet.

4

TAKE-OFF

Frank and Mike's meeting at the Bourbon and Beefsteak was to shape the destinies of both men. They were roughly the same age, both looking for opportunities and both self-starters. They quickly became friends. Occasionally, Frank would arrive at the Bourbon, order a drink and for entertainment sit back and watch Mike and Bud King moving from table to table trying to offload blocks of Ocean Shores land to GIs on R&R. It was finely tuned American-style capitalism, which Frank had come to admire during his time in California.

In August 1969, Mike took a shareholding in a new company, Australasian and Pacific Holdings, along with ten other Americans, all of whom were employees of Air America or other CIA airlines.* The firm set out to develop an island on the Great Barrier Reef, but when the project stalled Mike Hand decided to loan the company's capital to his friend, Frank Nugan. Frank used the funds to start a mining firm, Meekatharra Minerals, and gave Mike fifteen thousand shares in the company as collateral. At the time, Australia was in the midst of a mining boom. Frank later claimed that he had made a substantial profit from the venture, reputedly in excess of $1 million. No one was ever

---

* The author tracked down one of the former Air America pilots to his home in Tampa, Florida. He recalled Hand signing him up to the real estate development business, but said that he wasn't actively involved and that he did not believe it had come to fruition.

sure if there was any substance to the boast, but Mike seemed impressed enough with Frank's business acumen to join him in other moneymaking ventures, including other real-estate developments and bullion trading. They also became major stakeholders in a plastics and rubber company, which produced a variety of products, including condoms.

From a skills point of view, Mike and Frank saw complementary qualities in each other. Frank lacked finesse, but he was the guy with a grasp of the law and big ideas. Mike, on the other hand, was stylish, measured and calculating, with a gift for salesmanship — a man who could sell a T-bone steak to a vegetarian.

In 1972, they began calling the US servicemen who had purchased land at 'Ocean Shores'. By now most had returned to their homes in America, married and started families. Even though their land had significantly increased in value, it was half a world away and they were unlikely ever to see it again. Mike came up with the bright idea of contacting the landholders and offering to take it off their hands for a quarter to a third of what they had paid. They would then put it up for sale through a Panama-registered company at full market value. It was callous and unethical, but brilliant salesmanship. Of course, there was only so much land to buy back, so they were still on the lookout for other high-return opportunities.

*

In 1970 Frank had married Charlotte Lee Sofge, from Nashville, Tennessee. Lee, as she liked to be known, later enrolled at Sydney University, Frank's alma mater, where she studied psychology. The happy couple domiciled in Bellevue Hill, one of Sydney's most fashionable suburbs — an address that spelled success. But Frank wanted more and was willing to drive himself hard to reach that fabled status of millionaire, which back in the 1970s actually meant something.

Other than the bookies and illegal casino operators, the people

4 Take-off

making the big money in Sydney were the international merchant bankers, who were moving into Australia and shaking up the conservative banking system. In June 1973, Mike and Frank met up with prominent businessman and racehorse owner John Needham to discuss setting up a company that could act as a merchant bank. Needham was the perfect partner; his family was well known in Sydney business circles and would give the firm an air of respectability. The company would be formed with a view to advising clients on corporate matters, arranging finance, giving tax advice, facilitating company takeovers and engaging in real-estate marketing.

On 6 July 1973, the trio incorporated Nugan Hand Needham and took expensive offices at 55 Macquarie Street, Sydney, overlooking the Harbour Bridge and a stone's throw from the newly completed Sydney Opera House. Frank installed his private secretary Patricia Swan to run the office and began to employ staff.

An assistant manager with a large firm of auditors, spent two days with the fledgling firm:

> I was sent down there on the basis that they wanted to have our firm sign off on a prospectus to raise funds. I met Frank Nugan. He was dressed in a brown suit and brown shoes and seemed very country, not the slick investment banker. He gave me some records, which indicated that he'd already raised funds from properties in Western Australia and it was all in cash. I couldn't understand why it was coming in from such a remote location. I went back to my managers and said these guys have already raised the money improperly and we don't want to sign off on this because it is illegal. It struck me that Frank Nugan must have been very naïve. Being a lawyer he should have realised this was the last thing an auditor would want to see. I have since wondered whether this was a money-laundering exercise.[1]

The first year of operation was so disorganized that John Needham asked to be released from the partnership: 'I could never find out any information about the company's activities. During my time with it, no board meeting was ever held of which I received notice. I just got fed up with the lack of information and it seemed futile to go on with any involvement.'[2]

Following Needham's departure, the firm was renamed 'Nugan Hand Ltd'. In late 1974, the firm's young accountant, Stephen Hill, introduced Frank to Les Callings, a tall, aloof career salesman who had just been released from a Philippines prison. Collings had been based in Manila, working for Fund of Australia, an international investment organisation. When the firm collapsed, Collings found himself thrown into a Manila jail, courtesy of some powerful customers who had lost their investments. By means unknown, Collings had engineered his release and taken the first available flight back to Sydney.

On the credit side of the ledger, Collings could separate a man from his money faster than a Dickensian pickpocket. He also had excellent business and banking contacts across Asia — a region where Nugan and Hand wanted to promote their merchant bank. From his time in Southeast Asia, Mike Hand had recognised that wealthy people needed a secure facility where they could deposit money or gold. Why not offer them that facility through Nugan Hand?

Frank and Mike dispatched Collings to Hong Kong to establish the bank's first international office. From a hotel room in the Wanchai red-light district of Hong Kong Island, he set about seducing deposits from traditionally wary Chinese businessmen. Business proved slow at first and fell far short of Nugan and Hand's demands, but Collings ultimately proved his worth when he convinced a solid Hong Kong bank to underwrite Nugan Hand's operations for a fee. With a reputable bank behind it, Nugan Hand began to see the money coming in.

Collings soon found himself at the centre of power, along with

4 Take-off

Nugan, Hand and Stephen Hill. The so-called 'gang of four' met regularly to plot the future of the bank. Mike Hand was particularly impressed by Collings' success, and this helped ferment in his mind the idea of setting up a truly international bank. In July 1974, Nugan Hand registered a new branch in Hawaii and started filing paperwork for another office in the Cayman Islands, a legendary tax haven.

In Australia, Nugan Hand wasn't a merchant bank and was never registered as such, but Mike and Frank got around that fundamental technicality by promoting themselves as 'merchant bankers'. Groups of well-heeled investors, including the financial administrators of clubs and local councils were invited to the Sydney office for introductory sessions.

Before each session, Frank would prime his staff. 'Don't forget, there could be millions of dollars in the room today looking for a new home,' he'd say. 'Make it welcome.'

Mike would do the introductions, then talk about the bank's operations and preach on the benefits of the bullion market. Frank would concentrate on the topics of tax avoidance and the money market. They later explained their philosophy to a journalist:

> We're not competing with the big banks. Our concept is low-key, a conservative operation catering for a narrow segment of the market — the elitists, people who prefer to get involved on a personal basis. We call it private banking. We ask our customers what we can do for them and we do it. If you want to talk about investments or tax avoidance, we'll even come to your home or office. When was the last time you saw a regular banker get out of his leather chair?[3]

Consistently, the discussion would turn to loans and interest rates. Mike would say, 'Nugan Hand doesn't lend money, but we make money for our depositors.' Frank would then play his wild card. 'We can offer you up to 2 per cent more interest than the market rate — a stupendous return.'4

According to NSW Corporate Affairs Commission investigator Rick Porter:

> Nugan Hand wasn't a bank as such and it didn't operate as a bank, it didn't have a licence here, so it basically operated as a money market–type operator. The staff didn't have any experience in that area at all. No systems were in place and it was a real haphazard-type operation in regard to attracting deposits from various people and making money on it. In fact our investigations would suggest that they were paying too high an interest rate, but that is why they attracted councils and various other people. 5

Despite Nugan and Hand's total inexperience, the strategy worked. In its first eighteen months, Nugan Hand attracted more than AU$50 million* in deposits. Frank and Mike were only in their early thirties but were already pulling in salaries higher than their phone numbers. Mike and Helene moved into a waterfront apartment a few floors below Bernie Houghton's penthouse in Elizabeth Bay. By now, Frank and his wife, Lee, were driving around in a top-of-the-range Mercedes Benz and were on the lookout for a waterfront home.

But in late 1974, someone from Mike Hand's past appeared from the shadows — someone who threatened to bring down the whole box and dice.

---

*   Approximately AU$400 million in 2015

5

THE MAN WHO FELL TO EARTH

Bud King never forgot a birthday. He wasn't sentimental; it was a simple fact that dates seemed to stick in his mind. He remembered the date in 1947 when he won a newspaper contest. The prize included a visit to Fort Richardson, in Alaska, as a guest of the 85th Fighter Squadron. From that day on, he dreamed of becoming a pilot. He also remembered the dates when he met his wife, Patricia, and the day she walked out on him, taking their son, Larry. These were days of historic importance.

On Mike's thirty-third birthday, 8 December 1974, Bud wrapped up a bottle of wine, wrote a birthday card and thought about heading up to the Nugan Hand office in Sydney. He called first, but Mike was unavailable, so he unwrapped the bottle and drank it.

Word had got around town that Bud was down on his luck. Ocean Shores had gone bankrupt and a finance company had repossessed his plane. Somewhere along the line he had become heavily dependent on booze and prescription drugs. To fund his growing addiction, he had started hitting on people for money. According to a secretary working for Ocean Shores, he turned up at Paul Stocker's office making threats about 'the shit going down at Ocean Shores' and how they owed him 'big time' and demanding money. He became so aggressive the police were called to remove him.[1]

On 6 January 1975, less than a month on from Mike's birthday, Bud was found dead. Four days later, Mike told Frank that he was resigning from Nugan Hand and quitting Australia for good.

Exactly what precipitated both events was never investigated. The only clue was a report of a telephone call discovered two years later among unrelated documents in a filing cabinet at the offices of the Federal Bureau of Narcotics, in Customs House, Sydney. According to the report, a Sydney lawyer had called the Narcotics Bureau in 1973 and spoken with investigator Russ Kenny. The lawyer asked Kenny if the department had any records of Americans by the name of Paul Stocker, Bud King and Mike Hand. When asked why he wanted the information, the lawyer alleged that they were 'involved in a drug-smuggling ring in the Brunswick Heads–Coffs Harbour area of northern New South Wales.' He added that he was acting on behalf of a woman and that he believed 'there may be blackmail involved'.[2]

The woman at the centre of the story was Bud King's Thai housekeeper, Arina, who had worked for King at Ocean Shores. When Ocean Shores went bust, Bud King told Arina that he could no longer pay her and had to let her go. Arina gratefully accepted an offer to work for Paul Stocker and his wife at their luxury apartment in Sydney's eastern suburbs. But in January 1973 Stocker called in the police, alleging that Arina had stolen his wife's jewellery. Arina protested her innocence, but to no avail.

A concerned Australian friend put her in touch with a young lawyer. He smelled a rat when he learned that the arresting officer was from the Water Police, not the regular police force.[3] The lawyer confronted the arresting officer, who said the theft charge against Arina would be dropped if she returned to Thailand in the next twenty-four hours. Such an offer was beyond the authority of any police officer. When Police Integrity officers later interviewed Arina, they believed her story.⁴ The arresting officer allegedly lost his job and the larceny case against Arina was thrown out of court.

Chauncey Holt, an American friend of Bud King's, suggests that Arina knew too much:

> [Arina] was certainly in possession of some dangerous facts … King had flown for Air America, Civil Air Transport, Southern Airways and Paragon Air Services, all proprietary interests of the CIA. King was involved in flying narcotics from Southeast Asia, an area he knew like the back of his hand, to other parts of the world.⁵

Both Bud King and Mike Hand had served in Laos, where opium production was prevalent throughout the Hmong highlands. Ultimately, Laotian opium ended up in the hands of American GIs on the frontline in Vietnam. By 1971, 11 per cent of US servicemen leaving Vietnam who were tested were found to have opiates in their urine.⁶ And as many of 45 per cent of servicemen interviewed admitted to having used either opium or heroin during their tour of duty.⁷

How did the drug get all the way from the Laotian mountains to the front line? Some of it arrived on CIA proprietary aircraft, such as Air America, and passed through the hands of Laotian, American and South Vietnamese middlemen. When allegations arose in the early 1970s that the CIA itself aided and abetted the movement of the Hmong tribesmen's drugs to keep them loyal to the war effort, the CIA firmly denied the claim. In more recent times, however, the CIA has admitted that Air America pilots 'may have moved drugs and that the agency had turned a blind eye to the practice.'⁸

In Laos, criminal syndicates capitalised on the opium trade by setting up clandestine heroin laboratories and a maze of international smuggling routes. By the late 1960s, Laotian heroin was being sold on the streets of American and Australian cities.*

Sydney was the epicentre of heroin importations into Australia and unequivocally linked to the needs of American soldiers on R&R. On arrival in Sydney, American servicemen were given a briefing about the rules of engagement with the Australian people and the authorities: 'Number one is narcotics. If you've brought any pot, hemp, LSD, marijuana, any type of junk at all, and you managed to get it through customs, get rid of it. Take it, smoke it, give yourself a shot, just get rid of it. Do not leave the hotel with it.'9

It was no coincidence that all manner of drugs, including heroin, were sought-after commodities in Kings Cross during the R&R period. Heroin, in particular, became a currency used in exchange for sex with the prostitutes of the Cross.

Immigration records reveal that both Bud King and Mike Hand returned twice to Laos from Sydney in the late 1960s. Mike Hand's visits were in defiance of his Australian visa requirements, which stipulated that he was not to leave Australia within two years of his taking permanent residency.10

Following his second visit to Laos, Bud King returned to Australia with the Piper Apache aircraft he'd purchased from the CIA. Back then, it was possible to fly undetected into one of hundreds of remote airstrips in the Northern Territory, unload contraband then fly to Darwin and proceed through customs before returning to the airstrip to pick up the contraband.†

The blackmailing of King's housekeeper and the involvement of an allegedly corrupt police officer suggested that something seriously

---

* In his book *The Politics of Heroin in Southeast Asia*, Alfred McCoy suggested that America's heroin plague was of its own making. He alleged that American diplomats and secret agents had been involved in the narcotics traffic by allying with groups engaged in drug traffic, covering up for the traffickers or active engagement in the transport of opium and heroin.
† Customs smashed such a drug importation plan in 1973 and intercepted another in 1978.

untoward was occurring.* Unfortunately, the Narcotics Bureau didn't follow up on the drug importation allegations against Hand, King and Stocker.

---

* When asked to comment on the allegations in 2013, Paul Stocker intimated to the author that King and Hand were involved in something untoward, but he could not talk about it as he was involved in a major international court case and did not want the publicity. Stocker died in 2014.

6

THE CONTRA

On Monday 13 January 1975, Frank Nugan picked up the phone at the bank's Hong Kong office and called his staff in Sydney. He told them bluntly that Mike Hand had resigned, that he would not be returning to Australia and that his name was to be taken off the bank's registration records by the end of the day. As to his partner's future, he reported that Mike had said that he was going 'turkey farming'.[1]

Frank allegedly became morose following Mike's departure. Losing the firm's chief salesman within eighteen months of starting the business was a disaster.

Corporate Affairs Commission investigator Geoffrey Nicholson had his team reconstruct the financial records from that period. It was evident that the embryonic bank had been outlaying far more money than it was earning:

> It became very clear to me that Nugan Hand had the trappings of a bank, but it was so much window dressing. There was 'smoke and mirrors' involved. A structure had been set up which was very impressive but effectively wasn't making any money locally and had false accounting entries, consuming millions of dollars of overheads.[2]

6 The Contra

To cover up the true financial position, Nugan had pressed his inexperienced internal auditor to move money from account to account and company to company, like a three-shell game. The Corporate Affairs Commission later reported: 'The more dominant character of Nugan persuaded the inexperienced auditor that the deceptions he wanted to employ were not deceptions at all.'[3]

*

From day one, Frank Nugan had deliberately recruited people he believed he could mould. The principal requirement, it appears, was that no one was to have any banking experience. In that way, nobody could claim to know better than Frank. His antidote for any concerns raised by his employees and executives was to pay them salaries far greater than their market worth. That bought loyalty. It was like the kings and queens of legend who trained young noblemen, conferred knighthoods on them and then expected them to happily lay down their lives to protect the crown.

Frank's noblemen typically fell into three categories: the inexperienced, the connected and the downright crooked. Five of his early recruits, including Les Collings, who was running the Hong Kong office, had been formerly associated with the Fund of Australia, an international fund-raising investment organisation, which collapsed in 1974. Another Fund of Australia recruit was Lebanese Australian George Shaw. Under Nugan's guidance, Shaw and others would perfect a unique act of financial wizardry that would propel Nugan Hand across the legal Rubicon.

*

In early November 1975, two Americans, one wearing a sports coat and cravat, the other wearing a silver suit and sporting a severe military-style crew cut, walked into the Nugan Hand office, unannounced, like centurions on a mission. They were not everyday bank customers. At reception, they introduced themselves as Duke Countis and Harry Wainwright. Frank Nugan greeted them as old friends and ushered them into his office. It was Countis along with Bernie Houghton, who had introduced him to Mike Hand. Frank had first met Harry Wainwright at Countis' restaurant and had since provided both men with professional taxation advice. But there was a great deal Frank didn't know about the two men sitting opposite.

George 'Duke' Countis was born on 23 August 1915 in New York and grew up in his Greek father's brothel in Ohio. From an early age his passion was gambling. In California, in 1951, he was arrested in an illegal gaming house. In the late 1950s, he ran a restaurant in San Francisco, where he befriended and became a business associate of Jimmy 'The Weasel' Fratianno, an infamous Mafia hitman. In 1967, Countis moved to Sydney, where he managed the Caprice Restaurant until September 1974, when he was declared bankrupt over gambling debts. By 1975, Countis was a regular patron at an illegal casino in Double Bay, a favourite haunt of drug trafficker Michael Moylan and former Olympian and detective Murray Riley, who was also eager to be involved in the drug business. Six months before this meeting with Frank, Countis had flown to San Francisco with Moylan and Riley and introduced them to Fratianno and a number of other crime figures involved in drug trafficking. The 'Moylan group' ultimately made between thirty and forty successful drug importations into Australia, using women employed as croupiers at Sydney's illegal casinos.[4]

Harry Wainwright's background was of a similar hue. Born in New Orleans, Louisiana, in 1923, Wainwright was a lawyer who had represented West Coast organised-crime figures. In 1968, he turned up in Sydney on the run from a US Grand Jury investigation into the

Mafia. In 1973, the FBI filed indictments against Wainwright for tax evasion and being part of a syndicate that had skimmed more than US$1.7 million from the takings of seven topless bars in San Francisco. That year, despite his criminal links, Australia's immigration department approved Wainwright's citizenship application. With a pile of allegedly ill-gotten cash at his disposal, he purchased a property at Telegraph Point on the New South Wales North Coast and allegedly began growing marijuana.[5]

★

Frank poured his guests a whisky and asked how he could help. Countis said that Harry wanted to make a deposit. Frank gave his usual spiel, 'Depending on the amount, we can offer up to 2 per cent higher than the average market rate.'

Wainwright cut Frank short. This was to be a short-term deposit; he wanted to access the funds in seven days. Confused, Frank said it was not worth their trouble. Wainwright said he wanted to pick the money up in Hong Kong and that it needed to be on the quiet.

Hong Kong? In the 1970s, it was illegal in Australia, as it was in many other countries, to move money internationally without seeking the approval of the Reserve Bank. Gaining permission entailed substantiating where the money came from and the reason for its transfer overseas.

With that, Harry and Duke upped and departed, leaving Frank pondering. There was nothing worse than money walking in the door and walking out again. So, within twenty-four hours, Frank Nugan and his staff came up with a novel but devious way to move the money from Sydney to Hong Kong without detection.

Joint Task Force investigator Clive Small later learned how it worked:

> When you looked at what they did, it was something quite ingenious, but so simple you'd say, 'Why didn't other people think of it?' They never transferred money anywhere. You would go to the bank in Sydney and say, 'I've got $50,000 here that I want transferred to Hong Kong.' So all they would do is ring their Hong Kong office and say, 'Mr X has deposited $50,000 cash with us in Sydney, we have the money, he's going to Hong Kong next week, would you give him $50,000 out of your cash reserve?' Hong Kong would then pay out $50,000 from there.[6]

Geoffrey Nicholson's corporate investigators dubbed the scheme 'the Contra':

> Those persons involved in sending money out of the country had a great desire, one would think, not to have been noticed by authorities; otherwise they would have gone through normal banking channels. Once that facility, known as a 'Contra', became available, I have no doubt that [it] was the main activity of the Nugan Hand group of companies. Obviously, they weren't doing it for love and charity. There was a substantial commission involved.[7]

Over the next six weeks, Wainwright and two of his associates used Frank Nugan's Contra system on three occasions.[8] Small amounts were deposited with George Shaw at the bank and withdrawn from Hong Kong one or two weeks later. There is no evidence to explain how the funds were to be used, but, in early April 1976, Wainwright again visited the Nugan Hand Sydney office with former policeman Murray Riley. Wainwright told George Shaw that if Riley and another associate wanted any of his money, they could use it. A week later

$15,000 of Wainwright's money was transferred by telegraphic transfer to Hong Kong.* A message sent from the Nugan Hand Sydney office to the chief executive of the Hong Kong branch, Les Collings, reveals the subterfuge in action, including the use of false names:

> A client of ours [the Sydney office] who will identify himself as Mr Murray [Murray Riley] will be calling into the [Hong Kong] office on 13 April to pick up the equivalent of $15,000 Australian. The money has been lodged in Sydney. It will be sent through the Bank of New South Wales to reimburse.⁹

Three days after the handover of money in Hong Kong, Riley returned to Brisbane with a large quantity of heroin concealed in a false-bottom suitcase.

The bank was soon actively promoting the Contra scheme, which was essentially a money-laundering operation, to all its clients, including politicians, radio and television personalities and powerful businessmen. Nugan Hand executive George Shaw was the scheme's principal promoter. Over a five-month period in 1976, one third of Shaw's deposit and withdrawal transactions were for reputed drug traffickers.†

---

* AU$15,000 is equivalent to approximately $102,000 in 2015.
† The Joint Task Force estimated that about thirty-five to forty drug dealers and syndicates ultimately used the Contra scheme to move funds.

7

TURKEY FARMING

Mike Hand's departure from Nugan Hand was a stunning development. He had given no warning and there was certainly no farewell party. According to fifty-year-old Dutch-born Wilhelmus 'Bill' Hans, who had only been with Nugan Hand for six months, Frank Nugan was upset at Hand's departure. He had given Hand a massive payout and said that his name was to be taken off all Nugan Hand company registrations by the end of the day.

Correspondence later unearthed by Corporate Affairs Commission investigators suggested there had been more to Hand's departure than Frank Nugan had let on to his staff. In a telex to Nugan, Hand had expressed concern that 'the project' he was working on was against US law and requested that his name be removed from the records of Nugan Hand in Hawaii to ensure that he would not have to include his bank account details in his US tax returns.[1]

As turkey farming has never been against US law, the question on investigators' minds was, 'What was Mike Hand really up to?'

*

In the ruins of the bank, the investigators uncovered an intriguing file labelled 'South Africa'. At first glance, the enclosed documents

7 Turkey farming

suggested that Hand had moved to South Africa to set up a Nugan Hand office and attract deposits from South African citizens. But why resign from the bank and then proceed to open up another office? And why all the secrecy?

At the time, South Africa's policy of apartheid made the country an international pariah. While most Western nations had implemented economic and military sanctions against South Africa, twenty major American companies had maintained interests in the country, which were not concealed from the US Government.

Handwritten notes in the file offered an intriguing insight into another motive for Hand's South Africa sojourn. Soon after his arrival, he had contacted Nugan by phone requesting the prices and availability of recoilless rifles, mortars, grenade launchers and machine guns, which were to be shipped to Africa. Hand followed up with a barrage of telexes, which included detailed lists of the arms he required. Each weapon was given a code name to be used in future correspondence.[2]

Other documents suggested that George Shaw asked staffer Hans to take over negotiations and attempt to fill the weapons order. Hans later told investigators that he was reluctant to become involved in arms canvassing. Nevertheless, he said he wrote to every gun manufacturer in the world asking for brochures and price lists and supplied them to Hand, who had insisted that he needed as many weapons as possible, as soon as possible.

In mid-May 1975, Frank Nugan sent Bill Hans to Rhodesia to meet with Mike and arrange the transfer of funds to him 'through a corporate structure' that could never come back to haunt Nugan Hand.

While in South Africa, Hand registered a company called Murdoch Lewis Proprietary Ltd. In the late 1970s, branches of Murdoch Lewis would be registered in the United States to two other military men, Admiral Earl P Yates and General Edwin F Black. By then Admiral

Yates would be president of Nugan Hand and General Black the bank's Hawaii representative.

On arrival in Rhodesia, Hans found Michael Hand fixated by the weapons issue. He told Hans they were needed by whites in South Africa and Rhodesia, whom he said 'were concerned at the possibility of civil commotion'.[3]

According to a senior CIA officer overseeing the agency's Africa desk, John Stockwell, 'South Africa in 1975 was in a dangerously beleaguered position. Its blacks were increasingly restive, its whites emigrating, the white buffer states of Rhodesia, Mozambique and Angola were threatened and its economy was sagging.'[4]

If the buffer was breached, the South African and Rhodesian governments, and their white populations, believed that their own black populations would try to topple both apartheid regimes. The only answer to their problem was to arm the white populations of both countries.

Bill Hans told Michael Hand that when he made enquiries in Sydney he was told that the export of weapons from Australia or the United States to the apartheid governments of southern Africa was banned outright. Hand said that he had a way to overcome the legal roadblocks: ship the weapons through third party countries, like Singapore, Germany and Yugoslavia. He also confided in Bill Hans that his plans involved establishing a helicopter squadron in Rhodesia, which suggested that he was dealing with government and military officials, not merely white farmers.

The timing and urgency of Hand's mission related to events in nearby Angola. After centuries of Portuguese colonial rule and fifteen years of bloody guerilla warfare, Portugal had decided to hand Angola back to its people. The day of independence was set for 11 November 1975. In January 1975, a transitional government was established and the country's three competing liberation movements began preparations for elections in October. But in February, the transitional government disintegrated when forces of two of the movements, the FNLA and the Soviet backed MPLA, clashed in northern Angola.

In Washington, US Government military advisors believed the Soviet Union was backing the MPLA in order to facilitate a communist takeover of the country that would, in turn, allow the Soviets to exploit its extensive mineral reserves. The South African Government shared the same fears and moved a small contingent of soldiers into Angola, posing as mercenaries.

John Stockwell, whom the CIA made head of its Angola mission, believed that the South African Government was playing a dangerous game: 'With scarcely a friend in the world, it was inviting further condemnation by intervening in a black African country. And it was forced to run its program covertly, concealing it from its own people.'[5]

The US Government had no appetite to help South Africa, but the CIA was sympathetic to its plight. In fact, the CIA was already providing intelligence to the South African Bureau of State Security without the US Government's approval.

In mid-1975, US Secretary of State, Henry Kissinger, and CIA director, William Colby, put together a super-secret proposal, which was backed by the US National Security Council, to intervene in Angola and support two Angolan liberation movements, the FNLA and UNITA, by providing both with military hardware and training. Eighty-three CIA officers, headed by Stockwell, were soon spread across Angola, Congo, Rhodesia and South Africa, running a paramilitary operation, code-named IAFEATURE.[6]

The US Government wanted no Americans to be involved in the fighting in Angola, but the CIA ignored the government and set up training schools in neighbouring countries run by its paramilitary experts, who for cover purposes posed as 'intelligence gatherers'.[7]

The CIA's objective was not to win the war, but simply make life difficult for the Soviet Union and its allies, Cuba and North Korea, who were pouring crack troops and weapons into Angola. According to John Stockwell, CIA officers were also supervising the trans-shipment of arms directly into Angola, despite it being illegal to do so.

*

During his month-long stay in southern Africa, Bill Hans travelled into Angola with Mike Hand. How they were able to enter the war-torn country, when journalists and travellers were being denied entry, is unknown. Logically, the only explanation is that they were aided and abetted by Hand's former employer, the CIA.

On 20 August 1975, US President Gerald Ford authorised the purchase of more arms and ammunition for Angola. The arms were to be untraceable foreign weapons. That's where Michael Hand fitted neatly into the equation. Hand was a former CIA paramilitary officer and the bulk of his weapons communication with Nugan Hand occurred after August 1975, when the CIA began its paramilitary operations in southern Africa, centering on Angola.

Was Hand back working for the CIA or was he operating as a 'freelancer' on very good information supplied officially or unofficially by someone within the agency?

Hand certainly had connections right to the top of the CIA. In Laos, he had served under William Colby, who was now the agency's director. He had also served under the CIA's deputy director in Laos, Thomas Clines, who was now head of the CIA's 'dirty tricks' department. Clines was a friend of both Bernie Houghton and a former CIA officer dubbed 'the Great Gatsby of the spook world', Edwin P Wilson. In the early 1970s Wilson had been seconded to the US Office of Naval Intelligence (ONI) to run Task Force 157, which set up front companies around the world as cover for America's various

7 Turkey farming

spy agencies. While working for ONI, Wilson had amassed a tidy fortune selling weapons and explosives to rogue states without ONI's knowledge.

It was the Wilson–Houghton–Hand connection that would later have Australia's Joint Task Force investigators salivating. They believed that Houghton and two other Australians acting on behalf of Nugan Hand went to Washington DC and met with Ed Wilson to discuss obtaining weapons and munitions: 'As a result, Wilson used the cover of Task Force 157 proprietary companies to obtain weapons and munitions, which were subsequently delivered to someone in Africa, probably Michael Hand, who then delivered them to US intelligence–supported forces in Angola or Rhodesia.'[8]

The operation was carried out, the Joint Task Force suggested, as a result of 'private entrepreneurial activity as opposed to one officially sanctioned and executed by US intelligence authorities'.[9]

Wilson was certainly a double-dealer and a moonlighter. He made sure that for every deal he ever carried out in the name of Task Force 157, or the CIA, a percentage went into his pocket. At the same time, he was setting up his own business, supplying arms to rogue states.

There can be no doubt that Mike Hand had access to excellent intelligence, to which even members of the US Congress were not privy. This intelligence could only have come from within the CIA. If Mike Hand's arms trading exercise had been simply 'freelancing', it could not have happened without the CIA's imprimatur and logistical support.

For much of 1975, the American public and its elected representatives in Washington knew nothing about the CIA's activities in southern Africa. When allegations appeared in newspapers in September 1975 that the CIA was providing weapons to Angolan groups, and that Americans were involved in the fighting, CIA director William Colby denied them outright.[10]

The truth finally emerged at year's end when Colby was called to testify at two top-secret intelligence review hearings in Washington. During questioning at the Church Committee, headed by Senator Frank Church, Colby admitted that the CIA was secretly involved in the Angolan war. It was a sensational revelation. Astonished committee members complained that it looked like America was getting itself into another war like Vietnam.*

The Church Committee concluded that the CIA was running covert operations in South Africa and Rhodesia to prop up the apartheid governments — exactly what Michael Hand had admitted he was involved in to Bill Hans — activities that ran counter to US foreign policy and were illegal.

In January 1976, more details of Colby's in-camera testimony leaked to the press, leaving President Ford no option but to shut down the CIA's covert operations in southern Africa. Two weeks later, on 1 February 1976, Mike Hand contacted Frank Nugan by telex to say he was returning to Australia immediately 'as the political unrest in southern Africa was worsening'. Eight days later, the CIA acknowledged defeat and began to withdraw from southern Africa. Soon after, President Ford sacked William Colby.†

Three years later, Mike Hand recruited Colby as Nugan Hand's Washington-based legal advisor.

*

The abiding question is, how successful was Mike Hand's gunrunning exercise? Corporate Affairs Commission investigators later uncovered

---

* Members of the Church Committee scoffed at Colby's 'alarming and exaggerated' statements about the significance of Russian influence in Angola. In the opinion of Senator Church, the two factions in Angola were making use of both the Soviet Union and US in a civil war for their own purposes. 'Whichever side wins it will be Angolan, not Russian or American.' Church added, 'We don't belong in Angola.'

† President Ford originally fired Colby in November 1975 but re-hired him until he could find a suitable replacement.

an abundance of weapons-related telexes between Hand and the bank's Sydney and Hong Kong offices. Investigator Rick Porter and his colleagues attempted to follow the local weapons trail:

> We interviewed George Shaw. He suggested to us that he had participated in talking to a gun dealer in Foveaux Street, Surry Hills, in regard to the moving of guns, mainly hand pistols, to South Africa via Singapore. One day we decided to take a trip to Foveaux Street and came across a gun dealer called Loy. We went up and saw this funny office and saw this Mr Loy and said, 'We are investigators into Nugan Hand and we are here to talk to you about their gun dealing.' With that, this bloke ruffled his desk, and he had papers on his desk from six years earlier that dealt with the Nugan Hand approach for guns. So it was pure luck that we came across him.[11]

The investigators learned from the dealer that an order had been placed for twenty thousand handguns, but such a quantity was unable to be sourced from within Australia.

The investigators were not able to determine how many, if any, of the weapons deals went ahead, which was exactly what Mike Hand had intended. But, in 1987, *The New York Times* quoted an unnamed American who alleged that 'Mr Hand was involved in deals, including the profitable 1976 shipment of ten million rounds of ammunition and three thousand weapons, including rifles and machine guns, that went from Boston and were eventually delivered to US intelligence–supported forces in Angola.'[12]

In its second full year of operation, Nugan Hand had involved itself with gunrunning and money laundering for drug traffickers. In time, such activities would be revealed not as aberrations, but pivotal steps in the merchant bank's global expansion.

8

THE RETURN

One morning in March 1976, Bud King's former housekeeper answered a knock at the door of her Bondi flat. A smiling Mike Hand greeted Arina like an old friend. He asked if she'd like to come down to the street and sit in his car for a chat. Naively, the middle-aged Thai woman agreed. Hand said he had been away and only on his return had he heard about Bud King's death. He then asked how she was dealing with the loss of her friend.

Arina recalls Hand being charming. But when he asked about her financial position and whether she needed money, she sensed his power at play and felt a similar fear she had experienced three years back when she had been arrested.

Arina explained to Hand that she had a new job and was fine financially, then extricated herself from the car. She never saw Mike Hand again, but he remains a lingering menace in her mind to this day.[1]

*

A week or so before his visit to Arina, Mike Hand and his wife had flown back into Sydney from South Africa. Mike walked into the Macquarie Street office, handed back to Frank Nugan his original settlement cheque for $500,000 and officially rejoined the Nugan Hand bank. It was if he had never left.

Mike would have noticed a considerable change in Frank. On the positive side, Frank's Tennessee-born wife, Lee, had just given birth to a son. On the negative, he was only thirty-four, but looked ten years older. He had put on weight; most of it had lodged around his waist. It was rare these days to see him without a glass of whisky soda in one hand and a cigarette in the other. On his desk, a pack of king-sized Dunhill cigarettes was always within reach, along with a flipbook of matches, monogrammed with the Nugan Hand gold logo.

Mike returned to find that the bank was facing a liquidity crisis. Frank's increasingly lavish lifestyle was at least partly to blame. Against the advice of staffer Stephen Hill, Nugan had just exchanged contracts for the purchase of a waterfront home in the exclusive suburb of Vaucluse. Smack in the middle of Sydney's 'millionaires' row', the two-storey 1920s harbourside mansion, named Green Gables, featured a private beach, a jetty and a pool.

According to Les Collings from the Hong Kong office, on the day of settlement Frank turned up at the real estate agent's office with $450,000 in $20 bills, all of which was unsecured depositors' funds. Another staffer quipped that Frank had created a bank and then decided to rob it.

★

A disgruntled Nugan Hand executive later claimed that Michael Hand knew about as much of Nugan Hand's finances as he did about needlework.[2] Justice Philip Woodward, who questioned Hand in 1980, believed otherwise: 'He struck me as a man of quick, acute and aggressive intelligence, who would not meekly allow his business interests to be managed by others without his detailed knowledge and active guidance.[3]

Indeed, evidence suggested that Hand was immediately impressed with Frank's red-hot Contra scheme. Moving money around the world without detection offered all manner of possibilities, some of which he was eager to explore. In his absence, Frank had become the money launderer of choice for Australia's drug traffickers, helping to facilitate the movement of heroin, marijuana and hashish from the Far East to Australia and the United States.

At the Bourbon & Beefsteak, Mike Hand caught up with Bernie Houghton and his American compatriots, Harry Wainwright and Duke Countis. Wainwright was thankful that Frank Nugan had helped him move his money, but considered him a big drinker and a bigger talker and didn't trust him to 'keep mum' about his dealings with the bank. Hand must have appreciated the problem. He told Wainwright to come directly to him in future. He would oversee Wainwright's account, and those of his associate, Murray Riley.[*]

Wainwright and Riley were about to head off to the Philippines, ostensibly to work as extras on Francis Ford Coppola's epic Vietnam War movie, *Apocalypse Now*. Wainwright told people that he was a friend of Coppola. Off camera, Riley would put into play an ambitious plan to move drugs from Southeast Asia through Australia to the United States. Wainwright allegedly remained in the background as a middleman, while Duke Countis acted as facilitator between Nugan Hand and his friend Jimmy Fratianno, the Mafia hitman, and other American underworld figures.

★

---

[*] Interviewed at the Royal Commission into Drug Trafficking in 1980, Hand categorically denied that Nugan Hand had offered a facility to move funds from Australia to Hong Kong and claimed that he did not know of any method of moving money without Reserve Bank approval. Harry Wainwright contradicted Hand in his testimony. The royal commission believed Wainwright.

8 The return

In October 1976, Mike Hand moved to Hong Kong to drive Nugan Hand's global expansion. Four hundred people responded to newspaper advertisements to staff new offices in Kuala-Lumpur, Bangkok, Singapore and Manila. Mike asked Bernie Houghton to help him with the bank's international recruitment drive.

One of Bernie's old friends, retired US Rear Admiral Earl P Yates, was appointed as the first president of Nugan Hand International and as director of the Cayman Island branch. 'Buddy' as he liked to be called, had impressive credentials. He had captained the US aircraft carrier *John F Kennedy* and had been chief of staff for strategic planning for US forces in Asia and the Pacific. When it came to banking, though, Buddy Yates knew little more than how to empty a moneybox.

Yates introduced another financial novice, retired Brigadier US Army General Edwin Black, who became the bank's Hawaii representative. A string of other retired US military officers came along for the ride, including Dale Holmgren, Flight Services Manager for the CIA airline Civil Air Transport, who would run Nugan Hand's Taiwan branch.

Frank Nugan enthusiastically embraced the new recruits. They were high-calibre appointments and gave the bank both cachet and a semblance of credibility. But it was plainly evident that Mike Hand was looking more to Bernie Houghton than to Frank Nugan to chart the bank's future direction, as Joint Task Force investigator Clive Small later noted:

> Houghton was responsible for introducing what we called at the time 'the explosion of military personnel' within the bank. Houghton was clearly very influential with those people and I think it raises some interesting questions about what was actually Michael Hand's relationship with Bernie Houghton. You really start to believe, when you look at all the facts, that Hand felt subservient to Houghton, or that Houghton was a person to whom he had to give deference.[4]

9

WHAT HAPPENED AT THE CIRCUS

In late 1976, Mike Hand's army buddy Doug Sapper arrived in Hong Kong. Thirty-four years old, with closely cropped hair now permanently grey, the former Special Forces jungle fighter and sometime soldier of fortune had teamed up with a journalist to establish a trading company in the busiest import-export hub on the planet. For the first time in thirteen years, he felt he could find some normalcy, make a little money and take life a bit easier:

> The next thing I know I am in Hong Kong and I go down to buy this Chinese junk that I'd heard was for sale. The sign on the outside said to call the Nugan Hand bank. I thought, 'Strange name, Nugan Hand', but I didn't put two and two together. I called the number on the sign and talked to a man named Collings. He said, 'You need to talk to our head guy, his name is Michael Hand.' I said, 'Michael J Hand?' And he said, 'Yes, do you know him?' I said, 'If it is the one I am thinking of, I do.'

By now Nugan Hand had moved from its drab office on the wrong side of town to the eleventh floor of the impressive Connaught Centre, opposite the Star Ferry terminal on Hong Kong Island. With its distinctive circular windows, the Connaught was one of the most

9 What happened at the circus

desirable financial addresses on the island. Sapper recalled: 'I went up there and Les Collings took me into the office and there, sitting behind a desk, was Michael. Now that was a surprise. I was impressed. Here he was running an international bank!'[1]

From that day on, Sapper spent much of his free time with Mike at the gym, sailing on the harbour and socialising, and began to see Mike Hand in a new light:

> Michael was a kind of a dichotomy. If you saw him walking around in civilian clothes, a pair of Levis and a shirt, you wouldn't get the image of this self-made banker, this millionaire, but that was the image that he portrayed when he put on the suit and the tie and he was on stage. He was a salesman and he strived to be a good salesman. He wanted to know all of the psychological nuances of a prospective customer: body language, the timing. He could have built the Ark, if he was so motivated, and he would have got you involved in it. You just wanted to be with Michael, you wanted to help him. You wanted to be on board.[2]

Over a buffet lunch at the Hilton Hotel, Sapper realised that his old army buddy was sizing him up for something.

'Well, well, Douglas A Sapper III from Mount Vernon, Illinois,' Mike quipped with a curious smile. Sapper told him to spit out whatever it was he was chewing on. Hand said he had heard reports about his escapades in Cambodia and elsewhere, and now wanted to hear it from the horse's mouth. Sapper did his best to deflect the question.

'Hell, that's like asking me what happened at the circus.'[3]

★

Sapper had certainly seen a great deal of drama since he had last seen

Mike in Sydney back in the R&R days. In fact, it was a miracle he was still alive. In the early 1970s, after leaving the army, he had taken a position as vice president of Southeast Asia Air Transport, a contract CIA airline based at Pochentong Airport in Phnom Penh, Cambodia. With Cambodia in the midst of a drawn-out civil war, his primary responsibility was the security of a fleet of twenty-five aircraft, including US military planes, which carried out clandestine mercenary transport sorties for the CIA inside Cambodia and across Laos. The United States and South Vietnam were propping up the Khmer state in its conflict with the forces of the Communist Party of Kampuchea, known as the Khmer Rouge. But with the Vietnam War all but lost, and the Americans looking to cut their losses in the region, the Khmer Rouge rose to the ascendency and looked set to take over the country.

By March 1975, the Khmer Rouge had encircled the capital, Phnom Penh. Activity at the airport was chaotic. Sapper camped in his small office, where he laid awake night after night, listening and waiting for the inevitable attack. It came on 5 March in the form of massive rocket and shelling assault on the airport, which destroyed dozens of aircraft, including one of Sapper's DC-4s. In the eerie quiet the next day, two Cambodian men approached Sapper as he left his office. He'd never seen them before, but by the looks they were giving each other, he assumed they were intent on killing him, there and then. When the lead fellow looked to his associate as if to say 'Now!', Sapper pulled out a pistol and shot them both dead.

At the peak of the bombing raids on the airport, Sapper arrived at the gate of the US embassy in Phnom Penh dressed in shorts, sneakers, a baseball cap and a T-shirt depicting Richard Nixon as Superman. In his right hand, he was carrying a double-barrelled shotgun; in his left, a military-issue khaki body bag. The bag contained the torso of an American pilot of a DC-3, which had crashed at Pochentong a few hours earlier. Sapper had taken it upon himself to extract the young American from the burned-out wreckage in order to arrange a decent burial. Journalist Anthony Paul witnessed the event. 'Risking one's life to accommodate a dead stranger and his distant parents suggested old-fashioned, higher qualities,' he wrote.[4]

In April 1975, the US Congress forced President Gerald Ford to end assistance to the Cambodian Government. Ford ordered the closure of the US embassy in Phnom Penh and the evacuation of all Americans and some Cambodians, including Acting President Sau Kham Khoy.

Sapper participated in the evacuation, code-named 'Operation Eagle Pull'. Close to nine hundred American nationals, Cambodians and third-country nationals were safely evacuated to US ships. As the last choppers flew out, the Khmer Rouge closed to within 1500 metres of the airport. Instead of joining the exodus, Sapper remained to look after employees of his firm, who weren't eligible for US evacuation flights.

Sapper later penned an article for a US newspaper about the evacuation:

> In those days, we saw people fleeing through the streets in panic, witnessed eerie scenes of a city of two million being cleared of its residents and heard of executions and the wholesale takeover of personal property by the tough new regime. Every day, there was gunfire throughout the city around us. I saw a country die and caught glimpses of a new Cambodia, one without traces of the more recent past. There were crowds of people on the rooftops and in the streets looking up to see the American helicopters do their air show in the sky. The Cambodians thought the US Marines were coming to save Phnom Penh. They didn't realise the American embassy was being evacuated and this was the end. I told some of those around me. It was like telling a kid that Santa Claus was dead.[5]

Following the evacuation, everything left behind was looted, including staff cars. The Associated Press quoted Sapper, who had lost 12 pounds in weight during the ordeal: 'I always thought my hometown was screwed up, but it's looking pretty good right now.'[6]

The American embassy was evacuated on 12 April 1975, and for the next five days until the government fell on the 17th, Sapper turned his attention to a little housekeeping:

> In that period of time I was a pretty busy guy. I opened up filing cabinets and dropped thermo-grenades in there. I put stuff in a 55-gallon drum and put aviation gas in it and torched it. I was shredding documents, because I realised we were going to get overrun here and anyone who worked for us was at great risk of getting their head cut off.[7]

By this stage, Sapper had become the eyes and ears of the US Government in Phnom Penh. His reports on the executions of high-level Cambodian Government officials were transmitted via the American embassy in Bangkok to the US Secretary of State in Washington. During that period of total mayhem, the rebels were moving into Phnom Penh, taking the city street-by-street and house-by-house. One morning, American freelance journalist Lee Rudakewych ran into Sapper's lodgings shouting that the Khmer Rouge forces were coming. Sapper grabbed some clothes and hopped into a car for the 800-metre dash to the French embassy:

> There was firing in front of the embassy and B40 rockets were going off nearby. We did one of those crouched runs across the street, pounded on the gate and then jumped over the compound fence. Bullets were ricocheting off the embassy walls. Things began to happen fast. The Khmer Rouge was all over the place.

There was intense firing and then all of a sudden you heard cheering and saw people running out of bushes and from behind walls. Motorcycles started driving up and down the street in front of us with guys on the back waving white flags. It built up into a crescendo, with people dashing around and embracing the Khmer Rouge soldiers in a carnival atmosphere. There was still sporadic firing but strangely nobody flinched or ducked. It wasn't long after that about half a dozen top government leaders arrived at the French embassy compound. The president of Cambodia's National Assembly was searched for weapons; the searchers found two in his briefcase. The French diplomats let the Cambodian officials stay in their compound but said they could give them no assurances of safety. In the afternoon there was a sudden commotion and hundreds of people started coming over the fence. The French were trying to shove them back but it was useless. There were more and more and they were spreading out and running like ants.[8]

Succumbing to a sudden surge of defiance, Sapper said he was planning to take a machine gun and storm up to the roof of the US embassy to raise the American flag and 'kill as many Commies as I can'.[9] On realising that he could have been shot on the spot, he wisely decided simply to burn the flag to prevent the Khmer troops using it as propaganda to humiliate the United States.

Meanwhile, the French ambassador had negotiated an exit with Khmer leadership. Sapper and two newspapermen — the last three Americans in the country — were chosen for the first convoy out of the capital: 'Three and a half days after leaving the French embassy we reached the border. I felt an indescribable happiness walking across that bridge into Thailand, but there was also sadness. I left behind too many people who I knew would not come out well.'[10]

At the border, Sapper gave American officials a statement about what he had seen, the countenance of the Khmer Rouge and the fate of some of the Cambodian officials. Sapper's detailed report was instrumental in the US Government convincing journalists to hold back on reporting the evacuation until everyone trapped in the French embassy had been convoyed to the Thai border.

Later that day, Sapper and an American journalist rented a car and drove to Bangkok and moved into the Trocadero Hotel, which Sapper knew from his times on R&R during the Vietnam War. He was home free, or so he thought.

The following year, the Thai military staged a coup d'état, ousting the elected civilian government. The military raided hotels popular with foreign nationals. At the Trocadero, which Sapper had maintained as his base, they discovered a trove of weapons in Sapper's name in the hotel storage and believed that they had foiled a revolutionary plot to overthrow the monarchy. Sapper was charged with sedition and thrown in jail with hundreds of other suspects. Three days later, he was inexplicably released from custody. Back at his hotel, he was 'dragged over the coals' by a person Sapper simply described as his 'handler'.[11]

By the next morning, Sapper had decided to extricate himself from the handler, get out of Bangkok and head on up to Hong Kong for good. Douglas A Sapper III from Mount Vernon, Illinois, was now looking for a fresh start.

★

Over their lunch at the Hong Kong Hilton, Michael Hand said he could use someone with Sapper's security background, someone he could trust for various purposes, 'who won't blow it out of the water'. Sapper liked the idea, especially when he was to be paid cash for his trouble:

You could say that I was the confidante and the trusted friend that Michael could call and say, 'I've got something for you to do. Go out to the airport and meet this guy, he's bringing in money. Make sure it gets back here to the office.' One day, Michael and I went to the airport to pick up some money that was being shipped in. In Hong Kong you can't have any weapons; you couldn't carry a machete and you'd never want to get caught with a gun in Hong Kong. So before we went to the airport, we went and bought a couple of hockey sticks and took them with us. I'm thinking, 'Oh yes, a bunch of guys are going to run up like they do in the movies and are going to grab these packages from us and we are going to be flailing them with hockey sticks.' [laughs] I used to refer to that as the 'hockey stick play.' [12]

Sapper witnessed a lot of money coming and going from the Nugan Hand bank. One of the most memorable deposits was handed over by a Chinese lumber merchant:

I think the amount was about $10 million and he just tossed it on the table and told Michael to do something with it and turned around to leave and Michael said, 'Don't you want a receipt?' and he said, 'Why? If you are going to fuck me, you are going to fuck me whether I have a receipt or not. I'll be back in two weeks.'

When you see several million dollars in hundred dollar bills on top of a table, you go, 'My God!' You want to take your clothes off and roll in it, like a dog rolling in a dead rabbit, or something. It is very seductive and it's very hard to walk away from. You just get so intoxicated with the power and the money.[13]

Sapper quarantined the cash he earned from his trading company books in a deliberate attempt to keep his dealings with Nugan Hand from his business partner:

> I wasn't a full-time Nugan Hand employee. I had my own business. I never told my partner about Michael and all the other shit, because he was a journalist, foremost. Although I trusted him, I didn't trust him with operational information because he was a little bit flaky when it came to keeping his damn mouth shut.

*

Under British rule, Hong Kong was a kind of Far East Disneyland for Western businessmen. The sweetly pungent air, thick with incense; the narrow alleyways crowded with stalls; the squawking of caged fowls; the unexpected bursts of fireworks; the clattering of mahjong tiles; and the harbour busy with sampans, fishing junks and ferries — all had a hypnotising effect on many a grey-suited, 'big-nosed' *gweilo*.*

At night, below the clutter of Chinese-lettered neon signs, girls wearing ruby-red lipstick and glitter dresses tempted the wealthy foreigners to let their reptilian instincts take hold. From his days on R&R in Hong Kong, Sapper could tell the difference between the locals, the refugees from the mainland and the international five-star escorts. Such knowledge was gold, especially now that his responsibilities included being the bank's social secretary:

> I was the official pimp for Nugan Hand. When somebody

---

* Foreign devil

came they wanted to impress, I arranged the pussy for them. That was a great job. Michael would call and say we need to get some girls for so and so. In most cases they were call girls — there was a Jamaican girl we used quite a bit. I think it's the old story — power corrupts.[14]

As social secretary, Sapper also got to eat out at some of the best restaurants in the colony and hobnob with the greats and near greats in the Nugan Hand circle:

I remember Frank Nugan came to town and Frank was smoking big cigars and kind of playing the Godfather. He was always a little bit larger than life. You know, he's kind of like a 600-pound gorilla; he sleeps where he wants to sleep. If you stood in Frank's way he became very threatened and belligerent. Then again, wherever he went around the world it was his opportunity to tap dance, to tell great stories and make everybody laugh and sell them the Frank Nugan brand. In Hong Kong he probably had more of a power aura than he had in Australia: 'Oh, yes, that is Frank Nugan in Hong Kong. Big man on campus.' I think Frank was very much into making himself something other than he was. He was a lawyer, his family was in the fruit business and that is a somewhat nefarious trade. But I think Frank was trying to hold onto that edge, that 'Hey, I come from a rough side of town but I'm also polished and suave and wear expensive shoes and smoke big cigars, and, oh, by the way, those are my two Mercedes.'[15]

According to Sapper, following the boardroom meetings and the glad-handing, Frank was on the prowl:

> He was rocking and rolling. He wasn't a bad-looking guy, just big, gregarious, crude in many ways, reeking of cigar smoke, but I tell you what, there were a lot of women who found that very, very attractive. What helps is the patois, the syntax and diction of the game. You are talking money, you are talking investments, you are talking stocks: 'Oh, yes, I had lunch with the Shah of Iran two days ago,' or, 'I just had lunch with Imelda Marcos,' or whatever. A lot of people who having nothing else going on in their life go, 'Wow, this guy is a real power player.' Of course, you have women who think, 'If I can just land this guy I'm on easy street.' [16]

Sapper also got to meet a number of the bank's new high-powered recruits:

> Most of them were ex-military. Okay, you [Admiral Buddy Yates] were the commander of an aircraft carrier; we are going to make you the president of the bank. You were the commander of the base in the Philippines in Clark Field [General Leroy Manor]. I never asked to see their resume, but from what I could make out none of them had banking experience. If I'm not mistaken the marquee over the door in gold letters said, 'Nugan Hand Bank'. I am amazed they didn't have Chinese fry cooks working there. I'm not even sure that speaking English might have been a requirement. I am just being humorous, but, truth be known, who had any banking experience?

Indeed.

10

THE HUB OF GOOD AND EVIL

During the mid-1970s, barely a week passed in Hong Kong without a new skyscraper rising from nowhere to punch its way through the South China Sea haze. Hong Kong was transforming itself from a bustling manufacturing centre into a financial powerhouse. More than half a million locals, who traditionally hid their hard-earned cash in their mattresses, were now investing in stocks. Soon, there were more brokerage houses and banks in Hong Kong than sampans on the harbour. While the big international firms vied for supremacy in the market, small, often unscrupulous, operators scrambled for the crumbs. Enter Nugan Hand (Hong Kong) Ltd.

According to law, banks were required to have minimum capital of HK$5 million. For the first two years of its operations Nugan Hand simply flew under the radar, collecting deposits and facilitating Australian drug traffickers' use of its money-laundering Contra system.

In 1976, the authorities passed an ordinance that forced smaller, deposit-taking, non-licensed bank entities, like Nugan Hand, to register with the government and have paid-up capital of HK$2.5 million. By stripping funds from its other international branches, Nugan Hand fudged the books enough to present 'a picture of affluence'. According to Australian corporate investigators, the paid-up capital in Hong Kong was a 'cosmetic contrivance' and 'no more than a sham'.[1]

In reality, they were walking a financial tightrope that could snap at any minute. To make Frank Nugan's Contra system work, the bank needed to cover the demand with funds from local Hong Kong depositors. According to Rick Porter, if an Australian trafficker turned up and the money wasn't available due to a shortfall in deposits then things would get ugly back in Sydney:

> It is dangerous, obviously, especially when you are dealing with members of drug syndicates. If anything went wrong it could have dire consequences because they wouldn't be going to court to sue Frank Nugan. I think they would pursue him personally and extract vengeance out of him if they didn't receive their money overseas.[2]

In Hong Kong, Doug Sapper found that Michael Hand was not overly particular about the calibre of the bank's depositors:

They have gangs in Hong Kong called Triads and in many cases they have tentacles into China. They control prostitution, drugs, illegal gambling, and for these guys using the word unsavoury would be an upgrade. They didn't announce who they were. It is not like they had business cards that said 'Triad Incorporated', but just from their looks and demeanour you knew these guys were not noodle merchants from the alleys in Hong Kong.[3]

When Nugan Hand opened its office, Hong Kong was experiencing a tidal wave of Triad-related crime. Some of the Triad networks had moved into exporting prostitution and drugs around the world. When the United States started cracking down on Hong Kong's role in the growth of the illicit drug trade, the Triads became more sophisticated in how they operated. They evolved corporate structures and employed financiers to seek out legitimate-looking enterprises that could move money undetected by any law-enforcement agency. According to Doug Sapper, Nugan Hand was one of those enterprises:

> It wasn't like they littered the lobby of Nugan Hand every day. But every once in a while you'd see a couple of them leaving or coming in. They weren't dressed like dock workers, but there are some rough edges you can't polish off. They just didn't look like they fitted into those suits they were wearing. They are the underbelly. So you can get a little concerned when they are around.[4]

Investigators later came to believe that Michael Hand first connected with Hong Kong's crime syndicates in 1976 via Murray Riley, after Riley started using Nugan Hand's Contra scheme to facilitate his drug deals. Riley's partner in the drug business was John Doyle, an English-born Australian citizen who had lived in Hong Kong since 1960. Doyle had developed close relations with senior members of at least two major Triad groups that had connections with major drug figures in Thailand, Singapore and Manila.[5] Coincidentally, Nugan Hand proceeded to open offices in those three countries.

After a dozen years moving around Southeast Asia, Sapper's contacts reached far and wide. 'In the Philippines, I introduced Michael to the wealthy family of Imelda Marcos, the wife of President Marcos. And I introduced Nugan Hand to a lot of the shadier characters in that area because I had some inroads and contacts.'[6]

In early 1977, Hand called by Sapper's apartment and asked him out for a meal. 'Michael and I were having dinner and talking and he said, "Hey, do you know anybody in Chiang Mai? We're going to open up an office there; can you introduce us?" I said, "Yes, I know somebody."'[7]

Sapper had contacts all the way up and down the Thai food chain; he warned Hand of the obvious perils of setting up business in that part of the world:

> Chiang Mai is the Wild West, the hub of good and evil, but mostly evil. You've got everybody from Burmese agents, the people in the Shan State Army, the Karen Army, the Thai intelligence community. You've got everybody running around, and you have to be very careful. That landscape is extremely volatile and it is extremely dangerous, and so, if you are going to go in there and muck around, you need to know the players and you need to know the *game de jour*.[8]

The danger stemmed from Chiang Mai's location — it's the gateway to the infamous Golden Triangle, which since the Vietnam War has produced much of the world's opiates.

> When I was in Chiang Mai, I could find an opium den faster than a McDonalds. You have the Golden Triangle, the underbelly of Burma and Laos and China on the Thai border, and the opium was being smuggled over the border and would go to several different places to turn it into heroin then be shipped all over the world through Bangkok, a major trans-shipment point for heroin.[9]

Sapper knew more than a thing or two about drugs. His father and grandfather were both pharmacists. In the 1950s, they were both convicted in Illinois for supplying dextroamphetamine and other drugs without prescriptions. But it was thanks to his family background that Sapper was selected for medic training in the US Special Forces.

During the Vietnam War, he dished out drugs, legal and illegal, to his military colleagues and friends, including *Rolling Stone* journalist Hunter S Thompson. In his book *Fear and Loathing in America*, Thompson included a letter he penned to Doug Sapper: 'Doug … This is just a quick note to say thanx again for The Help, as it were in Bangkok. At 50 cents a hit, that shit is the cheapest miracle on the market — except maybe for that 25 cents a pound weed those dope-addict bastards were smoking up in Laos.'

Sapper introduced Mike Hand to people he knew and trusted in Chiang Mai:

> Because of my contacts in the Golden Triangle area in Thailand and Laos, I also put Michael in contact with the opium smugglers. These guys up in Burma had money coming out of their fucking wazoo. And you can't spend it up there in the mountains; 'rice and pussy' is pretty cheap. So they would have had to have a way to move it. What better way than Nugan Hand bank? Then, of course, I facilitated helping Michael move money around.[10]

Nugan Hand employed thirty-eight-year-old Neil Evans to run the Chiang Mai office.[11] The hard-drinking, hard-playing, hard-gambling Australian arrived in Chiang Mai in February 1977 on a tourist visa. He set up a temporary office in an apartment at the Rincome Hotel, before moving to an office building. He later told investigators: 'The whole thing was laid on the table. I was never under any illusion at any time that I was to go over there for any other purpose but to seek out drug money.'[12]

Nugan Hand's investment in Chiang Mai, according to Doug Sapper, was inversely proportional to the risk. 'This was a pretty much bare-bones cheap deal: a desk, some radios, hire a car and a driver, two guys working there. If you have to, you can turn out the lights, go out the back door and head for the airport. You don't have to be there the next morning.'[13]

NSW Liberal Party politician John Dowd flew from Sydney to Chiang Mai to investigate the Nugan Hand office:

> I decided to enquire about Australian connections with Thailand but particularly the Nugan Hand bank. I went up to Chiang Mai. Having an address, I walked up the stairs, looked at two adjoining offices, one of which was the Nugan Hand bank and on its left was the US Drug Enforcement Agency. I was gob smacked. Chiang Mai is not a small one-horse town; there had to be a connection and a deliberate connection.[14]

Evans later admitted that locating the Nugan Hand office next door to DEA was intentional. 'I couldn't see any point in trying to gild the lily with him [the DEA agent], so I landed right in his lap and told him that I was over there to seek deposits and I was going to meet a lot of very heavy people in the course of seeking those deposits.'[15]

Evans allegedly told the DEA agent that he would pass on any information that 'actually proved [people] were heavily involved in drugs'. Joint Task Force investigators later concluded that the offer of information was clearly wilful deceit:

> The tenor of his admissions is that the offer was a sham, the purpose of which was an attempt to ensure that he would not be impeded in his activities. Perhaps coincidentally, perhaps not, the Manila office of Nugan Hand was also in the same building as the US Drug Enforcement Agency office in that city.[16]

Joint Task Force investigator Clive Small interrogated Neil Evans:

Evans claimed that he shared secretarial services with the DEA and that he often socialised with them, in particular playing cards with them and also a CIA representative who was there. Neil Evans was a person whom we regarded with some caution. But if you look at the fundamental proposition of why the Chiang Mai office was set up, his version of that is consistent with what we were told independently.[17]

In February 1981, Evans appeared on a television current affairs program in Australia, where he justified his part in the movement of drug money:

> I realised from the start what I was doing was totally illegal, but my main consideration was to get in quickly and make what I could out of it and get out just as quickly. As long as I didn't actually step over the line and physically handle drugs I had no qualms about doing what I [was doing] … And what this bank did is in effect not very far removed from what goes on every day through the normal banking system throughout every country in the world. They've all got their fingers in the pie; the pie I am talking about is black money.[18]

The idea for setting up the Chiang Mai office was traced to Murray Riley, whose drug shipments of heroin and marijuana were sourced from Thailand and destined for major American crime syndicates. Says Joint Task Force investigator Clive Small:

> We were told that Riley had discussions with Hand about the establishment of offices in Thailand, in Chiang Mai, where drug money could be attracted and that it had a lot of potential, both in terms of getting money out of Thailand, but

also, importantly, getting money from Australia to Thailand for Australian-based criminals, who were entering into that country.[19]

Neil Evans later testified that only two people within the bank knew the real purpose of the Chiang Mai branch: Michael Hand and the executive from the Sydney office who recruited him.* For reasons unknown, Hand wanted Frank Nugan kept out of the loop.

---

* During questioning by investigators, the executive, who threatened legal action if he was named, denied he knew the reason for setting up Chiang Mai. Asked if he knew the significance of Chiang Mai and the Golden Triangle to the international drug trade he said, 'In 1977, I had no knowledge of any significance attaching to Chiang Mai and the Golden Triangle. I still do not know of its significance, if any.'

11

PAYMASTER

In mid-1977, Neil Evans and his Bangkok counterpart, John Owen, flew to Hong Kong and booked into the Excelsior Hotel. A message awaited them: 'Meet me in the lobby bar at 6.30, Mike.'

John Owen, a former career officer in the British Navy who worked for Nugan Hand from 1976 to 1979, recalled the subsequent meeting in his published memoir, *Sleight of Hand*:

> An enormous bulk of a man came barging through the revolving door of the hotel; he wandered up to us and by way of greeting said, 'Hi fellows! I'm Mike Hand, guess you're awaiting me?' He was dressed in creased cotton trousers, a see-through, dark blue fishnet singlet and thongs on his feet. His transparent singlet revealed rather protuberant breasts, like a dugong's, on a torso shaped like a beer barrel. Out of the corner of his mouth protruded a half-chewed toothpick, which he waggled up and down with his teeth. His small piggy grey eyes, button nose and mean mouth that could never smile properly, set Hand aside from other people. Evans' parting shot before retiring was, 'I'm not impressed by all that swagger.' How he had managed to make those millions eluded me.[1]

While in Hong Kong, Neil Evans attended a meeting at the Nugan Hand office during which Michael Hand made a startling revelation:

> He told me that he'd been successful in arranging a contract with the CIA, whereby the bank was to become its paymaster, if you like, for disbursement of funds anywhere in the world on behalf of the CIA, and also for the taking in of money on behalf of the CIA. The idea was that money would be deposited with the Nugan Hand bank by the CIA through various channels and also that the Nugan Hand bank would be the repository for funds coming in from various CIA enterprises, namely drugs in Thailand — marijuana in particular — and that the Nugan Hand bank would then be responsible for re-routing that money to an account in America with a New York bank.[2]

Of all the allegations that would be made against the bank, these were the most politically charged. The Joint Task Force investigators concluded, 'Their significance to this investigation is of course crucial, as they go to the fundamental question: who controlled Nugan Hand at the time of its involvement in illegal and questionable activities in, or affecting, Australia.'[3]

★

Neil Evans was taken aback at the idea of dealing with the CIA:

> Terrified, in a word terrified. As I was going down in the lift, I was thinking to myself, 'Well how in the hell am I going to get out of this gracefully?' because it was quite obvious to me that I had to get out, I couldn't become involved in this ... The CIA

are the heaviest people on earth, life was ultra-cheap to them. I just didn't want to be part of it.[4]

By mid-July 1977, Evans had resolved to extricate himself from the bank. He concocted a story that he was ill with hepatitis, which he backed up with a doctor's certificate. He then flew back to Australia 'for treatment' and never returned to Nugan Hand.

Evans later recalled that Mike Hand had told him that the CIA deal was not to be discussed with anyone, even Frank Nugan and warned him to have 'no contact whatsoever with Nugan about his dealings in Chiang Mai.'

If Mike Hand had grounds to mistrust his business partner, they were about to be amplified many times over in the months to come.

12

RICOCHET

No one came forward to say they heard the shots, but their impact ricocheted across Australia. On 15 July 1977, Donald Mackay, a small-business owner in Frank Nugan's home town of Griffith, disappeared from a hotel car park after having drinks with friends. The police found bloodstains on Mackay's van and on the ground nearby. His car keys were found beneath his vehicle. Drag marks, clumps of hair and three spent .22-calibre cartridges suggested Mackay had been assassinated on the spot and his body removed by the killer or killers.

Donald Mackay's murder had all the hallmarks of a political killing. He was the Griffith branch president of the Liberal Party and a staunch anti-drugs campaigner, who had caused the arrest of a number of locals of Italian descent.

Mackay's death stunned the nation. John Hatton, an independent member in the NSW upper house, told parliament that 'The Mafia killed Mackay.' Three weeks later, the NSW Government set up the Royal Commission into Drug Trafficking (also known as the Woodward Royal Commission after the judge who chaired it, Philip Morgan Woodward) to investigate the links between the Mafia, corrupt police and Mackay's disappearance. Clive Small was one of the investigators assisting the commissioner:

I think the history of Griffith is quite an interesting one and a unique one in many ways in Australia. It was largely developed by Calabrian migrants. They worked very hard but were never able to afford mansions. In the late 1960s, or by 1970 at least, Bob Trimboli, who'd had a number of financial problems, got into the drug trade and started growing a couple of small marijuana crops in western Sydney and a couple of other places. By 1972, Trimboli had introduced a number of Griffith families from Calabria into the drug trade. I am talking about Tony Sergi of the winery and others. Trimboli said basically, 'Look if I can grow a very small crop and make this sort of money imagine what we can do if you can grow one that involves acres.' It went from crops in back yards, to crops of 30 acres over a couple of years. A lot of money was made very rapidly and a lot of money was spent very rapidly. All of a sudden we had these huge houses being built. Money seemed no object. There were also a number of arrests made during those early-to-mid-1970s and it just tied the suspicion of Griffith residents back to certain families. The families flaunting all this money were connected with people who were being arrested, and so you have this link being formed. We also saw a number of these people pleading guilty and getting very lenient sentences and that caused a lot of anger and the flaunting of the money didn't stop. Don Mackay started raising questions about the issue, saying, 'This is disgraceful. There are a lot of honest people here, but the town is getting a reputation.'[1]

Small believes Don Mackay had become such an impediment and distraction for the cannabis growers that they came together and arranged for him to be removed from the picture. 'Bob Trimboli organised the murder, but others were clearly involved as well, in making the decision for the murder. That really pushed things over the top, that's when the government said, "We are getting such a beating here; we have to do something."[2]

As the Woodward Royal Commission began its inquiries, rumours surfaced that the Nugan Fruit Group was also going to be investigated. At the time, the Nugan family, which owned 50 per cent of the company, was at war with an insurance company and two other corporations, which together held a 30 per cent shareholding. Central to the dispute was Frank Nugan, a director, who was divisive and appeared to have personally benefited from a number of 'irregular' land deals that lost money for the group. With Ken Nugan's position as chairman under threat from the other shareholders, Frank reluctantly agreed to relinquish his directorship. But peace did not return.

Soon afterwards, the group's external auditors, Hungerfords, uncovered evidence of bank accounts in false names and suspected that Ken Nugan was offering payola to Woolworths' staff in return for the placement of orders. Hungerfords came to the conclusion that the Nugan Fruit Group was engaged in fraud.

Ken Nugan called up his brother in the hope that he could sort out the crisis. Frank's approach was to confront the nut with a sledgehammer, as Attorney-General Frank Walker explained:

> At that stage, the company started to behave very badly indeed. The first thing they did was to sack the independent directors who were screaming, 'What about this money?' The next thing we hear is that two ex-Breaking Squad detectives, with notorious reputations as standover men and hit men, had been employed as private detectives, Krahe and Kelly, to look after the matter.[3]

Fifty-seven-year-old Fred Krahe was considered the king of crooked detectives and one of the most feared figures in the Sydney underworld.

During his long police career, he had allegedly framed criminals and organised armed hold-ups and even murders.

Underworld figure George Freeman knew Krahe personally. 'Krahe was deadly and evil. It was a measure of the fear the man generated in both crooks and police that he was never brought to justice. Everybody was frightened of him. He had a feared reputation as a killer.'[4]

Krahe's partner, forty-four-year-old Keith Kelly was of a similar ilk. The police suspected Kelly of having links to drug trafficker and Nugan Hand client Murray Riley.

Under instructions from the Nugan brothers, Krahe and Kelly visited the homes of the auditors at night. The wife of one auditor answered a doorbell to find Krahe in the front yard, patting the family dog. When such intimidation failed to bring the desired results, the Nugan brothers decided to be rid of the auditors once and for all.

They called an extraordinary board meeting to be held in Sydney on 27 October 1977. Previous meetings had attracted no more than thirty shareholders. This time, 250 shareholders attended, of whom 194 were newly registered. The new shareholders voted en bloc according to the vote of Fred Krahe, who stood up and raised his hand in support of every motion put forward by Ken Nugan. On a show of hands, 81.5 per cent voted for expulsion of the auditors.

The following day, the outraged minority shareholders began analysing a list of the new shareholders. They discovered that two dozen of them were either directors or staff of the Nugan Hand bank, including Mike Hand and his wife, Helene. The register also included former policemen, criminals and two Sydney Airport security officers, both of whom were later investigated for alleged involvement with drug traffickers Murray Riley and Ken Derley.

Some of the new shareholders had not even attended the meeting. Krahe and Kelly had simply arranged for other people to forge their signatures to gain admittance to the meeting.[5]

State Liberal parliamentarian John Dowd was alarmed by the brutal actions taken by the Nugans to take control of their company:

> I was approached by a fellow I knew through the Liberal Party about the intimidation of Hungerfords, the auditors. I was a reasonably new member of parliament, but I investigated that story, including the fraudulent shareholder action. So I decided that I would raise this issue in the parliament.[6]

In a remarkable move, Dowd called on his political adversary, Labor Attorney-General Frank Walker, for support:

> I went to the attorney-general's office to give him a courtesy notification as to what I was going to raise in question time. I thought I'd get a more intelligent response. Frank Walker, with whom I had a reasonable working relationship, said, 'You realise of course that there are a couple of members of your party going to be brought out in this?' I said, 'You think I care?' and he said, 'Okay, thank you,' or words to that effect.[7]

In the coming weeks, a disgruntled Nugan Fruit Group company secretary went public with sensational allegations. The firm, he said, had handed over cash cheques to a company called Sergi, Sergi and Trimbole. Two of the company's principals were the convicted drug growers Bob Trimbole and Antonio Sergi, both of whom were being investigated by the Woodward Royal Commission and suspected of involvement in the murder of Donald Mackay.*

---

* In 1979, Justice Woodward found that a hit man employed by the 'Honoured Society', a Griffith-based cell of the 'Ndrangheta, a Calabrian criminal organisation, had murdered Mackay. In his final report, Justice Woodward concluded that the members of the 'Honoured Society' involved in Mackay's murder were Francesco Sergi, Domenic Sergi, Antonio Sergi, [another] Antonio Sergi, Francesco Barbaro and Robert Trimbole.

12 Ricochet

Frank Nugan's heavy-handed strategies of intimidating auditors and stacking the shareholder meeting had backfired and delivered a far bigger problem.

The Nugan brothers sought urgent advice from city solicitor John Aston. With the help of his well-connected law clerk, Brian Alexander, Aston had been building a sizable practice representing crooked law-enforcement officers, white-collar fraudsters and drug traffickers, including people on Nugan Hand's books.

Ken Nugan told Aston that the names on the cash cheques, Trimbole and Sergi, were simply code names for other people who wanted to remain anonymous for tax purposes. How Aston responded is unknown, but that explanation would later be met with incredulity by the courts, the minority shareholders and Attorney-General Walker:

> This was a case where I thought there was a lot of smoke and there was a lot of fire. There were crooked policemen, there were respectable auditors being removed and harassed from their positions, criminals being used to go to meetings to kick them out, money being paid to Trimbole and Sergi, so I thought there was a great deal of reason to investigate this case.[8]

On Remembrance Day, 11 November 1977, Walker stood up in the NSW Parliament and thanked his political rival John Dowd for raising the allegations about the Nugan Fruit Group. He then announced that he had ordered the Corporate Affairs Commission to investigate the company. Remembrance Day now not only marked the end of the Great War, it symbolised the beginning of a new war between the Nugan family and crime-busting politicians Frank Walker and John Dowd.

Ken Nugan called a media conference at which he strongly denied any association between his company and people named in the Royal

Commission into Drug Trafficking. He said that the development of his business was among the most creditable of migrant success stories; his parents, he explained, were Spanish and had arrived in Australia to get away from the threat of fascism and war.

Such protestations did little to persuade nervous Nugan Hand investors, who were soon contacting the bank. Frank insisted that he had nothing to do with his brother's problems and threatened to sue anyone who implied that he did.

In Thailand, John Owen had his doubts about Frank Nugan's declaration of innocence:

> Sitting in my branch office in Bangkok, I couldn't help but speculate about the disappearance and probable murder of Donald Mackay and I wondered just how deeply my employers were committed to the drug business. When I pressed Collings on this matter all he could say was 'Well do you know what I think? The NSW Attorney-General has got it in for Frank!' 'What do you mean?' I asked him. He said, 'Well, Frank moves in political circles and looks after the money of rich clients and is naturally regarded as an enemy by less successful socialist solicitors, such as the Attorney-General. He is on record as saying that he is out to get Frank.'[9]

Despite Frank Nugan's protestations, there was little he could do to counter the Corporate Affairs Commission investigation, which was about to run a forensic eye over the Nugan Fruit Group's activities and maybe a glance or two in the direction of Frank Nugan's bank. And, unbeknownst to Nugan, another government agency already had Nugan Hand in its sights and one of its officers was preparing an audacious plan to infiltrate the bank.

13

INFILTRATION

Anyone bumping into Phil Bailey in Sydney's Chinatown in the late 1970s, with his long hair and unkempt beard, would immediately have assumed that he was a down-and-out junkie. In reality, Bailey was an undercover officer working for the Federal Bureau of Narcotics, a division of the Australian Customs Service.

Before going out to meet the subjects of his inquiry, he would dilate his pupils with drops prescribed by his friendly optometrist. The glazed-eye effect was guaranteed to fool even the big-time dealers. 'My job was working on Chinese heroin importations. I went between surveillance of the targets to meeting them to make arrangements for buys of heroin off the importers.'[1]

Bailey's work was highly risky. In the mid-1970s, Sydney was the epicentre of Australian drug importation and distribution and an estimated 90 per cent or more of the drugs got through to the streets thanks in part to corrupt officers inside the Australian Customs Service and other law-enforcement agencies.

In late 1976, Bailey and a team of Narcotics Bureau investigators joined officers from the State Drug Squad on a raid of the Waterloo home of Chinese-Australian Andrew Lowe. Thirty-year-old Lowe was a trafficker allegedly associated with the Pak Yok Lin syndicate, whose tentacles extended throughout Southeast Asia.

The investigators uncovered a pound (0.45 kilograms) of heroin hidden under Lowe's kitchen sink. Elsewhere in the home they found thousands of dollars of cash. As the search continued, Bailey's colleague, Dennis Kelly, took Lowe aside to extract what information he could:

> Kelly had that gift of getting people to talk to him. He sensed Lowe would try and offset the problem he was in with the Drug Squad. In those days, the Drug Squad didn't have a good reputation and the Narcotics Bureau did. So Kelly felt Lowe would trust us more than the Drug Squad.[2]

As Kelly predicted, Lowe squealed like a cornered pig:

> You blokes think you are doing pretty good catching a few people with a pound or two now and then. I will give you the names of two blokes who are merchant bankers. Their office is in the same block as Premier Askin's. The names are Frank Nugan and Michael Hand. They are bigger than anything you have ever seen here in the heroin game and are said to be part of an American security organisation. If you caught these blokes all hell would break loose. This is spot-on information.[3]

Kelly asked how he knew about Nugan and Hand. Lowe claimed he had worked for the bank for a short period in 1974 selling bullion. He said he was 'shit at the job', but during that time Mike Hand had approached him and asked if had any connections in the local Chinese community. Lowe said he knew a lot of restaurateurs and businessmen in Sydney's Chinatown:

> I took quite a few people — about twenty-five members of the

13 Infiltration

Sydney Chinese community — up to meet George Shaw, Frank Nugan and Mike Hand and they deposited money. The money was handed over and put into an account. I don't know if it was in their right name or under another name, because some of them wanted money put elsewhere or sent somewhere else. There were quite a few occasions where one client would have brought up, say, $15,000. Another time it could have been $30,000.[4]

A number of Lowe's introductions included Chinese nationals visiting Australia on a visa. Lowe convinced them that it would look suspicious if they were to carry large sums back home on the plane to Hong Kong. He offered them a more secure way to remit their money — the Nugan Hand bank.

Following his short stint working for Nugan Hand, Lowe had taken over the management of an illegal gambling casino in Dixon Street, Chinatown, where customers played dominoes and fan-tan. The gamblers with the deepest pockets were Hong Kong drug traffickers, who ran high-grade heroin into Sydney. According to Lowe, one thing led to another and he became a middleman, receiving and distributing as much as 9 pounds (4 kilograms) of heroin at a time to local dealers. By his own admission, at one stage Lowe had a stockpile of 27 pounds (12 kilograms) of heroin.

In 1976, Lowe started introducing local drug traffickers who needed money laundered to Nugan Hand. For every introduction, the bank promised Lowe a spotter's fee. The Joint Task Force believed Nugan Hand staff knew they were dealing with drug traffickers:

> With one or two exceptions, it can be fairly said that in neither their physical appearance nor their mannerisms did these depositors have the appearance of legitimate successful businessmen. Indeed, one depositor was described by an employee

as frequently having the appearance of being affected by drugs on visits to the Nugan Hand offices.⁵

George Shaw's secretary became concerned about a client who visited Shaw 'maybe twice a week'. She formed the opinion that he was dealing in drugs:

> I was seventeen at the time, but I wasn't stupid. I could tell by the style of his living. During the time I knew him, he never had a job and yet he drove a new, red Mercedes Benz. He was always smartly dressed and he told me that he had sent his girlfriend on two or three cruises … He was quite often stoned when he came to see George.⁶

Invariably, these depositors walked in with thousands of dollars cash and walked out without any receipt or paperwork. The money was kept as cash in the Nugan Hand safe and not deposited into an account.

According to Clive Small, word quickly spread about Nugan Hand's special money-laundering services:

> George Shaw was dealing with around twenty-five drug traffickers all up. Amongst those were a number of syndicates. The reason he focused on them was simply because if the word spread, [Nugan Hand] had a chance of attracting a lot more money into the bank and stood to make large profits out of it.⁷

Andrew Lowe claimed that drugs were never mentioned during the exchange of funds until Mike Hand started showing interest in Lowe's activities:

> He didn't actually talk about dealing in heroin. Hand just

pointed out an example whereby he was coming back from overseas one time and he was waiting in the queue to go through customs and the customs officers came up and they just pulled one person from the queue, and pulled a quantity of heroin from the guy's tie. And that sort of got me wondering. If they don't know what I am doing, why should he bring up such a matter — you know, like, talk about heroin? And then after a time we got to know each other, and I just felt that possibly he was trying to pick my brains.[8]

Later, under formal interrogation, Lowe alleged that he had acted as translator at a meeting in the Sydney Botanic Gardens between Mike Hand and the notorious Burmese warlord and trafficker Khun Sa*, who had somehow slipped into Australia undetected:

Khun Sa said that he knew of quite a few Americans high up in the government who used to come and see him on a daily basis in the Golden Triangle area. There was a reciprocal arrangement. Khun Sa was selling them heroin, and these people high up in the American Government were supplying arms to Khun Sa to outfit his army.[9]

Lowe claimed that Hand had boasted to Khun Sa about working for the CIA in Laos during the Vietnam War and how heroin was shipped out of Laos hidden in the bodies of dead American servicemen.

During the meeting, Khun Sa brought up the problem of moving

---

* Khun Sa's real name was Chiang Chifu. He adopted the pseudonym Khun Sa, meaning 'Prince Prosperous'. In 1969, he was imprisoned in Burma for drug trafficking. He broke out of prison in 1974, fled to Thailand and organised both a drug network and an army. In the 1980s, he allegedly offered to sell his entire opium production to both the Australian and the United States governments, allowing them to end the heroin trade overnight. Both countries, he claimed, declined the offer.

heroin through Hong Kong. The Hong Kong police and customs, he said, had cracked down on heroin trafficking. He was now planning to streamline the process by exporting the drug direct from Thailand to the market.

Lowe alleged that the ultimate outcome of the meeting was a discussion about the importation of 500 pounds (225 kilograms) of heroin from Bangkok to the United States. Mike Hand, he claimed, was to arrange the delivery of the drugs and to finance the operation.

Phil Bailey read a copy of Lowe's testimony and recognised the name 'Mike Hand'. A few months prior, when putting some order into the Narcotics Bureau's operational files on a major drug investigation, he had come across some typed notes out of place. One of the notes was a précis of a phone call received in 1973 from a Sydney lawyer who alleged that four Americans, including Mike Hand, Bud King and Paul Stocker, were involved in a drug smuggling ring in the north of the state. The lawyer said he was representing Bud King's Thai housekeeper, who was being blackmailed, and wanted to know if the Federal Bureau of Narcotics knew any of the Americans.

Bailey briefed his senior officers. They agreed the Nugan Hand bank was ripe for investigation and that Bailey should take the lead. His first task was to learn how merchant banks worked: 'The drug scene, particularly the heroin scene, was mainly in the Chinese area and it hadn't got into the big business area, so it was a whole new ball game.'[10]

An old school friend introduced Bailey to Garry Allen, a successful merchant banker in Sydney. They met at a bar in Circular Quay, a few hundred metres from the bureau's offices. Over drinks, Allen said that his firm did business with a Swiss Bank, which had asked him why his firm was unable to offer the same interest rates as Nugan Hand. Allen replied that no one could understand how it was offering 2 per cent more than the market.

Bailey asked Allen why Nugan Hand would open a branch in Chiang Mai, in Northern Thailand:

> Garry Allen said that would make about as much sense as opening a merchant bank office in Griffith. If Nugan Hand was a trading bank, he could see some sense in it, but it wasn't a trading bank. If they were into the drug business, he would be able to understand it. Bearing in mind that Chiang Mai was the heroin capital of the Golden Triangle, that started to make bells ring.[11]

Allen told Bailey that he knew an ex-Royal Navy officer, Ron Pulger-Frame, who worked for Nugan Hand in Hong Kong. Before joining the bank, Frame had worked for the American-owned Deak & Company, one of the biggest international currency and coin exchangers in the world. By Frame's own admission, he had devised a system for Deaks to circumvent Australia's exchange regulations. Frame was now running a bunch of couriers for Nugan Hand, who would pick up cash deposits from places like Chiang Mai and Bangkok and physically carry them on commercial flights to Hong Kong or Singapore.

Bangkok executive John Owen labelled Pulger-Frame 'the bagman' and said his skill was moving money through customs by whatever means, including the payment of bribes.[12]

Garry Allen said Pulger-Frame was a family man with four teenage boys, and simply could not believe his friend would have anything to do with narcotics. But Pulger-Frame was already on the Narcotics Bureau files.

A few months earlier, the Thai consul in Sydney had told the Bureau he had received an anonymous tip-off that Pulger-Frame was boarding a flight in Sydney bound for Bangkok with thousands of dollars of drugs on his body. An investigator had noted that this was like shipping coal to Newcastle and suggested that it may have simply been an April Fools' Day joke, but that it was 'worth checking'.

Hong Kong Customs was also watching Nugan Hand's bagman. At the airport, while awaiting his departure for Sydney, customs officers took Pulger-Frame into a room, forced him to remove all his clothes and searched him internally for drugs. None were found, but the experience left Pulger-Frame shaken.

On arrival in Sydney, he took a taxi straight to Macquarie Street to inform Frank Nugan what had happened. Nugan, who was drunk, panicked. He picked up the phone as if to call someone, then slammed it down. Instead, he dragged Pulger-Frame into a cab and up to the Bourbon & Beefsteak to see Bernie Houghton.

Pulger-Frame had seen Nugan hammered before, but nothing like this. Within minutes of arriving, Frank was literally sitting at Houghton's feet, pleading for him to help. With his connections, Frank said, Bernie could get to the bottom of the matter. Bernie was disgusted by Frank's performance, but said he would make enquiries, if he let go of his Florsheim shoes.

*

Bailey made a search of Australian Customs records and discovered that Nugan Hand had made seven importations of canned foods, furniture and golf clubs and balls from Hong Kong and China — a somewhat strange and suspicious diversion from the normal services of a merchant bank.

In the bureau's records, he also found that during a raid on the premises of two separate drug traffickers, investigators had discovered Nugan Hand documents and business cards bearing the bank's logo and the name George Shaw.

The material already on file was compelling, but not strong enough yet for Bailey to place before the savage eyes of his superiors. Bailey needed to come up with hard evidence; otherwise the investigation would be dropped: 'Having received information from Andrew Lowe about Nugan Hand's laundering of drug money and then having got information from the merchant banker, my next aim was to infiltrate the bank by getting one of their employees to become an informant.'[13]

Bailey asked Garry Allen to meet with Ron Pulger-Frame on his next visit to Hong Kong. He wanted him to learn as much as he could about Nugan Hand. Allen agreed to do so. Bailey provided Allen with a typed list of Nugan Hand staff and asked him to subtly bring up their names with his Hong Kong business and financial connections to see if they had any knowledge of their respective backgrounds.

In November 1977, Allen flew into Hong Kong and went up to see Pulger-Frame at Nugan Hand's offices in the Connaught Centre. Pulger-Frame had no reason to suspect Allen of anything more than being a friend and colleague making a courtesy call. He showed him around the office and introduced him to Mike Hand and two other older Americans, Admiral Buddy Yates, the bank's president, and General Black, who ran the Hawaiian branch.

Allen quipped, 'Admirals and Generals? We're not going to war are we?' Buddy Yates replied, 'No, but we are running a tight ship.'

On his return to Sydney, Allen reported back to Phil Bailey:

> His opinion of the business itself was that it was shonky. Some of the people involved in the bank were not very wise in the workings of merchant banks. Quite a number were ex-military, and he questioned what they would know about merchant banking. The money coming in and the money going out and the interest rates they were paying just didn't make sense. And all of these things were like smoke. He didn't believe it was a true merchant bank — there was something more than a merchant bank there.[14]

★

That same month, John Dowd received an unusual telephone call at his parliamentary office from an Englishman who gave his name as Peter Wilcox. 'This fellow said that he was a British secret service agent and asked me to check with a UK member of parliament as to his genuineness.'[15]

Wilcox said he was flying into Sydney from his home in Hawaii and wanted to meet Dowd to discuss the Nugan Hand bank. Dowd agreed and offered to collect Wilcox from the airport. Short, plump and in his late forties with greying hair, this mysterious intelligence officer was no James Bond.

'On the way back to my office in Macquarie Street, we stopped opposite the office of the Nugan Hand bank,' recalls Dowd. 'You can't feign the genuine terror in this man that I had exposed him. He was genuinely afraid of this contact with the building.'[16]

Wilcox told Dowd that he had had dealings with Nugan Hand and intimated that British intelligence was concerned about the bank and the possibility of its involvement with the CIA. Says Dowd:

> Obviously Nugan Hand was a shonky operation. And obviously the British Secret Service wanted to keep tabs for their own interests to see what they [the CIA] were up to. They may exchange information between intelligence sources, but they also keep an eye on each other. He was also obviously trying to encourage me that I was on the right track and to keep going. He conveyed to me that he wanted to do anything he could to help me get them.[17]

Wilcox then flew to Melbourne, where he booked into Room 286 of the Commodore Chateau Hotel and awaited a knock at the door. When it came, he ushered in two agents of the Federal Bureau of Narcotics, who were armed with a portable tape recorder. Wilcox told

13 Infiltration

them that he had received press cuttings from friends in Australia about allegations that Nugan Hand was involved with drugs, and thought it would be useful to pass on his experience and knowledge of the operation to authorities.

He explained how six months earlier he had received an approach from an old American friend, Rear Admiral Lloyd Vasey*, on behalf of the Nugan Hand president, Admiral Buddy Yates. Vasey said Yates wanted to offer him a directorship of a subsidiary of the Nugan Hand bank called the Swiss Pacific Bank Trust Company Limited. Wilcox, who ran a small finance company out of Honolulu, expressed interest in the position.

On a business trip to Southeast Asia, Wilcox called at Nugan Hand's Hong Kong office. He was far from impressed. The local manager, Les Collings, took Wilcox to dinner. With a few drinks under his belt, Collings spoke of how they had set up branches throughout Asia and how they moved bundles of money across borders. But it was when Collings mentioned the bank's branch in Chiang Mai that Wilcox became deeply suspicious.

At Collings' suggestion, Wilcox flew from Hong Kong to Singapore, where he dined with Mike Hand and his wife, Helene, in their million-dollar penthouse. Over dinner, Hand told Wilcox that the bank handled black money. The following day at Hand's office, Hand introduced Wilcox to Kings Cross bar owner, Bernie Houghton, whom he said was also in the running for a directorship. Wilcox recognised Houghton from his earlier intelligence days, when Houghton had worked for a US intelligence group run by Admiral Vasey. Houghton told Wilcox he was still affiliated with the CIA.

---

* Rear Admiral Lloyd Vasey's military service included roles as chief of strategic plans and policies at US Pacific Command Headquarters; secretary to the US Joint Chiefs of Staff; deputy director of the US National Military Command Center in the Pentagon; and chief of staff for Commander US Seventh Fleet.

After he arrived back in Hawaii, Wilcox received a call from Frank Nugan, who said he was in Honolulu on business and would like to meet him at the bar of his hotel. Wilcox arrived to find Nugan in a drunken state.

'I want you for deep cover to infiltrate the other side,' Nugan told Wilcox.

Wilcox was taken aback by another statement, 'We, Nugan Hand, do the bastards over. Anybody that gets in our way, we can take care of. We put people away.'[18]

Wilcox was so disturbed by what he was hearing that he told Nugan, there and then, that he was no longer interested in working for his bank.

Peter Wilcox supplied the Narcotics Bureau officers with valuable information about his meetings with the moneymen who ran the Nugan Hand financial empire. What Wilcox did not know was that the bureau was already in the throes of attempting to infiltrate the bank.

A few weeks later, in late November 1977, Garry Allen called Phil Bailey and said that Nugan Hand's money mover Ron Pulger-Frame was coming to Sydney. Allen offered to set up a meeting in his office. This was an unexpected but welcome opportunity for Bailey to obtain first-hand information: 'We arranged that I would meet Pulger-Frame, not as a narcotics investigator, but to just have a yarn and try and pick his brains, with the idea that he might be a way into the inner workings of Nugan Hand.'[19]

Bailey was adept at passing himself off as a drug-addled dealer, but masquerading as a businessman with an interest in international finance was another matter entirely. The meeting took place in Allen's boardroom. Pulger-Frame was generally non-communicative and wary of answering questions regarding the bank's operations. Unbeknownst to Bailey, Garry Allen had met with Pulger-Frame at his hotel prior to the meeting and had shown him the list of names the Narcotics Bureau was investigating and recommended that he get out of Nugan Hand. Pulger-Frame was taken aback. He denied that he, or any of the people on the list, was associated with drugs. Of course, that would be the expected response from an innocent man or a guilty one.*

But there was another twist in the tale, of which Bailey was totally unaware. As well as running his own merchant bank, Garry Allen was the finance director of a small Papua New Guinea airline called Panga Airways Ltd. Panga Airways also had an office in Hong Kong, located in the same building as the Nugan Hand bank. Indeed, Panga Airways' phone number, 5-262323, went through the same switchboard as the Nugan Hand bank at 5-262321. The man Bailey had innocently asked for advice about merchant banking never mentioned what appears to have been a serious conflict of interest.

Following his meeting with Bailey, Ron Pulger-Frame went to see Frank Nugan and told him every detail of their conversation, including the bureau's belief that the bank was 'involved in money laundering for people involved in drugs'.[20]

Bailey's mission to infiltrate Nugan Hand had collapsed, and the bank had been alerted to the Federal Bureau of Narcotics' investigation.

★

In late December 1977, Narcotics Bureau officers became concerned that someone within their agency was deliberately subverting their investigations.

While awaiting trial for the heroin bust, Andrew Lowe called up his bureau handler, Dennis Kelly. Lowe demanded to know why Kelly's colleague, Phil Bailey, was checking up on him. Kelly said it

---

* During the Royal Commission into the Nugan Hand bank, Allen testified that Phil Bailey gave him permission to inform Pulger-Frame of the Narcotics Bureau's interest in him. Bailey denied that was the case.

was 'probably routine'. Lowe said it was 'no routine inquiry, it came straight from Canberra'.

Three weeks later, Lowe telephoned Kelly again. In an even more aggressive tone, he said he knew where investigator Bailey lived. Kelly asked Lowe where he got his information. Lowe responded, 'Listen mate, anyone who inquires into me, I check on them also. As I have told you, I have some big names in Canberra.'

By 'big names in Canberra', Lowe seemed to be implying he had an informant inside a law-enforcement agency, most likely within the Narcotics Bureau headquarters.

Indeed, the bureau was leaking like a sieve. Information was even reaching Frank Nugan via his solicitor John Aston, or more precisely his law clerk, Brian Alexander. A well-known peddler of information, Alexander had contacts across the criminal spectrum and inside law-enforcement agencies, including the police and the Narcotics Bureau.

★

On 14 February 1978, Frank Nugan flew to Canberra for a head-on confrontation with the Federal Bureau of Narcotics. He was ushered into a room where he met with bureau chief Harvey Bates and his brother, Brian, who was second-in-command. Their first impression of the merchant banker was that he was anxious and possibly intoxicated. Cutting short the usual pleasantries, Nugan said he knew the bureau had a large board in the building with a diagram showing all suspected drug dealers, which included Nugan Hand.

Harvey Bates pointed out that he couldn't discuss operational matters. Nugan vehemently denied any wrongdoing.

'We are upright citizens and honest bankers,' he said, 'trying to do our best in a very difficult business field. The legal troubles of the Nugan Fruit Group in Griffith had nothing to do with my bank!'[21]

13 Infiltration

It was a bravura performance, which had the Narcotics Bureau chiefs flummoxed. They were used to hoodlums, junkies and other lowlifes complaining about a bum rap. But a millionaire, chain-smoking, lawyer-banker, wearing a shiny suit and professing his innocence placed them seriously out of their comfort zone.

As a parting shot, Nugan allegedly said he was happy to open up Nugan Hand's books to the bureau, but he would first need to contact his customers, which included a number of sitting politicians.

Nugan's visit sent shock waves through the Narcotics Bureau. Where was Nugan obtaining his information? That afternoon, a bureau officer cobbled together a report, which fingered heroin trafficker Andrew Lowe as the likely source, but sidestepped the question of where Lowe was getting his information. In March 1978, a secret minute was circulated inside the bureau which said, in effect, that no further action in relation to Nugan Hand was to be taken and that if any information was made available to the Sydney office it was to be reported to Canberra. According to Phil Bailey: 'The Nugan Hand file was locked away in the Intelligence Section in Sydney.'[22]

Five weeks later, Brian Alexander contacted Frank Nugan to say that the Narcotics Bureau had shut down the active investigation into Nugan Hand. Three months on, bank staffer George Shaw received a telephone call asking him to call by John Aston's office. On arrival, Alexander handed Shaw a brown paper parcel containing $10,000 cash. That same day, Shaw received instructions to open a Nugan Hand account in the name of Richard Spencer and to deposit the $10,000 in that account. Spencer was a senior Federal Bureau of Narcotics investigator.*

Bailey and his colleagues were furious that the Nugan Hand investigation had been pulled out from under them. One senior officer later

---

* The average yearly wage for a narcotics officer in the late 1970s was roughly $11,000, suggesting that the monies were derived from illegal sources. Spencer later denied knowledge of the account.

told the Stewart Royal Commission that his superiors 'went to water as a result of the visit of Frank and, in turn, the directive (to shut down the investigation) was a reflection of their going to water.'[23]

In response the bureau chiefs said they strongly resented the implication that they had gone to water and told the commission that they had good intent in deciding to not carry out an official or active investigation into Nugan Hand. They asserted that a 'passive mode' or 'watching brief' continued, meaning that if any information was supplied to the bureau about the Nugan Hand bank it would be inspected and filed.[24]

A number of Narcotics Bureau officers with an interest in the case suspected there was more to it when they were given new desks and telephones and told to wait for someone to call. According to Phil Bailey, the phone never rang:

> The real sad part of it from my point of view is that we were obviously getting so close to the truth without knowing it when the investigation was stopped. It would appear that one or two people were on the verge of breaking, but we didn't know that at the time, and the rest is history.[25]

14
THE PHANTOM

Frank had picked up a get-out-of-jail card. He put it down to his own brilliant strategy of confronting head-on the bastards down at the Federal Bureau of Narcotics. It was a lucky escape; if the media had caught on that the bureau had an interest in Nugan Hand, the bank would likely have collapsed overnight.

As it was, the Nugan Fruit Group issue remained an impediment to securing potential customers and the company's finances were in a perilous state. Frank had no option but to push his salesmen hard and himself harder. One of his strategies involved targeting business people with legal problems. He would offer them free or heavily discounted legal advice in return for handling their financial affairs. He also deliberately befriended wealthy people, such as his family doctor, Thomas Wall, who conducted a lucrative medical practice in Sydney's eastern suburbs. Over time, a personal friendship had developed; both men were keen chess players and regularly met for a game at Wall's home in Double Bay. Frank was soon acting as Dr Wall's solicitor and tax advisor. As Wall's practice generated a substantial amount of cash, Frank suggested he invest the cash and his surplus funds with Nugan Hand.[1] Wall agreed and ultimately invested $350,000 with Nugan Hand.

In 1974, Dr Wall then introduced Frank to his friend Dr Thomas Ogden, a Queensland surgeon suffering from a medical disability, who needed advice from a lawyer. Frank helped Dr Ogden obtain payment under a sickness insurance policy and then set about offering financial advice. Ogden's wife was particularly taken with Frank's charm and 'sincere interest' in her family. He'd often call up for a chat and on their occasional visits to Sydney the Ogdens would call over to the Nugan Hand office to discuss taxation matters. Mrs Ogden opined to a Nugan Hand secretary that she wished her daughter could meet someone like Frank.

Frank told the Ogdens that he had concerns about their finances. They were being poorly managed, he said. He suggested they consider investing with Nugan Hand. Dr Ogden respectfully told Frank that he saw him as his lawyer and not his banker. But over time, the surgeon formed the impression that Nugan was 'a reputable, interested and caring young solicitor.'[2]

In June 1975, Dr Ogden began investing his money with Nugan Hand. When both of the Ogdens' children died overseas in separate incidents, Frank stepped in and arranged for their bodies to be repatriated to Australia. It was a tactical triumph. In their despair, the Ogdens decided to retain Frank to handle all their affairs, both legal and financial. Frank told the couple that their money was absolutely secure, but never supplied them with any documentation. They had no idea that $35,000 of their funds had been funnelled through the account of a business owned by the deputy leader of the NSW Liberal party, Bruce McDonald, of which $34,500 was then transferred to Nugan Hand as a service fee.* Investigators subsequently deduced that those funds had been made available for Frank Nugan to use as he chose.

By 1978, the Ogdens had deposited their life savings of $650,000 with Nugan Hand.

*

---

* The Corporate Affairs Commission noted that Nugan Hand and Bruce McDonald's company, Macfield Corporation, 'had to some extent a business association,' but was unable to determine if the transaction was genuine.

14 The phantom

In early 1978, Nugan Hand's Bangkok representative, John Owen, began to see through Frank's scheming: 'Nugan, having worked a web of deception around himself and his "bank" and through the spending of other people's money, carried with him an aura of success, an aura in which he, himself, most fervently believed. He was a salesman wedded to his product: FJ Nugan and Nugan Hand.'[3]

On a visit to the Sydney office, Owen was taken aback by Frank Nugan's hubris:

> I was wheeled into Nugan's office at 9.30 one morning in May. Nugan's office had one large desk in it, in one corner, on which were heaped several piles of papers. Next to his office was that of his secretary, Patricia Swan, which had an interconnecting door. Underneath the windows ran a ledge about 18 inches wide, which housed air-conditioners and provided a readily accessible back-up to Nugan's heaped-up filing system. I sat down in front of Nugan's desk. Nugan was writing something. He stopped, looked up and peered at me around the corner of one of his heaps. He lit one of his Dunhill King Size cigarettes and Patricia Swan magically appeared with an early morning whisky soda. I couldn't believe my eyes. Nugan leaned back in his executive's chair, took a long swig from his whisky and then a deep pull on his cigarette, exhaling clouds of blue smoke. 'Why haven't you got any deposits for us then?' Nugan shot at me. I launched into a long dissertation about the problems in Bangkok during which another whisky soda appeared, and how, in any case, deposits notwithstanding, I had actually made the company some money. 'Humph' from Nugan, this time peering around another heap. The telephone rang. Nugan snatched it up and, puffing on his cigarette and taking swigs from his whisky soda, launched into a complicated bargaining session

on the telephone. He finally put the phone down and out came another 'Humph'. 'Well,' he said, 'I make the company money. There, that telephone conversation just made $80,000. I can do it, just on the phone. I do it all the time, why can't you do it?' I could see there was no logical answer to that question and decided to keep quiet. Another whisky soda came in fortunately to break up the silence. 'Humph' again. 'Well, John, I was going to tell you to pack your bags but I'll give you a chance. I'll give you three months to get in deposits. Then if you don't, you're out!' This was really just what I wanted, so I rose and gave Frank Nugan effusive thanks and said, 'I'll do my best, I'm sure that something can be done!' and then looking around the office at the piles of paper everywhere and Nugan smoking and drinking whisky at ten in the morning, it struck me that he was leading a very strange lifestyle for someone apparently so successful.[4]

Frank's alcohol intake fell into the category of 'excess is not enough'. He was drinking from breakfast to bedtime and consuming at least two bottles of whisky a day. By afternoon, his face would turn to jelly, his speech would begin to slur and he would slump into a morose state. Some nights he didn't go home; instead he would stumble up to a city hotel or simply collapse under his desk.

The booze had turned his belly to blubber and his face had ballooned, erasing his boyish features. As with most alcoholics, he had poisoned his brain. Staff whispered behind his back about his verbosity, pathological lying and decreasing ability to convey his thoughts in writing. Worst of all, he had become extremely abrasive, denigrating and insulting towards his secretaries and sales representatives. Even the office sycophants suffered the sharp end of his tongue. A concerned staffer telexed Mike Hand, complaining about Nugan's dipsomania. Hand preferred to ignore it, but on one visit to Sydney he was seen expressing his disapproval of Nugan's inebriated state by knocking his whisky glass from his desk.[5]

One evening, a young legal staffer asked Frank if he could catch a lift home with him. While driving down New South Head Road, Frank pulled up late at a stoplight. He backed up and ploughed into the stationary taxi behind. In a fit of rage, Frank got out of his bruised Mercedes and abused the taxi driver, demanding he pay for the damage. The young legal staffer came away from the incident convinced his boss had a 'split personality'.[6]

Frank's lavish lifestyle was legendary. His remedy to any problem was to spend money, lots of money. He took hundreds of thousands of dollars of Nugan Hand funds to decorate his waterfront home in what could only be described as a triumph of pitiable taste. Then there were the chauffeur-driven hire cars for visitors and a fleet of Mercedes Benz he leased for his executives. Legal staffer Graham Edelsten quipped, 'They gave me a car! They gave me a Mercedes! They gave everyone a Mercedes!'[7]

On his jollies in Southeast Asia, Frank played the international finance executive. He would rent the boardroom in the best hotel in the city and hire not one but two chauffeur-driven Mercedes. Both vehicles would sit in the hotel concourse with their engines idling.

*

Frank's vanity grew to such a degree that he believed he was a man of steel, impervious to failure. But on Friday 26 May 1978, his mettle was sorely tested. That evening, Yolanda Lee was preparing dinner at her Wahroonga home when the telephone rang. 'My husband called and he said something to the effect that, "Frank must have had a shocking row with his wife, he is awfully upset." He said he was going to bring him home for dinner.'[8]

Yolanda was the Deputy Mayor of Ku-ring-gai Municipal Council, which had over the previous two years invested $3.8 million with Nugan Hand. Her husband, Alexander, had a small accountancy firm a few doors down from Nugan Hand and often referred clients to Frank Nugan for tax advice. Recalled Yolanda later: 'Frank arrived for dinner. We poured him a whisky. He eventually took the bottle, he finished that bottle, he started a second one, he made two or three telephone calls after which we put him to bed. He wasn't in a fit condition to drive.'[9]

That afternoon, the police had issued warrants for the arrest of Frank and Ken Nugan, and the two former detectives Fred Krahe and Keith Kelly, in connection with a conspiracy to defraud Nugan Fruit Group Ltd and to defraud its shareholders. On hearing the news from his solicitor, Frank had made a hasty exit from his office to seek sanctuary with the Lees. According to Yolanda Lee, 'The following morning, when we got up, he was gone and we saw the headlines in the newspaper about the warrant for his arrest.'[10]

On the Saturday afternoon, Frank and Ken met with their solicitor, John Aston, to discuss a course of action. On Aston's advice, the Nugan brothers, Krahe and Kelly presented themselves on Monday morning to police headquarters in the city, where they were charged with two counts of conspiracy in relation to the removal of the auditors before the company audit was complete. They were then escorted to the Central Court nearby. After a short hearing they were bailed to await trial.

Implying that there would be no problem meeting bail, the presiding magistrate noted, 'You're a banker, Mr Nugan?'

Frank nodded sheepishly.

The magistrate smiled, 'We don't see many bankers in this place.'

To which a policeman quipped, 'There should be more of it.'[11]

Confronted by a swarm of newspaper and television reporters as they left the court, the Nugan brothers made a reckless decision: they ran down the street, with the media in hot pursuit. The story was front-page news the next morning. The accompanying, somewhat blurred, picture of a merchant banker and a giant of the Australian food industry on the run made them look guilty. Had they simply stopped and told reporters that the charge was a technical corporate offense that would be sorted out by normal legal processes, there would have been little story for the media to milk.

That evening, Ken Nugan appeared on ABC Television's current affairs program *This Day Tonight*. He said the decision to run from the court was a spur of the moment thing, which he now regretted. That said, he laid the blame with the attorney-general, Frank Walker, whom he claimed was running a smear campaign against his firm. The interviewer took the opportunity to probe Nugan about allegations, which had gained currency over the previous six months, that his Griffith fruit empire was involved in drug trafficking. Ken Nugan denied any involvement in drugs and claimed that the Woodward Royal Commission, which was looking into the drug trade, had shown no interest in talking with them.

*

Frank's arrest had serious consequences for the Nugan Hand bank. Depositors were soon turning up in person at the Sydney office wanting to withdraw their money. International deals evaporated and budding relationships collapsed, including one with Lloyds Bank in Manila. General Black telephoned Frank from Hawaii to say that he had had a big deposit fall through that morning. Black said that the accusations of drug and Mafia money connections were 'casting a long shadow right across the Pacific to Hawaii'. Frank replied that they were baseless accusations and that there was no connection between the Nugan Fruit Group and Nugan Hand. He advised General Black to tell customers that he had complete confidence in Nugan Hand.

In Hong Kong, Les Collings put out a press release from bank president Buddy Yates declaring that the bank had no connection to the Nugan Fruit Group. The *Business Standard* and *Business News* picked up the release. Collings attached copies of the media coverage in a letter to bank customers, conceding, 'It has been rather a rough week for Nugan Hand International. We have been heartened by the tremendous support which has been received by the Group from customers and friends here and around the world — and we thank you for that most sincerely.'[12]

Mike Hand was less sanguine. He warned Frank that the entire box and dice was on the line. The last thing the bank needed was one of its CEOs going to prison. Frank convinced Mike that it would never get to court and set about making sure that was the case.

The way Frank decided he would achieve that end was to destroy those who had instigated the corporate investigation into the Nugan Fruit Group. Staff in the Sydney office later recalled overhearing a furious Nugan thumping his desk as he dictated letters to his secretary Patricia Swan about Attorney-General Frank Walker and Liberal politician John Dowd. To his mind, they were the guilty ones.

Nugan set about using his powerful connections in both political parties. As a result, senior Labor Party figures confronted Frank Walker and told him in no uncertain terms to keep his nose out of the Nugan Fruit Group case. Recalled Walker:

> There were pressures certainly from the secretary and the assistant secretary of the Labor Party on me to desist in my investigations. The president of the Labor Party, Charlie Oliver, also tried to stop me prosecuting the Nugans in Griffith. And I had pressure from the Premier and Deputy Premier at the time,

who sent me what was virtually a 'no bill' application in respect of the Griffith prosecutions.[13]

Walker made inquiries and discovered unsettling links between his own political party and the Nugan Hand bank:

> The most difficult thing I had to deal with were the officials of the NSW right, which was the controlling machine in the Labor Party. They were closely linked to the directors of the Nugan Hand bank. Indeed, they were actually encouraging Labor Party councils, like Marrickville, Leichhardt and South Sydney, to put money into the bank.[14]

During the 1977 Australian federal election campaign, Frank Nugan held a fund-raising function for the Labor Party at his Vaucluse home, at which both the Deputy Leader of the Federal Opposition, Lionel Bowen, and Frank Nugan made speeches. Following his arrest, Frank Nugan changed his allegiance from the Labor Party to the Liberal Party, donating $2,030 for the 1978 NSW state election campaign. But the links went deeper. There were the millions of dollars in deposits Nugan had taken for the Liberal Party–controlled Ku-ring-gai Municipal Council, for example. On the credit side, back in 1975 Nugan had loaned the deputy leader of the Liberal Party, Bruce McDonald, $200,000 for a development project; this was significant not merely in terms of dollars, but also because Nugan Hand did not normally lend money to its customers.

When John Dowd made allegations about the Nugan Fruit Group on the floor of the NSW Parliament, a furious Bruce McDonald came to the defence of the Nugan company.[15]

In the lead up to the 1978 NSW state election, Frank Nugan made his move against John Dowd. At the end of a Ku-ring-gai Council meeting one evening, a man approached alderwoman Rae Kilkenny and offered her thousands of dollars to stand against Dowd at the upcoming state election in October. Kilkenny was in no doubt that Frank Nugan was behind the offer.

News of the approach reached John Dowd:

> I heard that there were people in town trying to get me out of the way, politically. I subsequently found out that they tried to get someone on Ku-ring-gai Council to stand against me to stop me investigating them. This was an organised-crime exercise, something I spent many years exposing.[16]

*

One Sunday morning in mid-1978, a former employee of the Nugan Fruit Group, Harry Bancroft, who had been preselected as the Liberal Party candidate for Murrumbidgee in the up-coming NSW state election, received an unexpected call at his Griffith home. The caller was Ken Nugan.

'Harry, it's Ken.'

'Ken?'

'Harry, you worked for us. You know these allegations against us are false.'

'I hope that's the case, Ken.'

'It would be to your benefit to have the investigation stopped.'

'My benefit?'

'You've got connections in the Liberal Party. I've got $10,000 here to help your election campaign. It'd be a win-win for both you and for Griffith.'

'I'm a lowly candidate, Ken. I don't have any influence in the party.'

'Incidentally, how is your family?'

'Fine thanks.'

'I understand you had a son since we parted company. He'd be about two years old now?'

'That's right.'

'It would be a terrible shame if anything happened to him, wouldn't it?'

'Ken, it would be a terrible shame and it would be a shame for you, as well.'

'What do you mean?'

'Listen carefully Ken because I will only say this once: if anything happens to any member of my family, I'll kill you.'

From that day on, Bancroft feared retribution from the Nugans.*[17]

*

Frank Walker later discovered that Frank Nugan had also enacted a devious plan around this time to destroy his political career:

> Nugan set up a bank account in my name — a Swiss bank account, the Union Bank of Switzerland, under the pseudonym 'The Phantom'. Now people may know that the comic strip character 'The Phantom's' name was Mr Walker, so that was a significant thing. A series of small amounts of money were put into that account; I think they were about $6,000 and $7,000, at the time, but $25,000 was supposed to be put in there, altogether. This suggested I was somehow having illegal dealings with the Nugan Hand bank. Here, on one hand, I'm investigating them. On the other, they are working for me, paying money into a Swiss bank account. Now there's only

---

* Interviewed by the author, Bancroft recalled the conversation in detail, which matched his testimony to the royal commission into the Nugan Hand bank.

two things you can think about that: either they were trying to blackmail me or that I was behaving very badly, indeed, as the first law officer of the state. So either way I was in deep trouble.*[18]

Frank Nugan's rabid determination to shut down the prosecution of the fraud case against the Nugan Fruit Group extended to a $50,000 bounty for anyone who could get rid of Walker. At the time, $50,000 could have purchased a quality inner-city apartment in Hong Kong, Sydney or New York.

It could also buy a hit man.

---

* Corporate Affairs Commission investigators discovered documents relating to the Swiss bank accounts in Nugan Hand's Hong Kong office.

15

THE BUSINESS OF MURDER

Doug Sapper and Mike Hand spent a lot of time going to dinner in the evenings in Hong Kong. Sapper was not on salary. He orbited the organisation like a satellite, picking up the occasional message and carrying out chores the suit-and-tie executives couldn't do. Sapper initially saw Mike Hand the merchant banker in a glowing light:

> If you met Michael in Hong Kong you would never know that this guy wasn't a graduate of Harvard or Yale. Michael just had one of those personas that you thought, 'Wow, this guy is cultured, he's educated, he's intelligent.' You never questioned that he was a blue-collar product. In fact, at that particular junction in his life, with his charisma and his ability to talk, Michael could have been the Pope in Rome, he could have been the head of IBM or he could have run for public office, he could have done anything. He just had that winning look and edge to his voice and that if you hooked your wagon to his star you were going to get whatever it was you were supposed to get.[1]

Hand never discussed with Sapper the problems Frank was experiencing in Australia. He was focused on making Nugan Hand International a success:

Michael hired a lot of people to advise him and to do certain things. He was the architect of all this and I give him full credit, he made it happen. From the outside it didn't look like anything was wrong but if you were near the centre there were some troubling things that just couldn't be explained and I don't think anybody wanted to ask Michael.

During one of their regular sessions, Mike asked Sapper if he would take a trip down to South Africa; a currency broker needed a large amount of cash moved. The job was not without risks; the international authorities were on the lookout for shady movements of money out of the apartheid country:

> I was offered a fairly sizable chunk of change and I went over to Johannesburg, took a suite at the Carlton Towers Hotel and I waited, and I waited, and I waited. I called back to Hong Kong and I said, 'Hey is there a particular month they are going to come by here?' 'No, no, no they'll get to you.' Then I get the word to go down to Durban. The package is ready. I rent a car and I drive down to Durban, but the package is not ready. So I go back to Johannesburg and I'm there six months. They finally said, 'We've got the package.' I go get it. Now I've got to figure how do I get it out of the country. I had bought a lot of hand-knit purses in Rhodesia, and some seriously large burlap bags, so I broke this money down and put a little bit of it in different bags. All the way to the airport I'm thinking this is going to turn out really, really bad.
>
> So I get to the airport, showed my passport, and they said, 'Where are you going?' and I said, 'Well I'm going to Hong Kong. That's where I came from.' They kind of smiled and said, 'How did you enjoy your stay in South Africa?' and I said,

15   The business of murder

'Beautiful country, I'd love to live here.' Small chitchat and I'm thinking these guys are trying to see if I'm going to get nervous or pee in my pants, or whatever. But he stamped the passport and said, 'Have a safe trip, sir.' They loaded the bags on the plane, nobody looked at them. I'm thinking: did I just dodge the magic bullet or is there a fix in here? Now smart money would say somebody got the word and said, 'Hey this guy is going to be leaving; he's going to have a bunch of things with him, do not check his bags.'

Sapper passed through customs at Hong Kong airport without a hitch. He then took a cab to the Hilton Hotel, as prearranged, where he rented a suite and waited for a phone call:

So I get a phone call from these two guys: 'Have you got the package?' I say, 'Yes.' They come up to the room, they look at the packages, they take [the money] out and they count it and they say, 'You've got a problem, pal, there's $50,000 missing.'

'Okay,' I said, 'Well, I don't have your $50,000,' and of course they got pretty antagonistic and I said, 'Look, if I was going to steal fifty grand why the hell didn't I just take it all? I didn't have to come back to Hong Kong. I could have jumped on a plane for Rio de Janeiro and been gone and I've got $500,000 cash with me.'

They were getting kind of edgy and I said, 'Gentlemen, you really don't want to close the distance in a close space with me, this will not turn out in your favour. You get on the phone and you call these rat-shit bastards and you ask them what the fuck they did with that money.' Well, they'd taken $50,000 out of the package to use in South Africa and didn't tell me, didn't put a note in it, didn't send a note to this currency trader, so we had a very tense hour wait. Finally, they called them and said, 'Hey, it's cool, get the money and leave.' But I had already planned on killing these two guys, I mean this was not going to end well and one of us was going to die, or two of them. I said to this guy when I finally got to talk to him, 'You guys are a bunch of amateurs at this. Not only that but you put people's lives at risk.' He said, 'I'm sorry, I didn't know they were going to keep the money.' So these are the kind of things that can happen that cause you to forget the training you had at the Dale Carnegie course.

It wasn't till after the mission that Sapper learned the apparent source and purpose of the money. 'It was money that the South African intelligence people were going to use externally for propaganda and advertising and who knows what. I'm thinking, here's the South African intelligence and you can't move money?'

Indeed, at the time, the South African government was secretly channelling funds from a special defence account to influence international opinion about the Apartheid government, or as the information minister put it, 'buy, bribe, or bluff its way into the hearts and minds of the world.'[2]

The propaganda war included attempts to buy the opinion of influential European and US newspapers. How and why Michael Hand became a party to this morally dubious exercise is unknown, but it reveals a willingness to tap into any source of money no matter how tainted.

Sapper wasn't squeamish, and certainly liked the remuneration, but with every new assignment he was becoming more and more concerned about the bank's dealings with the dark side:

> Money corrupts people. It's been that way since the beginning of time. When people are dumping money on a table, or giving

you a briefcase full of money, I think somewhere along the line you get caught up in the excitement, so to speak, and maybe what would have passed for really good intuition or very intelligent thinking gets trampled in the stampede.

Down at Hong Kong's Foreign Correspondents' Club, Sapper picked up a message to call over to Nugan Hand. Michael wanted him to meet Bernie Houghton, who'd just flown in to Hong Kong. Seeing Bernie was about the last thing Sapper wanted to do; when he'd met him back in Sydney on R&R, he hadn't been impressed:

I don't think anybody who knew Bernie Houghton in that era would have thought that he was just managing the Beef and Bourbon Bar [sic]. He wasn't just a meek-mannered pub keeper. He was always watching, always asking questions, always talking to people. If you ask me do I think Bernie Houghton was a gangster? Of course I do.

Sapper wasn't Robinson Crusoe in that respect. A lot of people had theories about Bernie. Indeed, his contacts were the *Who's Who?* of Australian and American organised and disorganised crime figures, crooked cops and corrupt politicians. As well as the Bourbon & Beefsteak, Houghton had set up two other iconic Sydney bars, the Texas Tavern and Harpoon Harry's Restaurant. In May 1976, Bernie's holding company had gone bust. As the liquidators moved in, the company books went up in flames when Harpoon Harry's burned to the ground. Arson was suspected but never proven. Following the fire, Frank and Mike stepped in to help Bernie with a $35,000 loan.* After a discussion with bank president Buddy Yates, Bernie agreed to repay the loan by assisting the bank to establish new branches in the Middle East.

---

* Approximately $250,000 in 2015

Sapper caught a cab down to the Connaught Centre, took a lift to the eleventh floor and moseyed into Mike's office, where he and Bernie were talking with two unsavoury-looking Australian men with bad haircuts. Mike introduced Bernie to Sapper as Nugan Hand's latest recruit, who had just flown in from Saudi Arabia. Bernie had a formidable memory. He remembered Sapper as one of the few customers he'd ever had at the Bourbon who abstained from alcohol. That was not a bad thing, he said, simply unusual. Recalled Sapper:

> Bernie had a couple of hard cases with him. Michael introduced them, 'Here's Bob. Here's Johnny.' Whoever those two Australians were, they weren't on the donation list for Christmas presents from the police. Michael told me I could trust them, but when somebody tells me I can trust someone, that's when I get a little bit suspicious.

Bernie asked Sapper to join them for a meal later in the day. Sapper arrived at the restaurant early. He ordered some Chinese tea and began pondering Bernie's surprise elevation from bar owner to Nugan Hand executive. 'Now he's a banker? How the hell did he get here? I just got the feeling that there was something radically wrong here. You know, it was like smelling a dead rat but you can't place your finger on where it is, but there is something in the air.'

The two Australians arrived at the restaurant without Bernie, saying he would be a little late. Over beers and noodles, they moved the conversation circuitously, but deliberately, from banter about the not-so-hidden talents of the local bargirls in Hong Kong's Lan Kwai Fong district to Cambodia and how they'd heard he had seen a bit of action at Phnom Penh airport.

Sapper realised these fellows were building up to something when the older one said, 'Mike says he's seen you in situations where lesser people would have folded. He's never seen anyone as proficient as you at clearing a room. Reckons you're the most violent human being he's met in his life.'

'I said, "Wow, I've got to use that line at a singles' bar sometime." But seriously, that kind of statement doesn't come from nowhere.'

The older fellow lit a cigarette, sat back and said there was a little job they needed doing back in Sydney that might be of interest to Sapper. His mate fashioned the shape of a pistol with his hand and mouthed, 'Pop. Pop.'

> It was suggested that I could help them with their problem. Somebody obviously said, 'Oh, this is this guy's background, he's a hard-nose, he can get this done for you.' They told me they could make arrangements to get me into Australia and that they'd get me out. And of course the red light went off in my head and I'm saying, 'Excuse me, you can't get this done in Australia? You can go down to Kings Cross and get a pimp to do this. Why do you have to come all the way to Hong Kong to try to find a hitter?'

The Australians intimated that there were two targets in the one location — NSW Parliament House. That rang warning bells:

> I didn't get involved in a lot of stuff around the world because I was stupid. Okay, you go down there, you don't even do the deal; they just shoot you through the head and leave the body in the lobby of the government building. They kill these two guys, throw the gun alongside of you and boogie. Okay, it won't take the Australian authorities very long to track my background down and say, 'He obviously did this.' So the police say, 'Well, it looks like the problem is solved.' I don't think they had any

intention of getting me out. The only way you can keep a secret is kill the other person who knows it. I just knew there was no cover, no protection and no guaranteed extraction.

Sapper needed time to think. He called over the waiter and ordered another pot of tea:

> I thought, 'Why should I get involved with this deal, which was fraught with quicksand?' So there were a lot of red lights going off on the panel. I didn't want to make them angry because these guys might say, 'Well we've told this son-of-a-bitch too much. He needs to go.' So I just said, 'Sorry guys, I don't have the skills to do that. You're talking to the wrong guy.'

The two Australians looked at each other, got up and left Sapper to pick up the tab. Bernie Houghton arrived minutes later asking about the whereabouts of his friends. Sapper replied, 'I don't think they liked the décor.'

> I didn't particularly feel warm and fuzzy towards Bernie Houghton. I was pretty knowledgeable about how things work in various organisations and Bernie had no loyalty to me. I was just a friend of Michael Hand's. He didn't have any reason in the world to protect me and, as far as I saw in this scenario, I was an expendable asset. I never had lunch with those guys again. I think they left Hong Kong the next day or the day after, and my exposure to Bernie Houghton was limited to seeing him when he came to visit Michael.

Sapper had no idea who the men were planning to kill. He had no inkling that Frank Nugan's political enemies, Walker and Dowd, fitted the bill or that Nugan had put $50,000 on Walker's head.

15 The business of murder

Sapper already had concerns about where Nugan Hand was heading, but they had been amplified by the thought that it was getting into the business of murder. 'There is always that option that when you become powerful and rich. You start believing you are omnipotent. You can't lose, you can't be hit, you are 9 feet tall and you are bulletproof, and unfortunately that is a very dangerous situation.'

From that day on Sapper sensed a change in Mike's attitude towards him. He decided to extricate himself quietly from Nugan Hand and concentrate on his own business interests. 'I had a feeling this was going wrong. In fact, I told Buddy Yates to get out of Nugan Hand. He was the president of the bank. He woke me one morning and I said, "Buddy you need to get out of this, this smells bad."'

Sapper took solace with a journalist friend down at the Foreign Correspondents' Club who wrote a puff-piece about him for syndication to American newspapers:

> Douglas August Sapper, ex US Special Forces jungle fighter, sometime soldier of fortune and presently Hong Kong businessman, says his love affair with Asia is over. After 13 years, he is thinking of going home to the United States. Well maybe not just yet — in a couple of years if his import-export business doesn't flourish.[3]

A few weeks later, Mike called Sapper to offer him a couriering job. He was back to his old ebullient, friendly self. At least it appeared that way; and Sapper wanted to believe the best of the man he still considered his closest friend in the world. 'Michael said there was a box of watches a friend of his wanted moved into Nepal. And while I was on this little exercise, I was meant to check out some people who wanted to get some money out of Nepal and India.'

Moving a bunch of watches to Nepal, he assumed, would be

routine; he had moved currencies and contraband across Asia and had never had a problem. Any hiccup, and a wad of US dollars would surely grease the way:

> It went real well until I got to Kathmandu airport. Somebody blew me in. Somebody used whatever influence they had with the customs people and said, 'Grab this guy and put him on ice.' Anyway, they put me in the Kathmandu Prison and I damn near died. Bottom line is that during this period of time there was some type of a rift between Michael and me, and I have no idea what it was.

Sapper got word to the US embassy in Kathmandu that he needed assistance:

> The first guy who came to see me from the embassy told me he was a consular officer. I said to him, 'Don't lie to me, asshole. I knew you in Vietnam. You were a fucking agency guy! You're a fucking intelligence officer. Well, that ended the conversation pretty quick. I figured the American Government did not have any interest in getting me out of there.

The Kathmandu court sentenced Sapper to four years in prison and fined him US$77,000. On appeal, the prosecutors argued that the sentence was too light. The judge agreed and increased the associated fine to US$85,000.

Sapper was certain that Michael Hand had set him up. What happened next only increased those fears:

> He sent this idiot over, George, who was written up like he was some kind of walking god and in fact he was an unemployed

arsehole who was working as a doorman at one of the restaurants. They have got him down as a CIA intelligence officer but he was none of the above. Anyway he came to Nepal, Michael sent him there with a belt full of gold Krueger Rands to try to see if he could get anything started to get me out. All he did was come visit me for a few days and then he told Michael he had spent the Krueger Rands on bribes and he went back to Hong Kong. He didn't do a damned thing for me, but he did tell me that Michael was planning to buy two Huey helicopters and get four pilots and some hard guys to come down and break me out of the prison. I said, 'This is bullshit. How much do you think that operation is going to cost? So where are we going, we are going to fly to India in the choppers,' because there is a limited range, 'and we are going to park them, get in vehicles and leave them on the ground?' I said, 'I don't know about you but you could buy me out of here for god knows what but it sure as hell wouldn't cost what that operation is going to cost and no bloodshed.' So I told him, 'You tell Michael I don't want anything to do with this. I'm not going to get a bunch of people that had nothing to do with my being in here killed.' So anyway George went back to Hong Kong, god knows what he told them. That is when Nugan Hand started going downhill.[4]

16

KILLING THE GOOSE

Doug Sapper was not the only person associated with Nugan Hand for whom 1978 proved a considerable disappointment.

In March of that year, Andrew Lowe, the former Nugan Hand bullion salesman turned drug trafficker, was convicted and sent to prison for ten years.

In May, police patrolling through North Sydney spotted a white Jaguar they suspected was transporting drugs. A pursuit ensued, during which one of the occupants pulled a weapon and opened fire on the police. The Jaguar was registered to a real-estate firm, whose four directors were current or former executives of the Nugan Hand bank. The alleged shooter, John Austin, was a gambling associate of Duke Countis and had been connected in business with Frank Nugan and Mike Hand in the early 1970s.[1]

In June, the police arrested drug trafficker Murray Riley, who had allegedly encouraged Mike Hand to set up the bank's Chiang Mai branch. Riley and ten other men were charged with importing 2.5 tonnes of Buddha sticks* from Thailand. Riley would ultimately be sentenced to ten years imprisonment. Two other Nugan Hand customers involved with Riley would also serve long sentences.

---

* A Thai variety of marijuana wrapped around thin bamboo splints, fastened with hemp string and dried slowly.

16 Killing the goose

In September 1978, the Nugan brothers attended the preliminary court hearing of the fraud case against them. The bank was not on trial but the name 'Nugan' was becoming so tainted that clients no longer wanted to be seen coming or going from the Nugan Hand building. Frank was forced to make arrangements for bank customers to leave their deposits at the office of solicitor John Aston, in central Sydney.

During the hearing, the Labor Party won the NSW state election in a landslide. Frank Walker was retained as the state's chief lawmaker and Liberal John Dowd was returned in his seat of Lane Cove. Frank Nugan's desperate attempts to destroy his political enemies had failed.

*

Following his court appearances Frank would invariably repair to his office, drown himself in Scotch and take out his frustrations on his employees and executives.

Meanwhile, Michael Hand was becoming increasingly concerned that someone would squeal to authorities about the bank's illegal activities. When the Nugan Fruit Group problems had first appeared in the media, he had put in place a coding system to improve the bank's security. Names were never to appear in bank records. Staffers and clients were allocated a number: Hand was 537, Nugan 536. Currencies were given code words: 'latex' represented US dollars, while Australian dollars were 'hide' and Singapore dollars 'glassware'.[2]

Clive Small recognised the strategy:

> Nugan Hand clearly took on board many of the practices that were adopted by the CIA. It was a very strong form of survival, not only for their clients, but also for the bank executives themselves. And it just permeated through the bank. That explains a lot of their thinking and the way they acted. In effect, they said

we can have two banks: one is the legitimate bank and the other provides all the services that criminals and others may want.³

The increased security was a wise move. The adverse publicity in Australia had encouraged the Hong Kong corporate authorities to put Nugan Hand on their watch list. In late October 1978, the FBI also opened a dossier on Nugan Hand when it received information alleging the bank was 'washing money for Australian and perhaps American organised crime elements, as well as corrupt Southeast Asian government officials and individuals involved in narcotics trafficking.'⁴

In a moment of apparent lucidity, Frank Nugan decided that the best way to counter the impression that the bank was spinning out of control was to spin harder. He and a staffer worked up a glossy brochure, which boasted that the bank had been in operation for thirteen years and had a turnover of a whopping AU$100 billion — equal to the gross domestic product of Australia in 1978. In reality, the bank had been in business only five years and its turnover was at best a few hundred million dollars.

Frank and Mike arranged for a series of full-page stories about Nugan Hand to appear in *Asia Week*, *Rydges* and the *South China Morning Post*. In Australia, they took out expensive full-page advertisements in the *Financial Review* newspaper. One advertisement featured the bank's president, Admiral Buddy Yates 'who administered the office that controls a powerful navy'. There was no mention in the ad that Yates had no banking experience.

The most remarkable advertisement featured a stylish wristwatch as its central graphic. Gold bars marked the hours, each engraved with the name of a city hosting a Nugan Hand branch. On close inspection, the watch face possessed not twelve but thirteen hours. Nugan Hand had well and truly entered the twilight zone.

★

According to John Owen, at the end of 1978 only three of Nugan Hand's branches were making a profit: Hong Kong, Bangkok and Sydney: 'The whole expansion operation was of course a charade — expansion caused money to be drained away in needless expenditure; money that wasn't Nugan Hand's. The brochure proclaiming Nugan Hand's worldwide services was just a façade for a fake bank.'[5]

Stephen Hill wrote to Michael Hand to warn him of the bank's dire financial position. Hand assured Hill that it was all under control and that he and Nugan could fix everything up.

Hand's optimism was inspired by what looked like becoming the biggest financial adventure in the bank's short history. At play was an astronomical sum of money — enough to put Nugan Hand 'on the map' and to make Mike and Frank wealthier than they could have ever dreamed.

17

COUP D'ÉTAT

This was big. Obscenely big. In mid-1978, word passed around the global banking network that someone in the Middle East needed money moved. It was no routine exercise; the funds involved were astronomical. The customer was the Shah of Iran who was making contingency plans to flee his country.

At the time, Iran was a country in turmoil. The capital, Tehran, was witnessing huge protests against the shah's dictatorial, oppressive and corrupt rule. When demonstrations turned to rioting, the whiff of an overthrow was in the air.

The shah and his family controlled a substantial portion of Iran's industrial base, including major interests in automobiles, aluminium, real estate and hotels.[1] To protect his wealth, the shah began looking for banks in various countries that could hold funds and keep his affairs secret, especially from other foreign governments. Most of the large international banks, including powerful Swiss banks, decided that moving the shah's money was akin to moving nitroglycerine along an unsealed road. Nugan Hand, however, saw it as an opportunity to make a killing.

★

17 Coup d'état

Through its office in Germany, Nugan Hand began negotiating the deposit of US$1.5 billion of the shah's loot to its Cayman Islands branch; the money would then be redirected to banks in America, Canada and Turkey. To disguise the identity of the lender, the role of Nugan Hand was that of a trustee bank. The commission payable to Nugan Hand was to be 0.5 per cent, a total of US$7.5 million.*

Mike Hand and the bank's German representative, Karl Schuller, a former insurance salesman, were doing the running, which included negotiating with the US Government. To secure the deal and prove its good faith, Nugan Hand offered to put up a deposit of US$100,000.

In November 1978, Hand and Schuller met with an Iranian princess and a Swiss financial broker representing the shah at the Sheraton Hotel in Zurich. The negotiations went well. Following the meeting, Schuller wrote to a colleague:

> Our worries will be over soon. Mike Hand has signed the papers. All papers are signed from the American Government and Mike has signed the papers to be a trustee bank for $1,500 million. Our only worry now is that the lender [the Shah of Iran] is satisfied with the borrower's security.[2]

Evidence discovered in Nugan Hand documents reveals that the US Government was keen to ensure that as much as possible of the shah's wealth would be moved to the United States. While the identity of the government department involved was not stated, the reason for America's interest in the shah's billions can be deduced from history.

Back in 1953, the CIA had planned and orchestrated a coup d'état in Iran. At the time, Iran had a popular and democratically elected

---

* In 2015, US$1.5 billion is equivalent to US$5.4 billion; US$7.5 million is equivalent to US$27 million.

government, which the US believed was a puppet state of the Soviet Union and 'threatened Western economic and geopolitical interests'.[3]

The CIA officers who orchestrated the coup worked directly with royalist Iranian military officers. They handpicked the prime minister's replacement, sent a stream of envoys to bolster the shah's courage, directed a campaign of bombings by Iranians posing as members of the Communist Party, and planted articles and editorial cartoons in newspapers.

On the night set for the overthrow of Prime Minister Mohammad Mosaddegh, little went to plan; in fact, CIA officials were poised to flee the country. It took several Iranian officers recruited by the CIA to seize control of the government. The intervention shored up the shah's power and influence and for the next twenty-five years he was one of America's most trusted Cold War allies.[4] For America the prize was oil. By the late 1970s, however, Iranians had had enough of the US-backed regime and were heading down the road to revolution.[5]

*

Why the Shah of Iran would trust such a small merchant bank with his money is difficult to fathom. The only certainty is that Michael Hand would have sold Nugan Hand on the credentials of its international executives, such as Buddy Yates and Ed Black, who were former high-ranking US military and intelligence officers.

As Nugan Hand was poised to take a slice of one of the largest money-laundering deals going, something went awry. In late December 1978, Nugan Hand's representative in the deal, Karl Schuller, arrived at his Frankfurt office one morning to find a disturbing message on his telex machine from Frank Nugan saying that he was sacked.

Nugan said that Michael Hand was no longer pursuing the shah's money and warned Schuller not to carry on any business in the Nugan

17 Coup d'état

Hand name. Schuller was understandably shocked and extremely upset at his sacking.

On 15 January 1979, Frank Nugan flew to Frankfurt, where he met with Schuller and told him that the shah's money deal was off because it was 'too political' and 'too hot to be touched.'[6]

While Frank was in Germany, news broke that the shah had fled Iran. Four weeks after the abdication, Frank sent another telex to Schuller, which Corporate Affairs Commission investigators considered was clearly designed to extricate Nugan Hand from any involvement in the transaction:

> We are not involved and are not to be involved in any international lending arrangements of the nature suggested as we are unable to satisfy ourselves of the genuineness or capacity of the lender. Schuller has been instructed to close the Frankfurt office forthwith and to go to the Singapore office.[7]

Frank Nugan may have been genuinely disenchanted with Michael Hand's pursuit of the shah's funds, but there are other possible explanations for his actions; for example, he may have been concerned about the possibility of Australian and international agencies investigating the shah's money-laundering exercise. Alternatively, Nugan and Hand may have been playing a double game to cut Schuller partners out of the deal.

Indeed, another series of telexes reveal that six months after the shah's abdication Mike Hand was still actively pursuing ways to move his money. In a short telex, Hand wrote that he was obtaining quotes for the sale of Iranian currency in price lots equivalent to US$100,000 per day.

In another telex General Black informed Hand, Nugan and Admiral Yates that he had a direct line of contact with the shah: 'Cobey arranging special dinner at our house 23 June for Chidiac and General Moinzadeh, senior member of shah's staff.'[8]

Exactly how much of Iran's wealth was secreted out of the country is unknown. The Iranians claimed that almost US$60 billion was missing from oil companies owned by the shah. Nugan Hand documents suggested the total was $100 billion.

In 1981, a Sydney newspaper reported that a Nugan Hand bank employee had told Joint Task Force investigators that hundreds of millions of dollars of the shah's fortune 'were stolen by employees of the collapsed Nugan Hand bank.'[9]

Corporate Affairs Commission investigators couldn't determine whether Nugan Hand did ever get hold of the shah's fortune. But if it had, the substantial fees it would have received would no doubt have been secured somewhere, such as Nugan Hand's Cayman Island branch, beyond the eyes of pesky investigators.

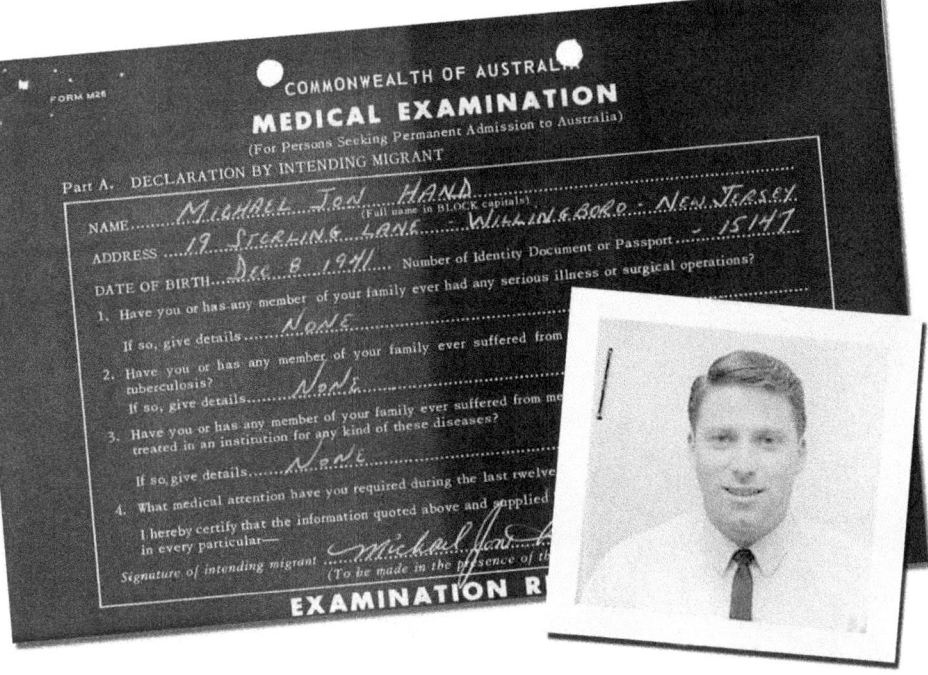

'At that particular junction in his life, with his charisma and his ability to talk, Michael could have been the Pope in Rome, he could have been the head of IBM or he could have run for public office, he could have done anything. He just had that winning look and edge to his voice and that if you hooked your wagon to his star you were going to get whatever it was you were supposed to get.'

Douglas A Sapper III

Michael Hand 1978

Michael & Helene Hand

PRIVATE BANKERS

Frank Nugan, 1978

'I remember Frank Nugan came to town and Frank was smoking big cigars and kind of playing the Godfather. He was always a little bit larger than life. You know, he's kind of like a 600-pound gorilla; he sleeps where he wants to sleep. If you stood in Frank's way he became very threatened and belligerent.'

Douglas A Sapper III

Frank Nugan, Griffith High School, 1956

'This was a very strange event for the senior executive of an international bank and naturally we were very concerned about it. Law officers, of course, are very suspicious about bank managers killing themselves. There is usually a big story behind that sort of behaviour.'

Frank Walker, NSW Attorney-General

Doug Sapper on the Thai-Cambodian border, 1975

Bud King & former wife Patricia

CIA pilot Bud King in Laos

Bernie Houghton
Middle East Representative

Admiral 'Buddy' Yates
Nugan Hand President

'These were serious crimes Nugan Hand had committed – and it wasn't just in Australia. It was all over the world where this bank was operating. Investigation may have led to cutting off some of these drug cartels around the world. I think it is a very pertinent question as to why nothing was done about it. I think the reason nothing was done about it was the nature of the people on the board of the Nugan Hand bank. They were very senior military officials from the United States of America and they certainly weren't going to be investigated by the American Government.'

NSW Attorney-General Frank Walker

General Edwin F Black
Hawaii Representative

William Colby
Retired CIA Director - US Legal Advisor

Nugan Hand International

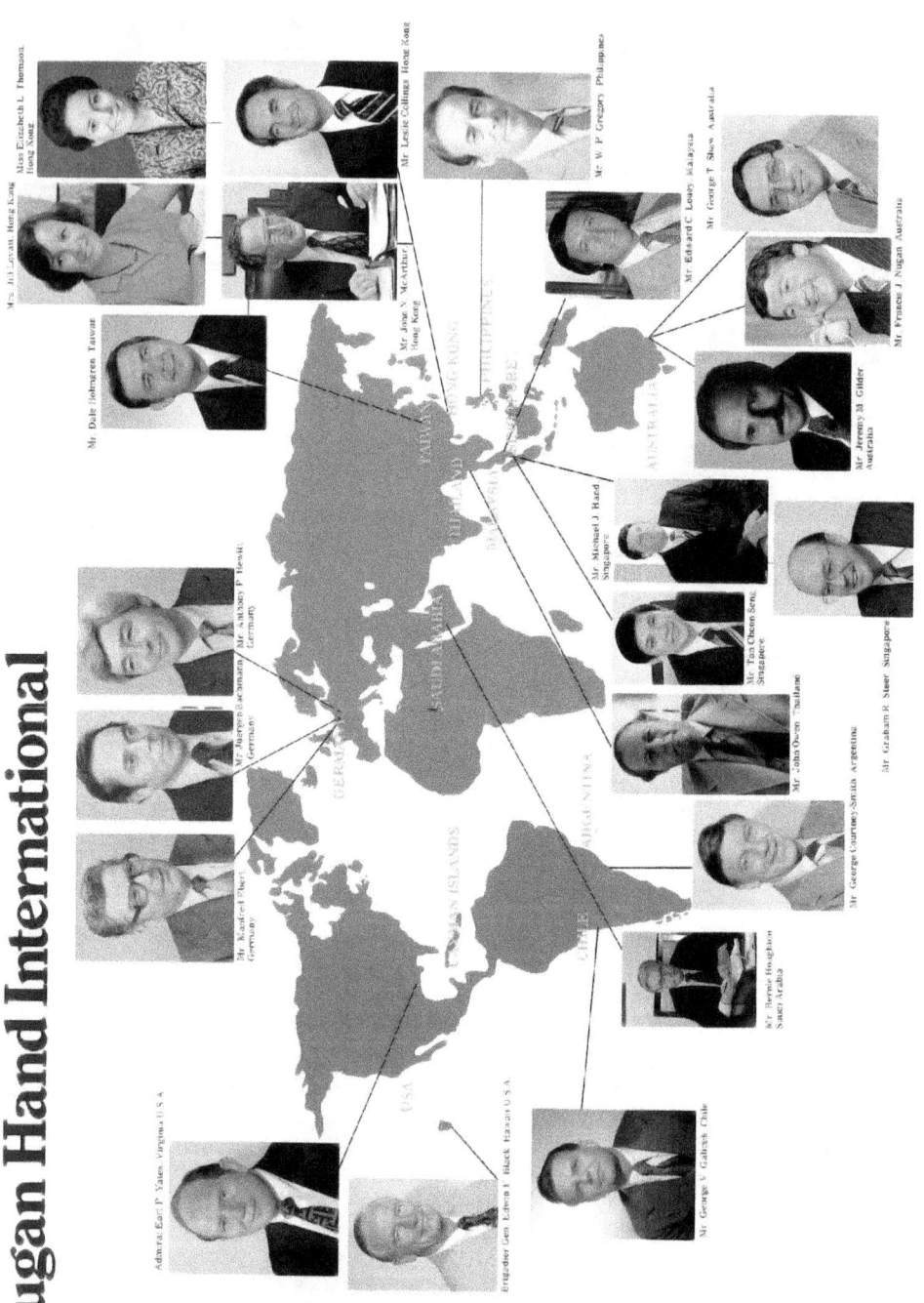

Michael Hand poses for a passport photograph wearing his disguise.

Prior to his disappearance, Michael Hand was holed up in a dank Pyrmont terrace, located two doors up from Bob Gehring's store.

Mr X

18

IN THE LORD'S HANDS

At every turn, Frank Nugan seemed to be running into potholes, each one deeper and more jarring. His behaviour became extremely erratic. Friends and acquaintances would speak of his many-sided character: the brash, arrogant and overbearing boss; the excitable, persuasive and knowledgeable lawyer; and the duplicitous moneyman.[1]

In April 1979 staff noticed a change in Frank. He had stopped drinking and had started attending church.

Paul Owens, a tall, blonde-haired lay preacher, befriended Frank at the Anglican St Andrews Cathedral in central Sydney:

> One morning I noticed this very debonair, very charismatic character in there, beautifully dressed, down on his knees and in deep prayer. And I suppose he watched me and I watched him for about a month. Then one day we were walking out of the church and for some reason I put my arm around him and said, 'It's not as bad as all that' and he said, 'Paul, what about lunch today?' I said, 'Yes, fine.' So, I waited outside the Town Hall where I worked and right on one o'clock came this big silver Mercedes Benz with Frank driving it. And he said, 'I'm going to take you up to the Bourbon Steakhouse in King's

Cross for lunch.' And so we had a very nice lunch and that was the beginning of our association.²

Frank was soon attending services at St Andrew's Cathedral up to three times a day. After one service, Frank asked Paul to call up to see him at the Nugan Hand office:

> The office was busy, people coming and going. The place was electric. And you sort of connected that there was something going on there that was pretty big. Frank told me he had gone over to Canada, had convinced the prime minister of Canada to invest. The Canadian Government was one of the clients. So, when you're getting all this, you are starting to see, here's a fellow that I've been privileged to associate with, that I've been privileged to be able to pray with, and to try and lead him in a certain direction. One particular occasion, when I was in his office, we were praying for this and that, and he said 'Have you ever seen a million dollars written out in a cheque?' and I said, 'No' and he said, 'Well there it is' and he wrote out a million dollars, took it out and gave it to one of the girls. So, I sort of wondered, 'What on earth have I struck here?' As far as I was concerned, the future looked pretty rosy. We looked like we were moving down the road for a Christian television show, which the Nugan Bank was going to finance, and everything looked terrific.³

One morning, Frank arrived at the office and told George Shaw that he had been to church and prayed for him and his family. Shaw later told investigators that he believed Frank had traded whisky for an intense interest in religion. Another staffer suggested he had 'embraced religion with a conspicuous intensity'⁴. He was carrying a Bible with him everywhere he went. Occasionally, he would take the Bible from his pocket and scribble notes or underline words or phrases.

During the police investigation into his death, the police attempted unsuccessfully to find the person who had inscribed 'To Frank, from Paul' on the inside cover. The Bible was, in fact, a gift from Paul Owens: 'It was a New and Old Testament, a lovely Bible. I bought it from Bible House, specially. He could put it in his back pocket or in his inside pocket. Often I'd say to him, "Never be afraid of your Bible. If you see something that's interesting in it, then you just underline it."'

Oddly, throughout his association with Paul Owens, Frank never mentioned his own wife or children: 'He never spoke about his family. No, I can't recall any of that, which was strange in a sense when you look at it. No, we never visited that at all.'

In August 1979, Frank's wife, Lee, returned to America with their young children and didn't return until mid-December for a short stay over Christmas.

Frank attempted to convince people that he'd found the 'road to Damascus', but not everyone was taken in. He continued abusing his staff, only now in a more sanctimonious tone. Meanwhile, the chaplain at his local church felt that Frank was 'going through the motions' and had 'no real understanding or affinity with religion'. Indeed, Frank Nugan's sudden conversion to Christianity appears less an acknowledgment of his previous indiscretions and more a desperate pursuit of divine intervention into his troubled business affairs. Inside the cover of his Bible he penned, 'God is our partner — GNH & Co,' which presumably stood for 'God Nugan Hand & Co'.

He also wrote, 'I place this day my life, my work, my loved ones in the Lord's hands. He is so good and it will be a good day, I believe. I believe this will be a glorious magical miraculous day, he is with me now, Jesus walks with me now. Visualise one hundred thousand customers worldwide, prayerise, actualise.'[5]

Despite this divine association, in less than six months, Frank Nugan would be dead.

19

THE FORTUNE OF WAR

While Nugan Hand was bidding for a slice of the Shah of Iran's money, the bank's international executives were also actively pursuing arms deals across the globe. There were two driving forces behind the bank's involvement in this activity: politics and profit.

In mid-1978, Mike Hand and Les Collings dispatched Ernest Wong, a director of Nugan Hand Hong Kong, to assist John Owen in the Bangkok office. The Chinese born Wong was an honours graduate of the London School of Economics, a staunch anti-communist and an alleged gunrunner.

Having grown up in Ceylon and as a former career officer in the Royal Navy, John Owen was a keen observer of Asian political intrigues and was suspicious of Wong's appointment. He later told investigators:

> I was against Wong's employment because of his reputation through his connections with the Shan States, which are remnants of the Kuomintang Army and are deeply involved in the heroin trade. In fact Wong was trying to raise arms for them and was their representative in Bangkok. I made both Mike Hand and Les Collings aware of Wong's connections, but they still went ahead and employed him.[1]

19 The fortune of war

On Wong's arrival in Bangkok, Owen learned that Michael Hand was interested in doing arms deals in Thailand. He later told investigators that Hand was involved in a deal to sell Swedish anti-aircraft guns and gunboats to the Thai military.

During the 1970s, shadowy arms traders, or so-called merchants of death, flourished. From back-alley warehouses, dealers sought out illicit channels to overcome arms embargoes, which were used as tools of Cold War foreign policy. Such operations were extremely dangerous, logistically complex and inevitably associated with bribery and corruption, but they were also highly lucrative. In 1975 and early 1976, Mike Hand had spent more than a year covertly working his way around international embargoes to get weapons into southern Africa. No one knows how successful he was. The fact that he maintained an active interest in arms trafficking suggests the odds for profit far outweighed any risks. And unlike his earlier South African interlude, he was now prepared to do it under the gold banner of the Nugan Hand merchant bank. Indeed, the deliberate recruitment of senior military officers to the bank's executive, encouraged by Bernie Houghton, who had experience in Vietnam of buying and reselling war surplus, suggests that arms dealing was now front and centre of Mike's vision for the bank's expansion. The only thing missing was an advertising pitch. 'Get more bang for your buck at the Nugan Hand bank', would have fitted the bill nicely.

Investigators would later find correspondence relating to weapons procurement, including a telex suggesting that Nugan Hand president Buddy Yates had pursued a deal involving NATO munitions and patrol boats for the Indonesian navy.

Neil Evans, Nugan Hand's former Chiang Mai manager, later told investigators that in mid-1977 he had attended a meeting in Hong Kong at which the infamous arms dealer Edwin P Wilson was present. The bank, he said, was in discussion with Wilson about acting as a financial intermediary for an arms shipment he was preparing for Saudi Arabia. At the time, Wilson was employing dozens of Mike Hand's former Green Beret paramilitary colleagues to train Libyan troops. Evans alleged that the Saudi transaction of US$200 million had been completed.[2]

On 7 November 1978, General Black sent a telex from the bank's Hawaiian office to Mike Hand and Admiral Yates about deals he had in the pipeline:

> 1. Regarding choppers for SA [South Africa], Hung Wai [Corporation] is checking to determine if seller already has his own established contacts in that country. Will advise.
>
> 2. Because of embargo, which I am told applies to US citizens as well as to US corporations, it might be advisable for buyer and seller to work through overseas channel, namely N/ H [Nugan Hand], rather than US nationals.
>
> 3. HWC [Hung Wai] also has reliable contacts with European munitions manufacturers who offer such items as aircraft frag bombs and ammo at attractive prices. Sai Ching has full details on these and plans to discuss with Mike in Singapore around 20 November.
>
> 4. Sai will also discuss possibilities of N/H arranging financial pages to accompany bids on Indonesian Government tenders. Frank worked with HWC and Sai on one such possibility while he was in Honolulu.[3]

While there can be no doubt about Hand's enthusiasm for gunrunning, General Black's telex prompted a fiercely negative response from Frank Nugan:

Please be specifically advised that the entire contents of points 1, 2, and 3 of your telex are mistaken and inappropriately sent to us. We have no interest, no facilities and no desire to assist in any situation like that outlined in your telex. I suggest any informal enquiries generated by yourself and your associates be immediately nullified. Our real business in trade and wholesale banking areas is totally time encompassing and we have no time for nonsense activities like those.[4]

The Corporate Affairs Commission came to an obvious conclusion:

Given the previous apparent involvement of Mr Hand in attempts to supply arms, it would appear that there may have been a division of opinion between Messrs Black, Yates and Hand on one side and Mr FJ Nugan on the other as to whether Nugan Hand ought be involved in that particular industry.[5]

But why had Frank changed his tune? Over the previous six years, Nugan had lusted after money. He was prepared to bend or break every law that stood in his way to launder money for drug traffickers and had entertained Mike's South African weapons deals. Now he was playing a holier-than-thou card. And he was doing it in writing. He could simply have picked up the phone and called Hand, Yates, Black and the other executives and told them to be careful. It was as if he wanted to put his antagonism to the deals on record, to demonstrate to the world that he was a straight shooter and that it was Mike Hand's idea to get involved in dubious activities.

Corporate Affairs Commission investigator Rick Porter saw Frank's response as a demonstrable act of self-preservation:

I think at that stage Frank Nugan had been charged in the

Nugan Griffith matter. I think he felt that the eye of examination was on the Nugan Hand group. I don't think he wanted to attract any attention to himself. It could incriminate him and that was why those telexes were sent overseas.[6]

Hand's next move appears to have been to deliberately cut Nugan out of the weapons deals. Company records reveal that Buddy Yates was made president of Murdoch Lewis Proprietary Ltd, the company Hand had set up to move arms into South Africa. Ed Black was made president of the Hawaii branch of Murdoch Lewis.

Buddy Yates liked Frank Nugan. On visits to Sydney, he attended church with Frank and socialised with his family. But their friendship and business relationship came under the microscope when agents of the FBI paid Yates a visit regarding allegations that the Nugan Fruit Group was involved with drugs.

Yates told the FBI that shortly after joining Nugan Hand he knew of the allegations. Aware of this, Frank Nugan had approached him and offered him 'the opportunity to leave the bank and rejoin after the matter was resolved'. Yates said he refused to leave. Instead, he hired an investigator to determine if there was any wrongdoing in the company.

As a result, Yates said he was convinced that Nugan Hand was in no way associated with the Nugan Fruit Group's problems. He said the Fruit Group's legal issues were a 'political case'. He noted that Attorney-General Frank Walker was a member of the Labor Party in New South Wales, Australia, which Yates considered 'a wing of the Communist Party and dedicated to the devastation of corporate business'.* Yates described Frank Nugan and Mike Hand as 'right-wing' and 'therefore a natural political enemy of the prosecuting attorney [Walker].' He told the FBI that Nugan had offered Australian

---

* Taken from partly redacted FBI files accessed under Freedom of Information by the author.

authorities an opportunity to review all the books and ledgers of its banks in Sydney, Hong Kong and Germany. Yates repeated his conviction that the bank was not involved in any illegal activities.[7]

Yates' FBI testimony is extraordinary. He appears to have fallen for Frank Nugan's protestations of innocence. He also chose to believe Frank's line that the Labor attorney-general was waging a political vendetta against the Nugan Hand bank, but ignored the fact that Liberal opposition parliamentarian John Dowd was also pursing the Nugan Fruit Group for using crooked ex-cops to intimidate auditors and stack shareholder meetings. If Yates had reviewed the bank's records, he would have found that Frank Nugan had been a regular donor to Walker's party — the Labor Party.

★

From his office in Bangkok, John Owen pondered Nugan Hand's true objectives. He knew of Michael Hand's attempts to carry out weapons trading and was continually being pressured 'to get deposits from local drug runners'.[8] He came to the conclusion that Hand had no scruples about where the money came from and believed he was a man completely without morals:

> Perhaps to be a successful Green Beret that is what you have to be. He is not clever but he is cunning, his brain could never have matched Nugan's. His physical presence could only be described as menacing. I could never understand how Hand could get his own way with Nugan; it was almost as if he had some hold over him — perhaps it was sexual.[9]

By early 1979, Nugan and Hand's friendship had been replaced by a mutual mistrust. In February, Michael Hand met with Admiral Yates and Bernie Houghton. Houghton later told investigators that Hand had come to the conclusion that Frank Nugan had to be eased out of Nugan Hand. Exactly how he would achieve it, he said, he hadn't yet determined.

20

BERNIE OF ARABIA

Reminiscent of a double-dealing bar owner in Hollywood film noir, Bernie Houghton was the most mysterious figure in the Nugan Hand saga. He was instrumental in Nugan meeting Hand in 1968, had acted as an advisor to Mike Hand in the early years of the bank's operation and was influential in the recruitment of US military officers to its executive. In 1978, he had formalised his relationship with Nugan Hand by agreeing to establish the bank's operations in the Middle East.

Under Islamic law the concept of 'interest' is forbidden, so there were no Western-style banks in the Middle East where people could legitimately deposit their funds. Bernie Houghton saw this not as an obstacle but an opportunity.

Bernie flew into Saudi Arabia and called on two friends from his days in Saigon during the Vietnam War, Colonel Marshall Inglebeck and Colonel William Prim. They introduced him to US Air Force personnel and private contract employees working in Saudi, who were making good money but had nowhere to spend or invest it.

A luxurious villa in Al-Khobar served as Bernie's office and residence. He soon opened two more offices in Jeddah and Riyadh and employed an American, Michael Murphy, the maitre d' from his other Kings Cross bar, the Texas Tavern, to run the Jeddah office. Three other Americans came on board, all friends of Murphy, to assist in deposit taking. On payday, they would turn up at construction sites and oil companies to collect cash from the American employees.

American plumber John Green and his father were working for a large US construction firm in Saudi Arabia when they were approached by a couple of Nugan Hand representatives. 'They said you are out of the country for some time and you're paid locally. If you put the money in a bank that's not in the US, there are advantages.'

Nugan Hand depositors were told that their money would be invested on the international money market, with the bulk invested in Australia. In fact, most of the funds went elsewhere in unidentified but suspicious circumstances.

The Greens became regular depositors, investing a sizable US$120,000. On one occasion, John Green was approached to see if he wanted to make another deposit, but this time Nugan Hand was offering fringe benefits: 'I met them and they showed me all these glossy pictures of girls. And I said, "What the hell are you doing here? I don't need girls. I take care of that myself." And they're showing me these pictures of these models. That was really weird.'[1]

*

While his acolytes were out in the stifling Arabian heat luring potential customers into quicksand, Bernie Houghton was having the time of his life in air-conditioned comfort, cozying up to Arab princes and politicians, extracting information and contacts, without anyone realising that they were being manipulated.

Doug Sapper got the measure of Bernie during his visits to Hong Kong: 'Houghton had inroads into areas that Michael would have taken twenty years to develop, if ever. He was a fixer and he had enough people in his circle of friends, contacts and associates who could get him into places you and I couldn't get into, even if we bought the building.'²

Within the first twelve months, seventy American investors had handed over US$1.5 million to Houghton. Another US$3.5 million came from wealthy Arabs. One investor recalled Bernie 'toting away the loot in plastic bags like some reverse Santa Claus'.³

Corporate Affairs Commission investigator Rick Porter saw a funny side to this:

> Houghton certainly was very successful in attracting the money in Saudi Arabia so he did have capabilities. But to my warped sense of humour, I think that was quite hilarious, because in Saudi Arabia if you steal things they cut your fingers off and Houghton had two fingers missing off his left hand and here he was in Saudi Arabia attracting deposits.⁴

By 1979, Houghton had gone from working part time for Nugan Hand to working full time. With all expenses paid, a 1.5 per cent cut of every deposit received, plus a $100,000 a year salary, it was money for jam.

★

In mid-1978, Houghton started opening serious doors for Nugan Hand when he contacted General Richard Secord, a serving member of the US Air Force, whom he had first met in 1972. Houghton said he was looking for ideas that would assist Nugan Hand's move into Saudi Arabia. Secord invited him to a meeting in Geneva with Thomas Clines, a tall, amiable former CIA officer who was director of training for the CIA's clandestine service and the agency's liaison officer with the Pentagon. Clines and Secord told him they were now establishing a company to ship US weapons illegally into Egypt with another CIA officer Ted Shackley, aka the 'Blond Ghost', who had run the agency's clandestine operations.*

Houghton told Clines and Secord that he would be interested in getting involved in the arms deals. At the meeting, Clines said he knew Mike Hand; they had met when he was chief of station in Laos during Mike's period of service. While in Geneva, they suggested Houghton talk with another former CIA officer turned international arms dealer, Edwin P Wilson, who was underwriting their weapons venture. Accompanied by his lawyer, Houghton went to Wilson's office, which he later described as 'extremely elegant and situated in Gustav on Lake Geneva'. During the meeting Wilson told Houghton that he was a former CIA agent and that his job had been to establish front companies for the CIA and other secret agencies. He had also been involved in weapons deals to Angola at the time Michael Hand was gunrunning to southern Africa.

In an interview for this book three months before his death, Ed Wilson recalled the meeting with Bernie Houghton: 'General Richard Secord told Bernie Houghton to contact me at my Geneva office. He arrived with the idea of me assisting selling mutual funds in Libya and other countries. Not only did I say "No" but "Hell no!"'5

According to Wilson, Houghton wouldn't take no for an answer and insisted he travel with him to Paris: 'We flew there in my plane and met someone. The guy in Paris at the airport was definitely about 5 foot 6, dark complexion, weighed about 160 pounds. I don't remember what the conversation was about. All I know, it was a total waste of time and money.'6

Wilson said he took a distinct dislike to Houghton because he had made a homosexual pass at his office manager in front of the manager's

---

*   Clines, Shackley and Secord would all become very big names in the Iran-Contra scandal of the mid-1980s.

wife.* However, telexes later uncovered by Australian investigators suggest that Houghton was a regular visitor to Wilson's Geneva office and that their meetings were not social. Houghton's mission was to sign up Wilson as a Nugan Hand client. The bank was offering a letter of credit totalling US$22 million to assist with a transaction involving weapons and military uniforms for Libya.

Wilson was later found guilty of a range of illegal operations including selling arms and explosives to Libya. In an interview carried out in his prison cell some years later, Wilson told a Canadian journalist that the Nugan Hand group was a big money-maker. 'It was on old concept — done before and will be done again.' The first big money, after Nugan Hand opened its base operations in Australia, was mutual funds from oil workers in Middle East countries. The oil workers, he said, 'didn't want American Internal Revenue to skim the cream off their income'. He also implied that he was directly involved with Houghton in deals involving the CIA. 'Then we got the military to invest, that kind of crap, so there were large funds swilling around to cover the CIA stuff.'[7]

During one of his meetings at Ed Wilson's office, Houghton asked Wilson's associate Peter Goulding about how he could obtain false US passports. He said that he needed such passports for his Nugan Hand customers, who 'might have been under scrutiny for their offshore banking activity'. Goulding said that this type of facility 'was not my cup of tea' and Houghton didn't pursue the matter any further.[8]

Joint Task Force investigators were curious about Bernie Houghton's desire to obtain false passports:

While the real purpose of this inquiry is not known, it is unlikely to have been for the purpose stated by Houghton, which most

---

* As a teenager, Wilson had developed a pathological hatred of homosexuals and he was known to use violence against them. Houghton was homosexual.

probably was an attempt to minimise the seriousness of the use for which they were intended. It is possible, of course, that Houghton was even at this early stage considering an escape route for Hand should such a course become necessary.[9]

From a deposit point of view, the Middle East was one of the few success stories for Nugan Hand. That success brought 'Bernie of Arabia' into the bank's inner circle, where he could influence the bank's future. Mike Hand clearly saw the dexterous, connected and cunning Houghton as a pivotal player in the bank's evolution.

Over the coming months, however, a series of events sent shockwaves through Nugan Hand, making Bernie's idea of escape routes and false passports less a contingency and more a necessity.

21

THE ARCHITECT OF FACT

In late March 1979, John Aston's law clerk Brian Alexander met with James 'Diamond Jim' Shepherd, a short, dapper man of slight build. Shepherd gave Alexander a substantial quantity of cash. This was a routine matter, one of many between the two men.

By his own admission, Shepherd was the financial administrator of the Mr Asia drug syndicate, which was run by a New Zealander, Terry Clark. In his tell-all book, *Mr Asia, Last Man Standing*, Shepherd wrote that he had paid Brian Alexander a monthly retainer to organise ongoing police protection for the syndicate. Alexander was also required to provide a daily report of the drug squad's activities and alert Terry Clark immediately if the squad was targeting any of the Mr Asia syndicate.

One of Shepherd's responsibilities entailed sending money overseas at least once a fortnight through a variety of banks. Alexander boasted excellent contacts in the banking world and, according to Shepherd, moved large quantities of money for the Mr Asia syndicate to Hong Kong, for which he was paid 2.5 per cent.[1]

On 26 March 1979, Nugan Hand's money mover, George Shaw, received a telephone call from Alexander's boss, John Aston, who told Shaw that he had a large deposit to be collected from his office. His emphasis on 'large' suggested security was required. Shaw called up his cousin, an alleged drug trafficker, who turned up with a tough Lebanese ex-policeman in tow. The three men drove up to Aston's office at 54 Park Street.

Aston greeted Shaw and said that he had some 'very good clients' who had given him some money to be transferred overseas. He stressed the necessity for secrecy in the transaction: 'We don't want this money to show up anywhere on the records and we don't want anyone knowing about it. If the matter is handled satisfactorily, then Nugan Hand may gain the depositors as clients.'[2]

Brian Alexander entered Aston's office carrying two overnight bags. Aston said they contained a total of $260,000 in cash plus $5,000 for bank fees. He said $130,000 was to be transferred to Germany, where a Mr Choo would collect it, and a similar amount transferred to Singapore for a Madame Ling Siew Eng. Aston gave Shaw written instructions, including the passport particulars of Choo and Ling.

Jack Choo or Chinese Jack, as he was named, was a seasoned trafficker responsible for blockbuster importations of drugs, including thousands of Buddha sticks into New Zealand, 400 kilograms of heroin into Australia and a similar quantity into Britain.

Returning to the Nugan Hand office, Shaw and Stephen Hill locked themselves in a room and counted the money. Some of the bank notes were covered in a purple stain, an unambiguous sign that the money was the proceeds of a bank robbery.

Hill took the $5,000 'bank fees' and then stored the rest of the money in the safe overnight. The next day, Hill and Shaw met with Frank Nugan. Shaw said he was worried about the purple dye. Nugan told him not to worry. Over the next few hours, Nugan carried out a complex sequence of deposits and transfers of the money across different Nugan Hand companies.

Under Frank's Contra system, the $260,000* was destined never

---

* $260,000 is the equivalent of $1.2million in 2015.

21 The architect of fact

to leave Australia. Instead, funds were to be taken out of deposits in Germany and Singapore. Nugan telexed Mike Hand in Singapore with the details of the clients and their passport numbers. Two days later, Nugan sent Hand a coded message about a change of plan; John Aston now wanted the full $260,000 to be transferred to Singapore to be picked up by Madam Ling Siew Eng in 'latex' — US dollars.[3]

Three weeks later, George Shaw called John Aston and advised that the transaction had been successfully completed. According to Joint Task Force investigator Clive Small, the Mr Asia syndicate used the funds to import heroin into Sydney, and that was only the beginning:

> This was probably the largest single amount of money that we identified coming from a major drug importation group. But we understand that much more money was deposited by the Mr Asia syndicate and in most cases handed to Brian Alexander and then deposited via Aston's office into the Nugan Hand bank.[*4]

Within days of the transfer to Singapore, AU$10,000 was deposited into a Nugan Hand account in the name of Richard Spencer, the Narcotics Bureau officer running the investigation into the Mr Asia syndicate. This was the second $10,000 cash deposit into Spencer's account via John Aston. Aston would later deny any knowledge of the deposit.

Aston's statement to George Shaw that 'We don't want this money to show up anywhere on the records and we don't want anyone knowing about it' suggests that Aston and Alexander were much more than legal advisors, and had become part of the Mr Asia machinery. By extension, Nugan Hand was assisting the syndicate by moving its money.

According to Corporate Affairs Commission investigator Rick Porter, George Shaw later admitted under examination that he was

---

* The Joint Task Force estimated that the Mr Asia syndicate laundered at least AU$3 million, equivalent to $14 million today, through Nugan Hand.

aware the money transfer was to facilitate a drug deal: 'I guess you could say Nugan Hand was aiding and abetting the drug trade in Australia. In that way the bank was complicit. If they didn't move the money to Choo and other members of the Mr Asia syndicate, they would not have been able to bring drugs back to Australia.[5]

*

In May 1979, two members of the Mr Asia syndicate, Douglas and Isabel Wilson, were found dead in shallow graves on a vacant lot in Rye, Victoria. They had been executed for informing on the syndicate. Back in June 1978, Queensland State Police and Narcotics Bureau agents had interviewed the Wilsons in Brisbane. The couple had claimed that the syndicate boss, Terry Clark, had been responsible for half a dozen murders, and that the syndicate was paying a Federal Bureau of Narcotics officer $25,000 a year for information.

In June 1979, a combined police group made up of New South Wales, Victoria, Queensland and federal officers began investigating the Wilsons' allegations. Four people came under the microscope for supplying information to the Mr Asia syndicate: John Aston, Brian Alexander, and two Narcotics Bureau officers, Richard Spencer and Wayne Brindle. Spencer was running the bureau's Mr Asia syndicate investigation and was a Nugan Hand customer.

On Monday, 1 October 1979, Frank Nugan arrived home from an extended business trip to North America. On the Tuesday morning, the receptionist buzzed him to say that the deputy director of the Federal Bureau of Narcotics, Brian Bates, was on the line. A year and a half had passed since Frank had confronted the bureau, an action which he believed had precipitated the cessation of its investigation into Nugan Hand. Frank took the call, during which Bates asked if Frank could be available the next day for an interview. The following

21 The architect of fact

morning, 3 October 1979, two senior members of the Federal Bureau of Narcotics arrived at the Sydney office of Nugan Hand to interview Frank. The details of the interview are not known. However, that afternoon, Frank called an extraordinary meeting of the Nugan Hand legal division.

Nugan told those assembled that he wanted to change the image of Nugan Hand and to steer all of its companies away from criminal activities. The meeting was recorded:

> We will have to go through quite a lot of files and find all the secret bank accounts that are secret for reasons unacceptable to us. We are even thinking of passing most of the illegitimate clients off to other banks. I know of many of these that you people don't know of, so there's more to get rid of than you would think, simply because I have been the main guilty party for some reason in years gone by. But what little you people have assisted me with we will also cut out, so that we don't have any. Look, if you are shocked, let me tell you that I am determined to achieve this at whatever cost. This company costs about $10 million a year to run — Nugan Hand — and it's going to toss off a lot of illegitimate cash flow and business, and hopefully I can get legitimate work.

As well as admitting to illegalities, Nugan laid the blame on himself:

> The problems in the firm basically stem from the top, rather than from the bottom. We've got people who at present get away with murder and never give a damn, because at one time or another you were either inside a bottle of Scotch or in a church, or whatever, in this period. We are reborn. Those sons of bitches who were passing under our name, prior to today, including

me, we are different people. I am bigger and smarter than Alan Bond.* High-quality people like me get paid $100,000 a day to work something like that out ... I can't do anything that would be unprofessional or infamous conduct. I have a theory that I espouse, but it may be inaccurate, or I may be hallucinating, but I operate with a fragmentation theory of thinking ...† but I am probably wrong because I have been wrong on so many things all my life and maybe my theory is just vanity ... I am an architect of fact.[6]

The following Thursday, 11 October 1979, Mike Hand flew into Sydney. On his arrival at Nugan Hand's Macquarie Street office, a concerned staffer handed him the recording of the recent legal department meeting. The contents provided an alarming picture of both Frank Nugan's admission of illegalities and his delusional state of mind. In the hands of a law-enforcement agency, or the media, the tape recording could have single-handedly destroyed Nugan Hand.

In the short term, there was little Mike Hand could do. Over the coming days, fifteen of Nugan Hand's international executives and some well-connected intelligence operatives would be arriving in Sydney for a conference. Heaven forbid if the self-proclaimed 'architect of fact' started hallucinating in their presence.

---

* In the late 1970s Alan Bond was on the way to becoming a high-profile business tycoon. In 1983, Bond's yacht *Australia II* won the America's Cup. In 1992, Bond was declared bankrupt with personal debts totaling AU$1.8 billion. In 1997, he was sentenced to four years' jail after he pleaded guilty to defrauding Bell Resources of $1.2 billion.

† By referring to a 'fragmentation theory of thinking' Nugan may have been alluding to a theory put forth to explain how, under hypnosis, some people can compartmentalise pain and prevent pain from reaching their consciousness. Equally, he may have been hallucinating.

22

THE LAST SUPPER

In mid-October 1979, two dozen Nugan Hand executives and guests bowed their head in prayer as Mike Hand asked God to look favourably on Nugan Hand, its staff and the important work they were doing around the globe. The venue was the Gazebo Hotel in Kings Cross. The event was designed as a forum to discuss a range of issues affecting the bank's international organisation.

That first session, Mike welcomed everybody and introduced the bank's recent recruits, including Dale Holmgren, Roy Manor and Walt McDonald. Dale Holmgren had managed a secret CIA airline out of Taiwan before setting up the bank's Taipei branch. Retired Air Force Lieutenant-General Roy Manor was the former chief of staff for US Pacific Command and US Government liaison with the Philippines' president, Ferdinand Marcos; Manor was now running Nugan Hand's Philippines branch. Walt McDonald was a CIA veteran of twenty-five years, who was now representing the bank in Washington.

Frank announced that Admiral Buddy Yates, his most important counsellor for the previous three years, was standing down as bank president in favour of Donald Beazley, a recent president of the Great American Bank in Miami. Buddy Yates said that he had been romancing Beazley for more than two years, hoping he would join Nugan Hand to give it extra credibility.*

Don Beazley, the only person in the room with legitimate banking experience, addressed the delegates:

'Listening to Buddy and Frank and Mike, I was able to make the decision that I would want to be associated with this group. It was an opportunity and a challenge that I think is probably one of the best ones I've ever made, decision-wise. I am looking forward to a long and fruitful relationship. It is a privilege and an honor for me to be president.'[1]

At each session of the conference, which was recorded, two or three executives addressed the assembly and spoke candidly about their parts in the business, legal and illegal. A number of the Asia-based executives openly discussed their involvement in the bank's illicit activities in the Philippines, Taiwan and Malaysia.

Michael Hand, too, made it clear that Nugan Hand was still actively pursuing illegitimate and covert business, but it was nevertheless essential to embed all activities deeply behind a firewall of secrecy. Information, he said, was only to be passed to certain employees on a need-to-know basis.

'Think for just five seconds about the various people each and everyone of us know, who for a multitude of reasons would prefer not to give out information. They don't want to be legal.'[2]

Bernie Houghton concurred: 'In Saudi there is more money moving under the table than on top of it. We get garbage bags full of cash! The clients say, "I've been trying to move and deposit money anonymously for a long time, so once I see a vehicle like Nugan Hand, I'm happy. I've been looking for something like this all my life!"'[3]

Hand reiterated, 'Internal security is a major issue. We have

---

* A year later, Beazley's former bank, Great American, found itself at the centre of a $100 million money-laundering scandal involving a Colombian cocaine cartel. While Beazley was never implicated, other staffers were imprisoned.

obligations to all our clients, even if they're not clandestine or they're not even very secret deals. Walt, how does our security hold up?'[4]

Walt McDonald pondered the question.

'To be honest,' he said, 'when I came to Nugan Hand it was like trying to divine the inner workings of the KGB. I had to draw on my days in the CIA to simply understand how the organisation was structured.'[5]

If there were any doubts about Nugan Hand's future direction, Admiral Buddy Yates put that to rest.

'For those of you who don't know Walt, until recently he was the director of the CIA's Economic Division. Walt's acknowledged in this world of grass politics, drug events and battles and it starts generally in the area where Walt is going.'[6]

*

Such statements were in perfect misalignment with Frank's desire to rid the bank of illegal activities. Frank said he didn't want sensitive clients to show up on the books. If Nugan Hand was to handle such clients, he said, 'we should simply take a service fee and pass their deposits onto other banks.'[7]

Their contrasting attitudes set the partners at odds and, according to one conference attendee, the tension between Mike and Frank was palpable.

Late on the second evening, Mike convened a closed meeting with Bernie Houghton, Walt McDonald and Admiral Yates. Frank Nugan was not invited. One can only speculate about the purpose of the meeting, but everyone in the group had previously expressed concerns about Frank's behaviour — how he had turned up at a meeting at a Manila hotel, leaving two Mercedes running out front; his boasting about moving money for the Marcos family; how the Filipinos thought he was crass; and his taking exception to the helicopter deal General Ed Black had been working on and calling it 'nonsense'. Also, while in the United States, Frank had dictated a letter to Walt McDonald's secretary attacking the Bank of New South Wales in Sydney for providing the media with false information about Nugan Hand and his family's fruit company. McDonald had directed his secretary not to send the letter; in his opinion, Frank was 'unbalanced'.

Frank put proof to that notion throughout the conference. His presentations drifted from self-aggrandisement to incoherence. In one rambling, embarrassing speech, he bragged about his own leadership qualities in dealing with the run on the bank in the wake of the fraud allegations. Thirty per cent of all depositors' funds, he said, were lost; one client alone took $4 million out of Hong Kong. But despite that crisis, Nugan Hand had survived, thanks to his efforts.

Bernie Houghton blamed Frank Nugan's legal problems, which in his opinion were hanging around Frank's neck like a skunk. The name Nugan was now poison and its possessor was the firm's greatest liability. McDonald concurred; he and Beazley had tried to introduce their own contacts to the bank, but the bad publicity had scared them off, completely.

Houghton's view, which Mike now apparently shared, was that it was time to pull down the shutters on the Sydney office and hightail it out of Australia altogether. But if anyone knew Frank Nugan it was Mike and he believed Frank was proud of what he'd built and wouldn't take that option lying down.

There was one certainty: Mike Hand's loyalty to Frank had been all but expended. His overriding fear now was letting Frank travel outside Australia. Everywhere he went he had left a trail of problems and sullied the brand. From now on, Mike decreed, Walt McDonald would accompany Frank on all his international business trips and handle the negotiations. A twenty-five-year veteran of the CIA was now the designated nursemaid to a dipsomaniac.

22 The last supper

The following day, an American guest at the conference couldn't help but notice Frank's entrance: 'Nugan arrives at the meeting, shining eyes, saying, "Oh I feel so good, I have been to church. I took communion. I feel really good."'[8]

During one session, Frank fronted the delegates and announced that he was stepping down as the chief legal advisor for the organisation. That position was to be handled by Mr Beazley. 'Beazley is now the boss' he said. 'He's taking the responsibility for hiring and firing throughout Nugan Hand'. Three outside 'legal counsels had also been appointed, including William Colby, the former director of the CIA.'

Power had now been transferred to the Americans. Indeed, if the Australian delegates had looked around the room they would have come to that conclusion. Virtually everyone in a leadership position or advisory role was an American with either a US military or CIA background.

For all intents and purposes, Frank Nugan had lost control of the firm.

*

In the final session, Mike thanked everyone for coming, but there was a sting in his concluding words: 'I've been asked in recent days by some of you how we are placed should there be an unexpected run on the bank. There has long been a contingency plan in place for two people to take over should anything happen to Frank or myself. And now a new contingency plan is being developed and will be completed within the next day or two. Frank and I will have substantial insurance policies equivalent to 75 per cent of the value of Nugan Hand to meet any run that may occur in the event of … well, let's call it misadventure.'[9]

A group photo was taken and the delegates repaired to the bar. Frank meanwhile followed Mike and another staffer into an anteroom.

According to the staffer a conflagration of insults and accusations deteriorated into an isometric tangle of fists and smashed furniture.*

On hearing of the altercation Doug Sapper reflected on what it meant:

> Regardless of what it said in the recipe book, the plot was thickening. Michael could be the best friend that you've ever had or he could be the worst enemy you could pick and you definitely didn't want to be on Michael's bad side. But marginalising Frank Nugan was a bad plan. The more he was marginalised the more he felt like he was out of the loop, and I would not put it past him that at that point he became a little bit unstable. And that could lead to Frank trying to dump everybody in the shit. It played into his dysfunctionality, like giving a drunken monkey a hand-grenade. It was not a question of 'Will it go off?' but a matter of 'When?'

Two days after the Nugan Hand conference, Mike Hand flew out of Sydney bound for Hong Kong. Hours later, Frank Nugan and Walt McDonald boarded QF3 bound for Honolulu, where they were to brief Ed Black on the conference, before flying to England and Germany to negotiate the purchase of two banks.

While in Germany, Frank received confronting news from his brother. The pre-trial magistrate had declared that as directors of the Nugan Fruit Group they had a case to answer. They had been committed for trial at a date yet to be set. The bribes, standover tactics and the AU$1 million plus, which Frank had taken from bank deposits to pay legal fees, had achieved nothing.

On 29 November 1979, Nugan received even more disturbing news. The police had arrested Brian Alexander at his home. That same

---

* The eyewitness to the incident would not disclose what was said during the Nugan vs Hand encounter.

morning, the police had staked out the Customs House building in Sydney and arrested Narcotics Bureau officers Richard Spencer and Wayne Brindle as they arrived for work. All three had been charged with conspiracy to pervert the course of justice. Spencer and Brindle had allegedly supplied information to Alexander about the Wilsons. Alexander had then passed it on to Mr Asia boss Terry Clark, who in turn had ordered the murder of the Wilsons.

For Frank Nugan, this was far too close to home. Brian Alexander worked for the law firm that was defending his fraud case, and bank customer Richard Spencer was allegedly involved with a murderous drug syndicate for which his bank had provided its illegal money-moving service.*

If Alexander or Spencer decided to unburden themselves to investigators, the bank's complicity with drug traffickers would be outed. Worse still, the knowledge Frank had of how the murderous Mr Asia syndicate moved its money, and to whom, made him a potential target of violence. In the organised-crime business everybody knew that the most knowledgeable, and therefore dangerous, person in their midst was the accounts man: he knew the dates, the names, where the money came from and where it went. And when the 'shit hit the fan', the accounts man was usually the first to end up dead.

---

* In 1980, the charges against Brian Alexander and Narcotics Bureau agents Richard Spencer and Wayne Brindle were controversially dismissed in the Court of Petty Sessions. In 1983, the Stewart Royal Commission found 'The Commission doubts that the decision [by the magistrate who dismissed the case] was a proper exercise of magisterial function in a committal hearing. Unfortunately, it would appear that at times the magistrate lost control of his own court.' The commissioner also found 'that Mr Clark and his associates used the services of Mr Brian Alexander, a Sydney law clerk employed by Mr John Aston, a solicitor, to obtain information from police and the Sydney office of the Narcotics Bureau'. The commissioner noted that 'the evidence points strongly to Mr Spencer being one source of Mr Alexander's information.'

23

ETERNITY

When lay preacher Paul Owens called at the Nugan Hand office to see Frank, he was surprised at the change in his physical appearance: 'He had lost a lot of weight. Whether that was a diet, I don't know. I never asked. But he seemed very tired, very drained, and ... I just took that as heavy work.'[1]

They prayed together, as usual, and on his departure Owens posed a question to the merchant banker: 'I said to Frank, "Where will you spend eternity? You've got a choice. Where will you spend it?" And that hit Frank very hard, as it does most people. I said, "You've got a choice. When are you going to make it?" That had a dramatic effect on Frank.'[2]

★

Frank Nugan had returned to Sydney in mid-December 1979. His wife, Lee, and the children arrived two days later for the Christmas holidays from Tennessee. Frank was so distracted he'd forgotten he had invited Guy Pauker and his family to stay with him over the Christmas–New Year break. Pauker worked for the Rand Corporation, an American think-tank and was an advisor to Henry Kissinger, the National Security Council and the Pentagon. His associates, such as former Pentagon official, Fletcher Prouty, believed Pauker was on the CIA payroll: 'I worked with Pauker a lot in my job as CIA liaison officer. There is no question in my mind that he worked for the agency with Rand as a cover.'[3]

Pauker first met Frank Nugan and Michael Hand in Hawaii in 1977. In mid-1979, Pauker had met them again at a Nugan Hand–sponsored conference in Manila, where he agreed to do some 'isolated consulting work for Nugan Hand'.* He later told the Stewart Royal Commission that during his Christmas stay 'Nugan and his wife seemed to be not on very good terms, and he was definitely clearly depressed.' He also observed Frank with his children: 'He would bounce that little girl of theirs on his knees very wistfully and talk to the little boy ... The way he was talking to those children, in particular, almost in retrospect of course, looked as if he was saying goodbye to them.'[4] He came to the conclusion that Nugan was no longer 'a man of sober judgment, but a man with a very unbalanced mind'.

Lee Nugan later denied Pauker's depiction of the family. She told journalist Jonathan Kwitny, 'Frank did not want him there. He asked him, but then he changed his mind.'[5]

In early January, a female member of the St Andrew's Cathedral congregation expressed concern to Paul Owens about Frank Nugan, who had attended the morning service: 'She told me she was sitting behind Frank and had heard him crying, and [had seen him] red-eyed after the service was over.'[6]

In the first week of January, Nugan Hand's accountant and auditor confronted Frank with further bad news. Unless AU$5 million in internal bills were repaid, he would be forced to 'qualify the accounts', exposing the Nugan Hand bank as bankrupt.[7]

Corporate investigator Rick Porter recalls:

---

* Following the collapse of the bank, Pauker denied any involvement with the bank, even though the bank's publicity boasted that he was now an advisor to Nugan Hand on international affairs. He was also listed on the bank's register, with an internal code number of 509.

The bank was insolvent and it was generating paper to cover the hole, but the hole was getting bigger. Nugan had disguised the insolvency for quite some number of years. His auditor had told him that he was going to qualify the report, which would have rung all the bells and whistles. I think he had become aware that Nugan Hand was going to be opened up to public scrutiny.[8]

Frank was in trouble. Public scrutiny would reveal not merely the bank's insolvency but the depth of its illegality.

On 7 January 1980, American Congressman Bob Wilson, a Republican member of the US House of Representatives Defense Subcommittee, flew into Sydney and dined with Bernie Houghton at the Bourbon & Beefsteak. Wilson's successful election campaigns owed much to donations from defence contractors such as Lockheed and McDonnell Douglas. He was also a determined supporter of the CIA's right to engage in clandestine activity, including the destabilisation of foreign governments.

Bob Wilson later claimed that the dinner was purely a social occasion, but that Houghton, whom he described as 'a kind of typical Texan bullshitter', only wanted to talk about business. Wilson denied that they discussed 'military or defense', despite the fact that both men had interests in that area. Four days later, Wilson dined with Michael Hand in Singapore, which suggests that Nugan Hand and Wilson were indeed exploring areas of mutual interest.[9] (Intriguingly, Bob Wilson's name, along with that of former CIA director William Colby, would later be found on a piece of meat pie wrapper on Frank Nugan's body.)

On 9 January 1980, Frank Nugan flew out of Sydney on a US-bound flight with his wife and children. On arrival in Nashville, he gave Lee a file of legal documents and an insurance policy on his life.[10]

Frank then flew to Florida to see Don Beazley, the new chairman of Nugan Hand International, to discuss taking an interest in a US bank. Beazley recalled that Nugan said he was thinking of moving to the United States. Indeed, while in Miami, Frank began inspecting expensive homes in the Palm Beach area. Nugan then flew to Europe, where he met with Mike Hand, Walt McDonald and Bill Colby.

Frank returned to Sydney on the morning of Friday 25 January 1980, drained from the flight. Over the previous two weeks he had dragged himself onto and off more than a dozen aircraft, woken up in six different time zones and emptied hotel bar fridges with abandon. After a few hours sleep, he arrived at the Sydney office, where senior executive Stephen Hill confronted him over the company's indebtedness. Together they drove in Nugan's car to Mrs Macquarie's Chair, a site overlooking Sydney Harbour, where they could discuss the matter in private. The external auditors, Hill said, were not going to sign off on the books. The problem related to Frank's use of depositors' funds to buy and renovate his home, to pay for the Nugan Fruit Group's legal fees and to purchase an orange juice company.

When Nugan refused to accept Hill's demands to 'man up' over the bank's financial problems, Hill offered his resignation. The men met again that afternoon. According to Hill, Nugan said, 'I don't know why I ever became involved in big business. I could have been more successful and made more money if I'd stayed with Freehills [a large firm of Sydney solicitors]. Sometimes I think I would have been better working on a mushroom farm like Alf [his half brother].'[11]

Frank's answer to most problems was money. His most pressing problem now was a lack of it. And so began his desperate attempt to plug a hole amounting to more than $3 million. That evening, 25 January 1980, he dined at the home of his friend Paul Lincoln-Smith. They had met while working at Freehills in the late 1960s and had become semi-regular fishing buddies. In many ways Frank had modelled himself on Lincoln-Smith, right down to purchasing a waterfront Vaucluse home, identically positioned on the next peninsula.

Over dinner, the conversation moved to a mining venture Lincoln-Smith had started. Frank soon turned the conversation to how Nugan Hand was on the up and up and in the process of taking over banks in Hamburg and London. Investors, he said, were excited by what they were offering in terms of returns. It was a loaded hook, but Lincoln-Smith failed to take the bait.

Lincoln-Smith told *Wall Street Journal* reporter Jonathan Kwitny: 'I never did any business with Frank. We didn't need each other. He was rich and I was rich. People who have money don't often do business with each other. We're looking for people with propositions. He was very excited about Nugan Hand.'[12]

Following dinner, Lincoln-Smith acknowledged the proverbial elephant in the room.

'I'm very sorry that the magistrate committed you for trial,' he said.

Frank sank into his chair and said he was thinking of going to live in the United States with his family.

'My business life is finished here.'

Lincoln-Smith recalled that Nugan drank a lot of wine and several glasses of cognac and that by the time he took his leave he was 'laughing drunk'. Lincoln-Smith said they made a loose arrangement for Frank to return for dinner the next evening, but he never arrived.[13]

*

Saturday 26 January 1980 was Australia Day. That morning, Frank Nugan arrived at the office, hung-over, to meet again with staff. At 10.30, he called the meeting to an end and said he was going home to bed.

As Sydneysiders picnicked alongside the harbour or at the beach, the self-proclaimed 'richest man in Sydney' pulled another name out of a hat. He called successful merchant banker and film-industry figure John Darling. Nugan had recently made a $2.4 million offer for Darling's estate at Mulgoa, located 75 kilometres west of Sydney, at the base of the Blue Mountains. At the time, the property was one of the most expensive of its type in Australia. Darling invited Nugan to lunch at his estate the next day. Nugan agreed and gave Darling the impression that he wanted to firm up the offer, but he would never arrive.

That evening millions of Australian families settled down to watch the popular American cowboy series *Gunsmoke* on television. The story that night, entitled 'Blind Man's Buff', opened with a traveller and his horse resting beside a pleasant river. The peace was broken when two rough-looking cowboys rode up and decided to rob him. Shots were fired from a rifle, hitting the traveller in the temple. He appeared to be dead, but when the thieves were long gone he came to and sought help. He stumbled upon a homestead, where he collapsed into the arms of a lonely but caring spinster. He had no recall of his own name and his past — good, bad or indifferent — had been completely erased from his memory.

At 4.20am, the following morning, Sunday 27 January 1980, two uniformed police officers from Lithgow were out patrolling a stretch of the Great Western Highway, 140 kilometres west of Sydney. Passing through the sleepy hamlet of South Bowenfels, Constable Les Cross noticed through a clearing the parking lights of a vehicle sitting on a stretch of road the locals called Forty Bends. A few hundred metres further on, he took a turn-off to investigate. His partner, Sergeant Neville Brown, motioned to him to take it slow. Forty Bends was once a part of the highway with a notorious reputation for its blind corners, close proximity to a nail-bitingly perilous ridge and a propensity for ice. Countless travellers had come to grief over the years until the bitumen bureaucrats in Sydney finally decided to bypass the section in the early 1970s. Since then, it had become one of the district's popular lovers' lanes, witnessing little human drama other than the occasional unplanned pregnancy. But on this Australia-Day long weekend, Forty Bends was destined to make news across the country.

Around a sweeping a curve, the patrol car's headlights found the rear of a metallic-silver-coloured Mercedes parked on the wrong side of the road. A Mercedes in this part of the world was unusual; nearby Lithgow was a working-class coal town.

Through the rear window, Brown could make out the shape of someone in the driver's seat. He unclipped the torch from his belt and directed light along the passenger-side windows; they were spattered with what appeared to be blood. Cross gingerly opened the door to find a man in his late thirties dressed in bone-coloured trousers and a dark blue shirt slumped over the centre console. He had a military rifle in his hands and a massive, point-blank wound to his temple. Unquestionably, he was dead.

Brown radioed for back-up and an ambulance. At 4.45 am, Constable Owen Carter arrived from Lithgow. Composing himself, Carter carefully prized the barrel of the rifle from the man's left hand. Rigor mortis had set in. In the breach of the weapon, he found a live .30-calibre cartridge then another in the magazine. Only one shot had been fired, the remnants of which were lodged between the headlining and the roof metal. On the rear seat, Carter retrieved a rifle box and a smaller box containing forty-seven rounds of live ammunition.

Detective Sergeant Bill McDonnell was home asleep when the phone rang:

> The Lithgow police told me they had been patrolling in an area of South Bowenfels and had come across a car with its parking lights on, which looked suspicious. They'd made a closer examination and found the deceased person sitting in the car with his hand on a rifle and a massive sign of violence. He had been shot in the head.[14]

McDonnell was a former Australian middleweight boxing champion who ran a squad of investigators out of Orange, 120 kilometres west of Lithgow. With his regional superior on leave, McDonnell was required to head down to Lithgow and take charge of the investigation. On arrival, Sergeant Brown informed McDonnell that the body had been transferred to the local hospital mortuary, where the resident medical officer had pronounced life extinct.

McDonnell inspected the contents of the deceased's wallet. A driver's licence bore the name Francis John Nugan, born in 1942, a resident of Vaucluse, an exclusive Sydney harbourside suburb. McDonnell knew the surname; the Nugan family owned a major fruit and vegetable packing and transport firm in Griffith. Frank Nugan, he recalled, was connected with a bank down in Sydney. 'The deceased person was thirty-seven-year-old Frank Nugan. We had his licence, credit cards and numerous other cards found upon his body. The car was registered to a Frank Nugan and it was quite obvious to us that he had committed suicide.'[15]

No one answered the phone at the Nugan home. The Griffith police made inquiries and tracked down Nugan's brother to his Sydney apartment. At 3 pm, Ken Nugan and his wife arrived at Lithgow Police Station. He could offer no reason for his brother to take his own life. Frank was a highly successful businessman with a young family. McDonnell quizzed him about his brother's movements. A week after New Year, he said, Frank had taken his American-born wife, Lee, and their children to visit her parents back in Tennessee. Frank had then travelled alone to Miami and onto Europe for meetings with his American-born business partner, Mike Hand, and other international executives of the Nugan Hand bank. He had returned from Germany alone only two days earlier, on Friday 25 January. Ken said he had last seen his brother late that morning, when he had called in for a short visit on his way home.

McDonnell asked Ken Nugan if his brother had seemed troubled or morose:

> Ken Nugan said he saw absolutely no outward indication that Frank Nugan was in a state of mind to take his own life. He had only just arrived back in the country. He had put off a couple of meetings because of his tiredness, and made arrangements to have meetings in a day or two. But then of course they didn't materialise because he shot himself.

McDonnell drove Ken Nugan to the local hospital morgue to identify the body:

> Naturally, Ken Nugan was very upset when he came to view the body. The deceased was a hell of a mess. I said, 'Well you have to go through the procedure,' and he said, 'I can tell you something that his mother, father and myself are probably the only people in the world to know. Frank has a webbed left foot.' I went in and had a look and sure enough the middle toes of his left foot were webbed. I said to Ken Nugan, 'It's him but that doesn't negate us having to go through the sorry procedure of you having to identify the body.'[16]

The mortuary attendant lifted the sheet covering the man's head and upper chest. Ken Nugan winced at the sight of his sibling, his temple shattered, his hair and face spattered with dry blood.

Shaking his head, he said despairingly, 'He used to boast about being the wealthiest man in Sydney. Look at him now.'[17]

As they left the mortuary, McDonnell asked Ken Nugan to meet him that evening at his brother's home in Sydney to conduct a search for a suicide note.

23 Eternity

McDonnell and Constable Carter arrived at 7 pm. Ken Nugan, his wife and his half-brother, Alf, had arrived minutes before, along with two legal representatives, barrister Ian Strathdee and law clerk Brian Alexander.[18]

With security bars on every window and door, the dwelling looked more like a fortress than a home, and raised the question in McDonnell's mind as to whether Nugan had had reason to be anxious about his safety and that of his family.

With a key found in Nugan's car, McDonnell entered the property to find that the home's sophisticated alarm system hadn't been activated. He ordered Carter to check with the security company while he searched the house. McDonnell instructed the family and the legal representatives to accompany him to corroborate any evidence uncovered. As they moved from room to room, the house exuded a natural melancholy. Framed photographs throughout told the story of a family: a wedding in New York, a pretty blonde wife, two young smiling children — a boy and a girl. Their world was shattered.

*

According to Bill McDonnell, fifteen minutes into the search things went haywire:

> I could hear sirens heading towards the house. Not knowing whether they were police, ambulance or fire brigade, I didn't take a great deal of notice of them until they stopped outside Frank Nugan's home. They were police officers answering a call. I was very upset about the police doing that and asked them, 'Why would you have sirens?' They said, 'We were told there were police in trouble at this address.' I have never been able to establish where that came from. It was an anonymous phone call.[19]

The call had to have originated from within the house. Unbeknownst to McDonnell, Brian Alexander, who was on bail awaiting trial for allegedly perverting the course of justice by providing information to the Mr Asia drug syndicate, had peeled off from the group and was prowling about the home alone. In doing so, Alexander clearly had the opportunity to remove evidence and thereby hinder the investigation into Frank Nugan's death.

After seventy-five minutes searching the house, McDonnell found nothing to help his inquiries. There was certainly no evidence of violence or anything to suggest that another person had recently been in the home: 'We were there primarily to look for a suicide note or any other evidence to suggest that he had left home with the intent of taking his life. We found no note or anything else to explain why Frank Nugan had seemingly killed himself.'

Later that evening, Ken Nugan tracked down Mike Hand to a hotel room in London. Mike had already heard of Frank's death and said he was booked on the next plane back to Sydney. Before hanging up Mike allegedly barked, 'The little fucker, he's gone and got out of this mess and left me to clean it up.'[20]

24

THE TWILIGHT ZONE

Over the coming days, the incident at Forty Bends dominated talk in the corridors of the New South Wales parliament. Liberal John Dowd had doubts about the suicide finding: 'Execution was my immediate assumption. He didn't strike me as the sort of fellow who would commit suicide. I felt it was probably someone from within the Nugan Hand bank structure, but it may have been someone unconnected.'[1]

In his parliamentary office, Attorney-General Frank Walker chewed over the first newspaper reports and wondered whether the fraud case, which was soon to be scheduled for trial, had anything to do with Nugan's death. That notion receded when he received a briefing from his police minister about items found in Nugan's car and on his body:

> There was a ledger with names of people who were obviously clients of the bank. Twenty-six of those were drug dealers, including football player Paul Heywood, who was rotting in a Bangkok prison for heroin trafficking. There was also the business card of William Colby, a former director of the CIA, and a strip of meat-pie wrapper inside a Bible with the name of US congressman Bob Wilson and again the name of Colby scribbled in pencil.[2]

Pondering the names, Walker picked up the phone, called the head of the Corporate Affairs Commission and said he was going to call an inquiry into the Nugan Hand bank: 'This was a very strange event for the senior executive of an international bank and naturally we were very concerned about it. Law officers, of course, are very suspicious about bank managers killing themselves. There is usually a big story behind that sort of behaviour.'[3]

*

Nugan Hand's Sydney office reopened on the Tuesday following Nugan's death. The scene was one of chaos. Staffers were in shock, some were crying, the phones were running hot and concerned depositors were lining up at reception demanding to know if their money was safe. The bank's international executives were also phoning in asking what to tell their customers.

Mid-morning Mike Hand and outgoing Nugan Hand president Buddy Yates arrived from London. Half an hour later, Frank's wife, Lee, arrived from the United States and was ushered into the boardroom, crying and demanding answers as to what had happened to her husband.

Frank Nugan's attractive, hard-nosed private secretary, Patricia Swan, briefed Mike Hand on a disturbing occurrence the previous day, a public holiday. She had received an early morning call from staff accountant Stephen Hill to say that Frank was dead and to get over to the office. According to testimony later given in court, Swan said she had found Ken Nugan, Hill and another employee rifling through filing cabinets, pulling out desk drawers and looking for documents:

> Steve Hill told me to go through all the filing cabinets and drawers in my room and Frank's room and to 'take out anything that might implicate you or go against you.' I asked Steve if he could be more specific, as I had no idea what I was meant to be looking

for, and he just repeated what he first said. Not really knowing what I was looking for, I quickly went through the filing cabinets in my room as both Ken and Steve seemed to think the Corporate Affairs or the police might arrive at any moment. Steve was in his room putting papers in cartons — either cashbooks or ledgers or journals — and Dennis Pittard was taking them downstairs, presumably to put in a vehicle to take away.[4]

Patricia Swan said that, as she left the office, Ken Nugan repeated the warning that Corporate Affairs or the police would probably raid the bank the next day and that 'things wouldn't be easy'.[5]

The authorities had not yet appeared, but Mike Hand suspected that to be merely a matter of time. Hand and Bernie Houghton called the staff together. There were no heartfelt speeches about his friend and business partner. Hand simply introduced solicitor Michael Moloney, whom he said had been brought in to oversee the Sydney operations. It would require a 'crack-hot lawyer', Houghton said to forensically analyse another lawyer's modus operandi. The fact that Moloney was Bernie's personal lawyer suggested that Houghton was now pulling the strings.

With eyes of cold savagery, Hand scanned those assembled and warned them that if they did not cooperate and follow his and Maloney's instructions their wives would be seized, cut up and returned to them in brown paper parcels.[*]

*

Concerned investors were soon arriving at the bank. From his home in Queensland, Dr. Thomas Ogden telephoned Mike Hand. He had

---

[*] At a committal hearing of a conspiracy case involving the destruction of bank documents, an executive of the bank claimed that Hand had told staff that he was worried that 'his wife would suffer greatly and that she would be mutilated and sent to him in packages.' Other staff suggested that it was Hand who was making the threats to 'cut up wives'.

deposited more than $650,000 with the bank, more than any other individual. Hand assured him that his funds were safe. Dr. Ogden ultimately lost everything.

A suburban dentist with a substantial deposit at risk achieved a different result. He summoned George Shaw and staff lawyer Graham Edelsten to a meeting at a city hotel. The dentist sent a tough-looking negotiator to the meeting. After a few pleasantries, the negotiator grabbed Edelsten by the throat with one hand and punched him in the head with the other. The negotiator said he had a pistol in his car and was prepared to use it if his dentist friend did not receive his money within five days. The dentist received his money.[6]

*

In mid-February 1980, three weeks after Nugan's death, thirty-year-old legal barnstormer Geoffrey Nicholson led a three-man team of Corporate Affairs Commission investigators down to the Nugan Hand bank, took a lift to the eighth floor and came upon a crime scene:

> As we walked into those premises, they were in the process of actually shredding information. People were feeding documentation into the shredders and seeking to physically divert us, meaning: 'Come into the office, Maud.' But we didn't, and consequently we were able to observe the shredding of documentation and the identity of the people doing it. It was clear enough that it was a standing order to get rid of as much as possible. If I had any doubts that something was seriously wrong, those doubts evaporated on day one.[7]

CAC investigator Rick Porter witnessed the shredding: 'At that stage a solicitor called Michael Maloney was basically running Nugan Hand

and he was complicit in the destroying of the records and in fact was ultimately charged. It ultimately came out that they had burnt out a shredding machine destroying records.'[8]

The sanitisation of incriminating evidence had been in progress for almost three weeks. Staff later testified that Hand, Houghton, Maloney and Patricia Swan oversaw the operation. Even Admiral Buddy Yates had rolled up his sleeves and pitched in. Two dozen boxes containing vital files were removed from the Macquarie Street offices and placed in a van, which was then driven to a commercial car park and left there until a suitable hiding place could be found.

Joint Task Force investigator Clive Small suggests that amid the chaos and fear, clear heads ruled:

> After Nugan's death the bank entered this almost twilight zone of absolute paranoia and asking, 'Who's at risk?' and, 'What have we got to do to minimise that risk?' That means we've got to get rid of the records. We've got to check on who might give us up, who might have loose lips, or have records at home, or have something that can implicate us. This would have been going through all of their minds. Some would have been more capable of executing a solution than others — the likes of Hand, the likes of Houghton, the likes of the military — they would have had a more critical and objective approach to this than perhaps others who would have been running around like chooks with their heads cut off, not knowing where to go, not having been used to this before.

The role of Admiral Buddy Yates and his motive for involving himself in the destruction and removal of records later became of particular interest to Joint Task Force investigators:

Admiral Yates' presence at the meeting of 29 January and

involvement that evening in the removal of records certainly raises questions, which on the state of investigation to date cannot be positively answered. But the fact that he flew to Australia with Hand and his involvement in the affairs of Nugan Hand during this time suggest that he, too, had a vested interest in seeing that not all the records were made available to investigating authorities. Some support for this proposition is gained from the taped record of the conference of Nugan Hand executives in Sydney in October 1979, which he attended. The record clearly demonstrates that all those present were aware that Nugan Hand was engaged in illegal and clandestine activities, though the precise nature of those activities is not spelled out.[9]

Frank Walker was gobsmacked at the blatant illegality unfolding in the heart of the city's financial, legal and political precinct: 'There was virtually nothing left in the bank, which is amazing. There were no accounts, there were no documents of any significance left in the bank and that gave us great suspicion that something awful was happening.'[10]

In late February, Bernie Houghton's business partner, Bob Gehring, and one of his employees accompanied Bernie Houghton and George Shaw to the AMP building in Bridge Street, Sydney. They took a lift to suite 1709, where they removed documents, including journals and cashbooks, from five filing cabinets and placed them into fifteen boxes. The boxes were then loaded into Gehring's truck and driven to his butcher's shop in Union Street, Pyrmont, then a down-market inner-city area, where they were stored for two weeks. During that time, Houghton and Shaw had access to the documents. Gehring later moved them to his cold-storage facility a kilometre away in Ultimo. A room full of hanging pig and lamb carcasses was the last place anyone would think of looking for the entrails of a failing merchant bank.

24 *The twilight zone*

★

As the wheels of the Nugan Hand bank began to fall off, most of the executives, office staff and salesmen resigned. Some fled the country. The bank's Kuwait representative, Michael Miller, a former mercenary whom Hand had met in Rhodesia, simply upped and disappeared. The media found his white panel van abandoned outside his Sydney home. Investigators discovered evidence of a $40,000 HSBC account in his apartment.*

Having been a major participant in Nugan Hand's illegal operations, George Shaw feared for his life. He later told investigators:

> There were pressures applied by Michael Hand, [lawyer] Michael Moloney and others that I should go to the Philippines with great haste, so as to make myself unavailable for any interviews by investigators. I was threatened [by Hand] and warned, and with great pressure applied, involving injuries, not only to myself but also to my family, that under no circumstances should I identify any clients.[11]

Shaw called on Frank's lawyer, John Aston, for advice. Aston said he had a conflict of interest and could not act for Shaw, but went on to say that Frank had been involved in a number of questionable dealings with people of questionable background. Aston warned Shaw that no one should ever know about the cash transferred to Singapore on behalf of the Mr Asia drug syndicate, otherwise the lives of Shaw and his family would be in danger. Shaw took this as a death threat.

Aston also warned Shaw that if he was ever questioned he must give authorities as little information as possible. He demanded that Shaw destroy all files relating to his own transactions and those of

---

*   Approximately $165,000 in 2015

Narcotics Bureau investigator Richard Spencer. When Aston offered to destroy the files himself, Shaw said he would do it. After the meeting, Shaw returned to the Macquarie Street offices and shredded both the Aston and Spencer files.[12]

*

In late March 1980, the Royal Commission into Drug Trafficking summonsed Mike Hand to appear before Commissioner Justice Woodward. Two previous witnesses, American lawyer Harry Wainwright and convicted drug trafficker Reg Parkin had told the commission that they had used Nugan Hand to transfer money illegally to Hong Kong. Mike Hand told Justice Woodward that his bank did not provide the facilities for transferring money overseas as described by Wainwright and Parkin.[13] By giving false or misleading evidence and knowing it to be false or misleading, Michael Hand was now guilty of an indictable offence.

Hand walked out of the commission aware that the authorities were closing in on Nugan Hand's dealings with drug traffickers. He had to act quickly to neutralise George Shaw. He telephoned Shaw at his home and asked him to come immediately to the Nugan Hand office. On his arrival, Hand produced a number of photocopied documents about the transfer of money for the Mr Asia drug syndicate and said words to the effect of:

> Look what I've found lying in the office; this is very incriminating. There is enough here to put you in jail. You had better leave the country. You know what I mean, you transferred this money, you could go to jail for this. Take my advice and leave the country, sell up your house and take your family while you can and get out.[14]

At a subsequent meeting, Hand threatened Shaw. He said 'arrangements' could be made through connections of Bernie Houghton's to have him killed. Shaw ignored Hand's threats and wisely kept files of incriminating documents, which he felt might come in handy should the authorities come knocking.[15]

25

THE GAP

Three weeks passed before thirty-seven-year-old Frank Nugan was laid to rest in a private ceremony at Sydney's Northern Suburbs Cemetery. For his family these were the worst of days. There was still no satisfactory answer as to why he was dead. Why hadn't he left an explanation? Perhaps he hadn't taken his own life?

Following the burial, a convoy of funeral cars travelled across the city to Sydney's east for a memorial service at the Church of England Chapel at Watson's Bay. The location was a darkly ironic choice: nearby, a sheer ocean cliff, known as 'The Gap', was the suicide capital of Sydney, where desperate people jumped to their deaths.

Lay preacher Paul Owens took a few hours off from his work at the Sydney Town Hall to attend the service. Owens was stunned by Frank's death: 'Well, the first thing the ABC said was that he'd been shot dead and I just couldn't work it out. Was this a murder? I couldn't fathom in my own mind it would have been a suicide.'[1]

Owens had spent six years visiting Sydney's ill-famed Long Bay jail, ministering to some of the state's worst prisoners. He found that if Frank had something on his mind he would talk about it. No matter which way Owens looked at it, he could not accept the disparity between Frank Nugan's newfound religious faith and the way he had allegedly died.

25 The gap

The small chapel was packed; extra chairs had been brought in to accommodate the overflow. But the atmosphere seemed less a heartfelt celebration of a life and more an obligation for most people there:

> The funeral was strange. There was a big crowd; a lot of business people, but there was no coffin. I met Frank's wife. My impression was of a very beautiful lady, obviously very distressed. And while I couldn't give her much solace, I said, 'I'm Paul, I had a lot to do with Frank.' And she said, 'Yes, I know … thank you.' Then of course someone else came and gave her a hug. It was a terrible day.[2]

Following the service, mourners witnessed open animosity between members of the Nugan family and Mike Hand. A visibly aggrieved Ken Nugan confronted the burly American and jibed for all to hear, 'Now you can blame it all on Frank.'

Hand looked to an associate and half-smiled, as if to say, 'Another time, another place.'

26

WHERE THE BUCK STOPS

For Nugan Hand employees, Frank Nugan's death was a disaster. But for Bernie Houghton it was but a blip on the landscape. After assisting Michael Hand and the Sydney staff to destroy, sanitise and remove records, he flew to Saudi Arabia to assess the fall-out and found that Nugan's death had attracted little publicity. So he decided to continue raising deposits from American military officers, oilmen and construction workers. If anyone happened to query the death of the bank's founder, Houghton simply plumbed the depths of his Texan charm and said that Nugan Hand was sound and that their money was in safe hands.

Investigators later discovered that Houghton was shamelessly pocketing money. On one occasion he placed $100,000 of his depositors' funds into Frank Nugan's personal company, Yorkville Nominees, then moved the money across three other Nugan Hand company accounts then into a company called Leyte Pty Ltd, which was owned by Houghton and his friendly butcher, Bob Gehring. Those funds were then transferred back and forth between Leyte and Nugan Hand twice more before settling in Leyte. Bernie's customers would never see those funds again.*

When news finally filtered through to Saudi Arabia that all was not

---

* The Joint Task Force discovered that Houghton had used similar deception for a number of Australian customers, where their deposits ended up in his own company's account. The JTF noted 'there seems to be prima facie a case of misappropriation of funds by Houghton…'

right with Nugan Hand, Bernie gathered up all of his sensitive records and placed them in a suitcase. He then flew to Geneva and left the case at the office of international arms trafficker Ed Wilson for safekeeping. Australian police investigators later established that former CIA officer Thomas Clines and his business partner Rafael Quintero called at the office two months later. Wilson's assistant looked on as they went through the travel case and removed at least one document. During the search the name Major General Richard Secord was mentioned and Clines said, 'We've got to keep Dick's name out of this.'[1]

Ed Wilson told me a different version of the story:

> Bernie arrived at my office when I was gone and left a suitcase to be picked up later. Apparently, I had given him a calling card with my office numbers and addresses. This calling card somehow involved me in the later publicity. When everything ended in Australia and the United States, General Secord came by the Geneva office and inspected the bag Bernie had left. He took documents, leaving the bag in the office. Later, Bernie came back to pick up the bag.

Either way, the common denominator was Major General Richard Secord, who had overseen the operations of the CIA airline Air America during the CIA's secret war in Laos. At the time of the Nugan Hand collapse, Secord was director of international programs for the US Air Force, including weapons sales to the Middle East. In 1983, after allegations of improper arms dealings with Edwin P Wilson, Secord was forced to resign from the military. The nature of the deals Houghton was doing in Nugan Hand's name with Secord, Clines and the other rogue arms traders in the Wilson circle remains a mystery to this day.

★

On Mike Hand's instructions, the bank's Jeddah manager, Michael Murphy, returned to his office to destroy all depositors' files. In March, a Middle East newspaper reported that the bank's Hong Kong depositors were unable to withdraw their funds. Murphy panicked and called Mike Hand, who told him that 'everything was alright'. From where Murphy was sitting that was patently false. Customers were turning up and threatening violence.[2]

Fearing for his life, Murphy telephoned Bob Gehring, who advised him to get out of Saudi Arabia immediately. Murphy picked up the phone and booked himself and all the other Middle East representatives on flights to London and elsewhere. Murphy arrived at the airport with a suitcase brimming with depositors' funds. The Saudi police got wind of their movements and turned up at the airport, but Murphy and his associates were one step ahead: on arrival at the airport they had rebooked their flights to earlier times and different destinations. They escaped the country with an unknown amount of cash, leaving angry depositors pelting stones at the offices of the Nugan Hand branches. Calm only settled when armed US Air Force officers turned up to guard the Nugan Hand establishments.

On his arrival back in Sydney, Murphy confronted Houghton and Hand. He told them that his escape had been extremely close and it was no thanks to them. He wanted to know why he and the others were not given adequate notice. He received no reasonable answer. Six months later, Murphy returned to the United States for good.

The US Consulate General in Saudi Arabia wrote to the Department of State in Washington on behalf of one hundred victims of the bank. The letter outlined their demand that the US Government investigate the 'errant bank':

> Needless to say they are extremely anxious to recover their funds. Each has contributed to a $25,000 'war chest' to pursue

this and other goals. The 'Mid-East Charter Group', which they organised, includes a cross-section of Americans working here from heads of companies (Beck Arabia) and top military (Colonels) to oilfield workmen (some with 22-inch collars). Unless signs of US Government action are forthcoming soon, I foresee that the Group and its members will launch a barrage of letters to congressmen and Washington agencies. Perhaps you will agree that Treasury and Justice Departments would be the appropriate action agencies for responses to such letters. I hope we are not deluged with congressionals on it.[3]

When investigators interviewed Hand over the missing records from the Sydney office, he volunteered that they were being held at the law office of Michael Moloney, who had taken over the bank following Nugan's death. The investigators seized the records only to discover they had been totally cleansed of any sensitive or incriminating evidence.

At NSW Parliament House, Corporate Affairs Commission lead investigator Geoffrey Nicholson briefed Attorney-General Frank Walker. Astounded by the bank's blatant destruction and concealment of its records, Walker suggested Nicholson try to source information from Nugan Hand's branches around the world.

Nicholson, Porter and a colleague flew to Singapore. According to Rick Porter, they arrived at Nugan Hand's plush, waterfront office on Collyer Quay unannounced:

Michael Hand was impeccably dressed in a pure white silk suit. He had been away skiing and he had broken his leg, which was in a cast. We asked him if we could look at certain records. He said they were locked in his rosewood cabinet and that he didn't have the key. We pressed him and said, 'Well, look, we are only here for a few days, we really need these records.' And with that he got angry and he swung his leg round with the cast on it and put it straight through the front of the rosewood cabinet and said, 'Help yourself.' That revealed the mind of Michael Hand. I guess he was saying to us that he wasn't a person to be trifled with.[4]

Days later, the commercial crime division of the Singapore Police raided the office and arrested the local Nugan Hand director Tan Choon Seng for conducting banking business without a licence. Warrants were issued for the arrest of Hand and two other Australian employees, but they had skipped the country and returned to Sydney.

Frank Walker had also sought the cooperation of Hong Kong's law-enforcement agencies:

> The Hong Kong police impounded the books of the Hong Kong branch of Nugan Hand and that was the big breakthrough. When our investigators began to look through the accounts that is when we started to uncover things like huge payments going backwards and forwards to Australia without Reserve Bank knowledge. We discovered names in the books that were obviously drug dealers around the world. We gained a very strong impression that Nugan Hand was in fact the financier of the drug trade not only to Australia, but around the world.[5]

Buried in the Hong Kong records, Australian investigators discovered the Swiss Bank account in Walker's name. Walker took the principled but extraordinary decision to announce a special Corporate Affairs Commission investigation into himself: an investigation that was to be totally independent of his office. Walker's political opponent, John

Dowd, was certain of his innocence: 'They tried to set Frank Walker up because Walker is not the sort of attorney-general who was easily bought and they set up a false Swiss bank account to make allegations against him. That, of course, went nowhere and Walker survived that without any difficulty.'6

For Walker this was personal; he had received threats before, but this was an unbridled organised-crime exercise designed to make him look corrupt:

> I thought that I was in the middle of a spy movie or a Le Carré novel. Here I was with merchant banks in the international drug trade, the CIA and the Mafia involved. We had Swiss bank accounts and my belief is that the Nugan Hand bank was attempting to have me compromised. I was a very worried man at that time. I thought, what else is going to happen to me as a result of this?7

★

On his return to Australia, Hand tried to reassure concerned investors that 'everything would be all right'. Soon after, John Green, the American plumber working in the Middle East who, along with his father, had deposited $120,000 with Bernie Houghton's crew, arrived in Sydney on holidays:

> They said that if I was ever in Australia to stop by the bank. The building was right next to the Opera House and I go in there and Nugan Hand has its name on a piece of paper stuck on the door, and I go 'Oh, shit, this is really bad.' And Hand was there and he said let's go and talk a bit and he walked me around down by the Opera House and back, bullshitting, right.

And there is the head guy in the bank walking and talking to me. In retrospect, he wanted to allay fears because he knew he was going under. And I went back home and the offices in Saudi were closed and you couldn't get hold of anybody at that point. So I was probably in Sydney in the last week, or so, of their business.*8

Incredibly, local financial planners were still trying to sign up depositors for the Nugan Hand bank. Former advertising agent Rex McGowan, who had successfully turned his hand to property development on the Central Coast of New South Wales, happened to meet a financial advisor at a wedding in mid-April 1980:

The advisor suggested that if I had any money floating around that I should consider Nugan Hand. I'd never heard of Nugan Hand. Now this was a Saturday. This financial adviser arranged for me to meet Michael Hand at 1 o'clock the following Wednesday. He came with me to the bank's office in Sydney but Hand was unavailable. We chatted away with a fellow who said he was the general manager. I had no intention of investing at the time, but this fellow talked me round. I deposited $40,000. I was selling houses for that sort of money at the time, so it was quite a considerable sum of money.9

On Friday 18 April 1980, two days after Rex McGowan handed over his cheque, the Equity Court placed Nugan Hand into provisional liquidation with liabilities estimated at that time to be more than $7 million. That Sunday, Rex McGowan noticed a stark headline 'Millions at stake in bank collapse.' in *The Sun Herald*:

---

*   John Green's funds ended up in Nugan Hand's Cayman Islands branch. He received a third of his deposit back twelve years later.

26 Where the buck stops

'I opened the newspaper and it said Nugan Hand had gone bust. I was numb. I read that article six times to take make sure I was still part of this world. I rang the bank the next day, but they had already cashed the cheque.'

That same morning, as the liquidators began autopsying the corporate corpse of the Nugan Hand bank, the coroner Derrick Hand — no relation to Mike Hand — began his inquiry into the mysterious death of the bank's CEO, Francis John Nugan.

The question on the minds of those close to the Nugan Hand case: 'Was it suicide or murder?'

27

INQUEST

In mid-April 1980, Sergeant Colin Wedderburn drove from Sydney to Lithgow to prepare for the much-anticipated inquest into the death of Frank Nugan.

The job of the tall, imposing police prosecutor was to present the evidence in all its complexity to serve justice and allow the coroner to deliberate on an outcome: 'You go through the evidence, find out if there are any little anomalies that needed to be looked at more thoroughly. You discuss that with the police officers before the inquest starts, so you are not left with gaping holes in the evidence, then present the evidence to the coroner.'[1]

On reading the police brief, Wedderburn was immediately confronted by a series of conundrums:

> I had concerns from day one of this matter. There were two police officers patrolling a road at four in the morning. Where Frank Nugan's car was parked was quite deserted off the main highway. I wondered, quite frankly, what they were doing there in the first place, unless someone had raised the alarm. I would think that a .30-calibre rifle would make an enormous noise in the early morning hours; you would hear it a mile away. I asked the officers, 'Did anyone ring the police station and notify you

that they'd heard a shot?' But they said, 'No. We were just patrolling.' It was a miraculous find by the officers at that hour of the morning![2]

Another concern was a break from standard police procedure. Normally, the attending police deal with cases of suicide; detectives are not generally called.

> The detectives are only involved in matters if there is some area of suspicion, if things don't seem right. I said to the officers, 'You said you were convinced it was suicide, so why did you call the detectives?' The constable said the station sergeant called them in. It smelt of someone having known something other than what was in that brief.[3]

Wedderburn was also uneasy about the thoroughness of the scientific investigation:

> Now one of the things, especially where weapons are concerned, is that the police fingerprint the deceased and match their fingerprints up with the weapon. That is just basic investigation. No one fingerprinted the body! Normally, one would expect to find fingerprints on the weapon. But the fingerprint experts said that they couldn't find fingerprints on the weapon. Well, that would sort of indicate someone had wiped the weapon down.[4]

Investigators traced the origin of the weapon found in Nugan's car. They discovered that on 7 January 1980, nineteen days before his death, a man bearing a strong likeness to Nugan had walked into the Bondi Police station and applied for a shooter's licence.

The following morning, a man, again bearing a likeness to Frank

Nugan, and possessing a new shooter's licence in his name, walked into a city gunsmith and purchased a .30-calibre military rifle and an axe. The gunsmith said it was the quickest sale he had ever made; the man, who said that the purpose of the rifle was to go hunting, was in the store for no longer than ten minutes.

Colin Wedderburn was far from convinced that Nugan's intention was to kill himself: 'He purchased a rifle and a hatchet at the same time and I'm sure he didn't intend to hack himself to death. I don't believe that when he bought them he had the intention [of taking his life] otherwise he would have done it within the next day.'[5]

Detective Sergeant Bill McDonnell, who investigated Nugan's death, agreed that the purchase was peculiar: 'It is an unusual combination really, isn't it — a gun and an axe? I often thought at the time that perhaps Frank Nugan had purchased the gun for protection and in buying an axe also lends itself to that scenario. But it did not alter my original opinion that it was suicide.'[6]

Colin Wedderburn looked for a connection between Frank Nugan and the location where he was found dead:

> On leaving his home at Vaucluse, he could have driven for ten minutes and carried out the same exercise. But no, he drove all the way out to Lithgow. What was he doing at Lithgow? It doesn't make sense. It wouldn't be common to see a Mercedes Benz driving down through the streets of Lithgow in 1980. I can remember discussing this at the time with the coroner. So there was a hole in the brief and it couldn't be plugged.[7]

As expected, a large media contingent from Sydney packed out Lithgow Court House for the start of the inquest. The case had captured national and international attention and expectations were high that more headline stories would be in the offing.

27 Inquest

The coroner heard first from the two patrolmen who discovered Nugan dead in his car. In the witness box, Sergeant Neville Brown said that he found the body slumped forward in the driver's seat. The rifle butt was resting on the passenger side floor. Nugan's left hand was gripping the barrel just below the muzzle and his right hand was resting on the stock just near the trigger. His head was resting on his chest to the left of the barrel and below the muzzle.

One of the lawyers suggested that Nugan would have had to be a contortionist to receive the head wound while in that position.

Brown remarked, 'I don't know. At the time I discovered the body, I believed that was how he died.'

Sergeant Wedderburn questioned Constable Owen Carter who had attended the scene to collect evidence.

'Was there any consideration given, when you attended the scene, as to whether or not photographs should be taken of the deceased's body before the body was moved?'

'Yes, most certainly.'

'Was it you who made the decision that there was no call for photographs to be taken before the body was moved?'

'Yes.'

'What caused you to come to that decision, Constable?'

'I went to the scene with an open mind. From the enquiries that I made at the scene and from what I found I formed the opinion that it was a straight-out suicide and I had no reason to call in the scientific police or more senior police.'

'Right. You thought from what you saw and your enquiries as you have described them that the matter was beyond doubt?'

'In my mind, yes.'

Barrister William Hodgekiss, representing the provisional liquidators, quizzed Carter about his removal of the weapon, the spent cartridge and two live bullets found in the magazine.

'What about the necessity for fingerprint examination of those bullets?'

'I didn't preserve them for fingerprints.'

'So it would be fair to say that you formed the conclusion that suicide had occurred and there up you preserved nothing.'

'I had no reason to believe that it was anything but suicide at the time.'[8]

In further hostile questioning, Hodgekiss implied that Carter had dismantled the death scene too quickly before considering options other than suicide. The coroner came to Carter's defence, saying that as far as he was concerned there was no evidence to suggest that Carter had handled the weapon or other evidence without care.

In the witness box, Detective Senior Constable Jeffrey Devine said that he had examined Nugan's body and car and found nothing, aside from the gunshot that killed Nugan, to indicate any other form of violence or that another person, a murderer, had been involved in the tragedy:

> The murderer would have had to have been in the car when the rifle was discharged and it would have been extremely dangerous for him. I am satisfied that the evidence is consistent with the deceased self-inflicting a bullet wound to his right temple with the projectile exiting at the left ear and striking the metal roof of the car, before coming to rest in the roof lining.

Detective Sergeant Bill McDonnell, who took charge of the investigation, revealed that on Nugan's return from overseas, he had arranged to visit businessman John Darling at his Mulgoa estate on the Sunday for lunch but never arrived. Darling had learned of his death from Monday's newspaper. Nugan would have passed the Mulgoa turn-off on the Saturday evening as he drove toward Lithgow along the Great Western Highway.

27 Inquest

Sergeant Neville Brown told the coroner that among Frank Nugan's possessions found in his car was a business card of the former director of the US Central Intelligence Agency (CIA), who according to the card, was now employed by Washington law firm Reid and Priest. Brown also presented as evidence a small book of the New Testament and Psalms, which was found in Nugan's trouser pocket and contained two slips of paper. On one piece was written 'Bill Colby and Congressman Bob Wilson'. Brown told the court that Wilson was involved with military procurement for the US Government.

The newspaper reporters rushed to telephones to phone their editors, with the sensational evidence linking Nugan to the CIA.

*

On the fourth day of the inquest, the court was again packed, this time to hear the testimony of Nugan's mysterious American partner, Michael Hand. He was wearing a sports coat rather than a suit, and the coroner took this as a sign that Hand was relaxed, 'or wanted to appear so.'[9]

Sergeant Wedderburn quizzed Hand at length about recent allegations of missing money:

> I said to him, 'Mr Hand, there is millions of dollars missing from the Nugan Hand bank. Do you have any idea what happened to that money?' And he just looked me straight in the eye and he said, 'Frank Nugan stole it.' It was a pretty good answer when you think about it, because he has nominated the only person not around to defend himself. Michael Hand is a main player in the whole of this and we let him off the hook. He must have thought it was a bit of a joke really.[10]

Hand said there could be up to $3 million missing, which Nugan had lent to individuals and companies, whose identities were unknown or without formal documentation.[11]

In his memoir, the coroner, Derrick Hand, wrote of Michael Hand's performance at the inquest:

> As I listened to him, I thought it suspicious that all this money could go missing without Nugan's business partner or anyone else knowing about it. It did cross my mind that he was talking a lot of codswallop. However, he was the only one left who knew about what had been happening to the company.[12]

As the former deputy-chairman and now chairman of the bank, Hand knew that he was as legally responsible for the bank's financial position as Nugan. But prior to the inquest he had provided a signed statement to the police in which he blatantly minimised his dealings with Frank Nugan. It said: 'In 1975, I went to South Africa and returned in March 1976 to live permanently in Australia and from that time until the death of Frank Nugan, I had little to do with him both business-wise or socially.'[13]

Michael Hand was willing to lie through his pearly white teeth in order to distance himself from Nugan. But then, in an unexpected twist, he told the inquest that he didn't believe that Frank Nugan had taken his own life. While he had fraudulently misappropriated a vast amount of money from the bank, he was a very powerful and masterful man, 'a fighter', who revelled in what he described as 'the open combat of business'.

'He had the wherewithal to fight the problems that he created,' he said. 'He wouldn't give up the ship.'[14]

Hand didn't say it outright, but he was implying that his business partner had been murdered.

27 Inquest

Sergeant Wedderburn was suspicious of both Hand's hypothesis and his motive:

> There was a lot of pressure on one side to find that Frank Nugan had committed suicide. On the other side, people didn't want it to be suicide because there were million-dollar insurance policies. Two of them were within the thirteen months period, so they wouldn't be paid out if it was suicide. I think that is one of the main reasons they were pushing the various theories and rumours that Frank Nugan had been murdered.[15]

Indeed, the Nugan Hand bank and two of its major depositors had taken out insurance policies against Nugan's life. Nugan had also taken out a $1 million policy against his life with his wife as the beneficiary.

Bill McDonnell was subjected to intense grilling in the witness box over the assumption that Nugan had taken his own life. Had he considered that Nugan might have been killed and the crime scene set up to look as if he had committed suicide? But McDonnell didn't waver:

> There was overwhelming evidence that he committed suicide. We had his shooter's licence; we had the police officer, who made out the licence at the Bondi Police Station, who said, 'Yes, that is Frank Nugan. I made out the form and gave him his shooter's licence.' It would be very difficult to murder a person in a car with a gun that he bought himself. It would be difficult to be sitting in the passenger side and pull a person over and shoot them in the head in the manner in which Frank Nugan had shot himself. There is not much doubt in my mind that he shot himself, or committed suicide.[16]

The lawyer for the provisional liquidators, Bill Hodgekiss questioned McDonnell about Frank Nugan's state of mind.

'Have you ever had an interview with the deceased's wife?'

'Many of them; she often rang me, sometimes four times a day.'

'What information did she give you that might help His Worship in relation to manner and cause of his death?'

'Predominantly, the conversations I had with Mrs Nugan were in relation to her children and Frank's religious beliefs and his more recent turn to the Bible.'

'What do you mean by his more recent return to the Bible?'

'I think from my enquiries Frank Nugan had turned to the Bible or God in more recent times, in the last two or three years, perhaps.'

'And did Mrs Nugan suggest any matter which might assist His Worship in relation to the death of her husband?'

'No. I think it would be safe to say that it was a complete and utter shock to Mrs Nugan and she couldn't fathom it or understand the reason. She had travelled with him from Nashville to the point at which he connected with his international flight to leave America. She said he left her quite happy, he appeared to have no problem at all but was, to use her own words, "coming on strong with religion."'

'Now you have had a large number of discussions with Mr Ken Nugan, his brother?'

'Yes. I formed the opinion that Mr Ken Nugan thought that the second lot of charges laid against Ken and Frank weighed very heavily on Mr Nugan's worries at that time.'[17]

Hodgekiss also grilled McDonnell as to whether Brian Alexander, who had attended the home of Frank Nugan the day his body was found, was the same Brian Alexander arrested with two former narcotics agents, Richard Spencer and Wayne John Brindle, for conspiracy to disclose information relating to the importation and distribution of drugs. This line of questioning, which connected Nugan's death to the murderous Mr Asia drug syndicate, gave print journalists their headlines for the next editions. But the coroner stated that issues related to drug trafficking and other criminality were not within the purview of his court. His sole responsibility, he said, was to determine how Nugan had died.

Towards the end of proceedings, Mr Hodgekiss tendered a document found in Nugan's car, listing 190 individuals and companies. The names, which included two-dozen drug traffickers, a number of high-profile media personalities and a member of one of Australia's wealthiest retail empires, were not disclosed in court.

On 27 May 1980, following a month-long adjournment, the coroner returned to Lithgow to deliver his findings. He said that he was satisfied 'having regard to all the evidence that the deceased took his own life.'

28

THE MAGICIAN

On 31 May 1980, a silver-haired American businessman in his fifties flew into Sydney, took a cab to the Hilton Hotel in the centre of the CBD and walked up to the front desk clerk to check in. The American was Thomas Clines, the CIA's former liaison officer in the Pentagon who was now running an international gunrunning business with funding from his friend and former CIA colleague, Ed Wilson.

From his hotel room, Clines telephoned Bernie Houghton. That evening they met at the Bourbon & Beefsteak to discuss developments in the Nugan Hand investigation. News had just broken that the Royal Commission into Drug Trafficking was about to morph into a Joint Task Force police investigation into Nugan Hand and two of its notorious customers, Murray Riley and Harry Wainwright. Put in Bernie's unique Texan parlance, there was 'no point dancing while the enemy was circling'.

That evening Bernie and his ex-CIA chum went over plans for his exit from Australia — an exit that needed to occur before the cops made it impossible to do so. Two days later, Bernie boarded a Philippine Airlines flight to Manila. Tom Clines departed the following day on the same flight to Manila. Bernie's getaway went off without a hitch, leaving investigators scratching their heads.

28 The magician

According to Clive Small, Bernie Houghton's disappearance was a major setback for the Joint Task Force investigation:

> Not only had Houghton opened branches in Saudi Arabia, he had arranged for all these senior military personnel, or former military personnel, to get official positions within the bank. He was also using a military plane to leave Saudi Arabia. These connections don't happen if you are just an unattached citizen, or an ordinary citizen. There is more to it. We had spoken to Houghton a couple of times and had spoken to his lawyers at different times as well. But Houghton then basically disappeared and when we wanted to contact him we found he'd gone.[1]

*

A week later, in early June 1980, investigators learned of another setback. Following a tip-off, a television current-affairs crew turned up at a terrace in inner-city Pyrmont, owned by Bernie Houghton's American business partner, Bob Gehring. In a sparsely furnished bed-sit on the second floor, they found a wallet under a pillow containing Michael Hand's driver's licence and $70 in cash. Beside the bed, they found a briefcase containing Nugan Hand documents, micro-cassette tapes, Hand's Hong Kong passport and what looked to be a coded message.

'Now why would he leave and leave all this behind?' asked the puzzled reporter to camera.[2]

Lawyer Michael Moloney told the media that he was concerned for Hand's safety. He said that following the collapse of the bank his client had received death threats and feared for his life. The discovery of his possessions in the bed-sit left him in little doubt that Hand had been abducted and possibly murdered.

Rumour spread that a professional killer had been brought to Australia on a contract to kill Hand. A 'close colleague' of Hand told the *Herald*: 'I doubt if we'll ever see Michael Hand again. He's either dead or gone into hiding abroad, never to return.'³

A day after the sensational television story aired, Corporate Affairs Commission investigators and members of the NSW Fraud and Homicide squads arrived at the premises to investigate Hand's disappearance. No fruitful information was forthcoming, but the general conclusion reached was that Hand was still alive and that his disappearance had been staged to give the appearance that he was the victim of foul play.

★

The sign on the door of the tenth-floor William Street office, 'Harbour View Corporation', gave the impression more of a development firm than a Joint Task Force of twenty federal and state police officers, a team that had been assembled to tackle the increasingly political Nugan Hand saga. Some were investigating the bank's alleged links to drug trafficking, others were looking into its connections with the CIA.

The investigators were especially keen to establish the whereabouts of Mike Hand. Their focus, too, centred on Pyrmont butcher Robert Gehring, who owned the flat where Hand had hidden out prior to his disappearance. Gehring initially denied that he had played any part in Hand's departure, but an offer of immunity from prosecution later prompted him to come clean on what he knew.

The Joint Task Force report summarised Gehring's version of events thus:

> Following the death of Nugan, there was continual talk about the state of the Nugan Hand group and Hand's legal position in [Australia]. Houghton kept on saying that the 'best thing that

could happen was for Hand to leave the country,' but Houghton distanced himself from any talks about the means by which this could be achieved. About March–April, a plan was devised whereby Hand was to be smuggled aboard the cruise vessel *Ming Hua*, dressed as an employee of Gehring, whose firm Gehring Providores at Pyrmont, provided meat supplies to the vessel. Once on board, Hand was to stow away. The first port of call for the vessel on departing Sydney was to have been New Guinea, where it was intended that Hand would disembark. He was then to leave that country, by some back door arrangement, for the USA. But Hand failed to show up on the day the meat was to be taken aboard the vessel and the plan fell through. Told of the failure of the plan a short time later, Houghton commented, 'Hand has to go.'[4]

According to Gehring, Michael Hand had come up with another plan. He said that Hand approached him and said that he needed a false passport to leave the country. Hand asked Gehring to obtain a birth certificate from one of his employees, on the pretext that it was required for some taxation matter. About the same time, Hand contacted a former military associate in the United States, who flew to Sydney to assist with the passport. Gehring claimed that he only ever knew this person as 'Charlie'.

Charlie took passport photographs of Hand wearing a false moustache and goatee-type beard. Meanwhile, Gehring obtained the birth certificate of one of his workers. Hand then completed a passport application, which Gehring lodged with Australia's Department of Immigration. Gehring later collected the passport and made the arrangement for Hand's overseas travel.

Hand decided to test his disguise by approaching people he knew. A young staffer with the bank recalled walking through the city and sensing that he was being followed:

I turned around to see this fellow who looked like Inspector Clouseau from the *Pink Panther* movies. He had this goatee beard and an obviously fake moustache. It was Mike Hand! I recognised him immediately. He was taken aback and made off as quickly as he could. I used to think he was all teeth and savagery. After that, I thought he was absolutely nuts.[5]

But, on 14 June 1980, Hand, wearing his ludicrous disguise, successfully passed through immigration at Brisbane Airport using an Australian passport in the name of Alan Glen Winter and, in the company of his friend Charlie, boarded Air Pacific flight FJ716 bound for Fiji. Two days later, Hand entered the United States via Vancouver.

When the Joint Task Force learned of Hand's escape, the Crown Law authorities issued an arrest warrant for his use of a false passport and the making of a false declaration to customs officials on his departure from Australia. Interpol was also notified. But, despite worldwide alerts, Hand had successfully slipped the net.

According to Clive Small, the identity of 'Charlie' was a mystery:

Who was this person who Hand could just ring who would basically drop everything and fly from America, spend time in Australia, become involved in obtaining a false passport and would then leave Australia? The question is not only who, but who paid for it? Why would this person commit to such an expense, or was he compensated for it?[6]

Gehring told Australian investigators that the last time he had seen Hand was the morning he disappeared, but admitted to having been in contact with him in the United States seven months later, in February 1981. Gehring said that while he was in San Francisco his brother contacted him and gave him a telephone number and the name

'Charlie' and told him to make contact urgently. 'I rang the number, which was an interstate number. I asked for a man named Charlie and the person on the phone said, "There is no Charlie here." There was a pause and he said, "Wait a minute," and the man Charlie came to the phone.'[7] Gehring recognised the voice as that of the American who had helped Hand flee Australia.

> Charlie said that Michael Hand wanted to talk to me and asked for a phone number. I gave him the number of a pay phone and Mike rang me a few minutes later. He was looking for news about himself and the investigation over in Australia. He also asked me about Helene, his wife, and also if I had gotten into any trouble over the false passport.[8]

Later that year, Gehring said he met up with Bernie Houghton in London and they flew together to Canada. In Toronto, Houghton handed Gehring a suitcase he had brought from London and asked him to carry the suitcase through customs inspection into the United States. The suitcase was packed to the brim with $1 million in cash. Gehring passed through customs in Detroit without a hitch and met up with Houghton. They then flew to New York with the case. Gehring told investigators that he did not know the source of the money or its final destination.[9] But the money was likely destined for Michael Hand. His father, Oscar, still resided in New York and was known to be in regular contact with his son.

*

In August 1980, Doug Sapper, Michael Hand's Special Forces buddy and can-do-man in Asia, was released from Kathmandu Central Prison. Sapper returned to Hong Kong and started asking questions about the downfall of Nugan Hand. He was told that Hand was dead, then heard that a good friend of his had extracted Hand from Sydney.

> In Hong Kong, I heard Spencer Oswald went down there and got him out. Spencer and Michael and I were very good friends at Fort Bragg. Spencer was Special Forces and he went to work for the CIA. He had a photography background and you've got to admit it was a brilliant operation: he got Michael out before anybody even realised he was gone.[10]

James Spencer Oswald was born in Arizona on 22 September 1940. In the late 1950s, he majored in photography at Santa Monica City College in California. From 1962 to 1964, Oswald served in the Army Special Forces, after which he worked for the CIA. In the late sixties, with his surname being associated with the assassination of President John F Kennedy, Oswald changed his name to James Oswald Spencer and found work as an actor in the US television series *Star Trek* and *Gilligan's Island*.

According to Doug Sapper, Michael Hand had little choice but to leave Australia:

> I think Bernie Houghton was right on the money when he went to Michael and said, 'You've got a matter of days to get the hell out of here,' and Michael not being a stupid son of a bitch said, 'You are probably right, I'm gone.' I think Michael feared that the Australian Government was about to snatch his arse. He was afraid that they'd take his passport away from him and then he couldn't leave up and they'd put him in a cell somewhere.[11]

Sapper believed Hand called up Spencer because of his intelligence background:

There is a thing called 'tradecraft': the ability to do things like lose surveillance, how to get into a building and out of a building, the extraction of an asset from hostile territory. Spencer had to have had some prior warm-up for this. They just didn't call him up and say, 'Spence what are you doing, man?' 'I'm shoveling horse shit here.' 'Oh well, put the shovel down and get on a plane, here's where you're going.' This was pre-arranged, 'Go down and get Hand out of there.' Here's a moustache, change your hair colour, puff up your cheeks, a make-up job, click, click. Right, off to the airport. This was a great example of a magician doing a card trick. It worked flawlessly. I'm sure there were more than a few people in the Australian law enforcement community and the Corporate Affairs Commission and the Australian intelligence people that pissed down both legs because Michael was gone.[12]

Hand allegedly remained with Spencer for at least three months until September 1980 and continued to associate with him until late February 1981.[13]

It took until late 1982 for the Australian authorities to identify 'Charlie' as James Oswald Spencer. The Joint Task Force convinced the FBI to track him down and interview him on their behalf. Spencer denied helping Hand leave Australia and said that the last time he had seen him was 'several years ago when Hand was in the CIA'.[14]

Australian immigration records prove otherwise. Spencer had arrived on 22 May 1980 and departed Brisbane on the same flight as Hand on 14 June 1980, bound for Fiji.

The FBI's inability, or unwillingness, to press Spencer for the truth was a pattern that would frustrate its Australian law-enforcement counterparts throughout the Nugan Hand inquiry.

29

RESURRECTION

In late November 1980, with Frank Nugan ten months dead, Bill McDonnell took the most alarming call in his career as a detective. The chief of the NSW Central Investigation Bureau was on the line and he sounded distinctly unhappy.

'Billy, who the hell have you got in Frank Nugan's grave?' he barked.

If ever there was a question that came from left field, this was it. McDonnell had no idea what he was talking about.

'We've got information that Frank Nugan is alive,' his boss growled.

It had to be a practical joke; the last time Bill McDonnell had seen Frank Nugan he was dead on a slab at the Lithgow Hospital morgue.[1]

*

A few weeks earlier, an Australian businessman had returned home from the United States with an astonishing story. While on a visit to Atlanta, Georgia, he had borrowed a friend's car and driven to Lennox Square, a 30-hectare shopping centre in fashionable Northside. Arriving just after noon, the businessman wandered into a bistro and ordered a glass of white wine. Before leaving, he decided to use the bistro toilet. As he entered, a dark-haired man came out of the lavatory. The businessman recognised him immediately as Frank Nugan and said, 'What on earth are you doing here, Frank?' The fellow allegedly replied, 'Reaping.'

On his return to Sydney, the businessman contacted Corporate Affairs Commission investigator Geoff Nicholson:

> A person, whom I was satisfied was well acquainted with Frank Nugan to not be mistaken, came forward to say that he had met with Frank Nugan at a date in America after his burial. In those circumstances, I became concerned of the capacity of someone to have faked the death and drew that to the attention of the relevant police authorities at the time.[2]

The police referred the allegations to Attorney-General Frank Walker. Walker knew the witness as a justice of the peace and an influential member of the Liberal Party: 'The fellow was a respectable Australian businessman whose integrity was beyond question. He told us he knew Frank Nugan personally, he had dealings with the bank, and he was certain that the man he saw in the mall was Frank Nugan.'[3]

It was up to Walker, as the state's chief lawmaker, to decide what further action, if any, should be taken. When he suggested an exhumation of Nugan's body, the deputy chief of the Central Investigation Bureau, Geoff Hammond, exploded. He said he had full confidence in Bill McDonnell, who had investigated Nugan's death. There was no doubt in McDonnell's mind that Frank Nugan was dead. His own brother had identified the body!

The Sydney Morning Herald reported, 'The possibility of exhumation is the latest in a succession of cloak-and-dagger twists in the saga of the Nugan Hand bank.'[4]

A Sydney television station reported on the bizarre development from Nugan's grave:

A coroner's inquiry found that the death was suicide. The body was buried here at the Northern Suburbs Cemetery. Investigators from Frank Walker's department are checking a new theory, that the body is that of a missing Italian drug dealer. Backing up their suspicions are persistent reports that Nugan has been seen overseas and that money has moved in and out of a bank account in his name. This morning Mr Walker confirmed that investigations were underway. He is expecting a police report tomorrow and that's when he'll decide whether to exhume the body.[5]

Frank Walker received a call from Nugan's wife, Lee, who was back in Tennessee:

It was very hard for me because I had his wife on the phone saying, 'Don't dig up the body.' I understood why she was saying that and I didn't want to re-open this story because the coroner had found that it was Nugan's body. But I decided in the end that it was better to be safe and sure and I issued an order to exhume the body.[6]

The Western Australian *Daily News* featured an interview with Frank Nugan's mother-in-law at her home in Nashville, Tennessee:

'Why don't they just leave Frank rest in peace?' she said when told of the planned exhumation. Mrs Sofge said the family would be delighted if Frank Nugan was alive, 'But we know it's a lot of baloney.' She said, 'Frank adored his wife and children. Even if he was on the run from the law, he would have let them know he was all right.' Since her husband's mysterious disappearance last year, Charlotte [Lee] and her two children

29 Resurrection

have been living with her parents in Nashville, where she grew up. Her mother says Charlotte still has not recovered from the shock and will not speak about it. 'Charlotte has seen photostats of the autopsy report and pictures. There is no way she thinks Frank is still alive. She doesn't say very much but almost every night she can't sleep at all. She just sits there and cries.' Mrs Sofge said, 'Frank was the first man she ever loved and I think the only man she will ever love. I loved him too — he was everything you could ever want for your daughter. But we all accept the fact that he is dead.'[7]

Despite the pressure from the police and the Nugan family, Frank Walker decided to proceed with the exhumation. In drizzling rain, a front-end loader peeled away the first metre of earth from Nugan's grave at Sydney's Northern Suburbs Cemetery. Detective Sergeant Bill McDonnell watched on with his police colleagues as gravediggers then set to work shovelling away soil. Frank Walker stood with journalists under umbrellas and made small talk to take the edge off the macabre scene.

A sceptical journalist asked Walker, 'If there had been some sort of switch-a-roo and it's someone else in the grave, why didn't they just cremate the bastard? Nothing makes sense about this story.'

Indeed, nothing made sense.

After two hours of careful spadework, the gravediggers isolated the coffin, which was so badly deteriorated that the detectives and forensic scientists huddled together and argued over the option of examining the body there and then at the graveside. Due to the persistent rain and poor light, the decision was made to place the remains into a large wooden crate to be transported by a funeral director's van to the morgue.

At the city morgue, Bill McDonnell donned a protective gown and facemask and joined the forensic team as they began their unenviable job of extracting the remains from the coffin. The painstaking process of identification would continue throughout the weekend. Nugan's dentist was brought in to compare X-rays of the teeth with his dental charts. Fingerprints were taken and the Government Medical Officer, Dr Godfrey Oettle, looked for the known peculiarities of Nugan's anatomy, including webbed toes and plastic surgery to the nose.[8]

For Bill McDonnell the macabre exercise was highly personal. Having carried out the investigation into Nugan's death and then to be proven to have buried the wrong man would be catastrophic for his career.

> I attended the morgue where we carried out tests on the skull and teeth. Where the bullet had gone in was the same bullet hole in and same bullet hole out. It was still the same webbed toes on his left foot that we had seen at the morgue. It was still the same teeth, bullet hole and feet in the very badly decomposed body that we exhumed from his grave. That was a very dramatic part indeed of my policing career.[9]

The evidence was presented at a new inquest at which the coroner confirmed that the body was that of Francis John Nugan. In Parliament, Frank Walker's political opponents capitalised on his embarrassment:

> The Opposition was suggesting that there was a vendetta by me and my office against the Nugan family. Here we were investigating their Griffith company and suggesting there was drug involvement. We were also investigating Frank's bank and now we were digging up his body. There was some truth in all these facts, but there was no vendetta. It would have been a crime not to investigate it.[10]

30

LISTED ASIO

The grizzly spectacle of Frank Nugan's exhumation was a morbid sideshow for the corporate and police investigators who were forensically examining the remains of the now-defunct Nugan Hand bank. While the stench of corruption was patently obvious, getting to the bottom of some of the bank's international dealings required the assistance of ASIO. But obtaining the spy agency's cooperation was proving frustratingly difficult.

Australian investigators were particularly interested in Bernie Houghton's activities and background. They discovered that the wily and secretive Texan had had military intelligence experience during World War II, after which he gravitated to war zones, including Korea and Vietnam. He then turned up in Australia in January 1967 and set up American-style bars — with apparent foreknowledge of the US decision to select Sydney as an R&R destination, even before that decision had become public.

In January 1969, Houghton visited California, where he had once managed a restaurant before heading off to Vietnam. Exactly why Houghton had returned to the United States is unknown, but during his stay he was arrested and charged with 'forging cheques, resisting arrest and fraudulently disposing of chattels.' In court, he had offered to pay restitution and was given twelve months' probation.[1] Remarkably, once restitution had been made, the charges were dismissed and he returned to Australia.

In March 1981, the Joint Task Force approached ASIO with a request for information on eighteen people associated with Nugan Hand, including Michael Hand, Frank Nugan and Bernie Houghton. ASIO said it had no records of anyone on the list. The Joint Task Force had evidence to the contrary, in the form of travel records in Bernie Houghton's name, which were stamped 'LISTED ASIO'. The Joint Task Force investigators concluded that ASIO was either inept or involved in a cover-up.

The most intriguing piece of evidence the investigators uncovered related to an incident involving Bernie Houghton in February 1972. Following an overseas visit, Houghton had hitched a ride back into Sydney on a US military plane and had fronted up to immigration without a valid re-entry visa. The immigration officer's report stated that he had been allowed back into Australia, and had been vouched for by Leo Carter — the chief of ASIO in New South Wales. Carter not only gave Houghton immediate clearance to re-enter Australia, he supplied an 'A' stamp rating, which, in effect, guaranteed Houghton trouble-free and unlimited re-entry to Australia on future occasions.[2]

Joint Task Force investigator Clive Small recalls: 'ASIO denied any knowledge of Houghton. When we asked how come his immigration record was stamped with an ASIO clearance, they could offer no explanation. And they could offer no explanation as to how Leo Carter, who signed him into Australia, might have known Houghton.[3]

When a story linking Houghton to ASIO appeared in the *National Times* newspaper, the prime minister's department placed an urgent call to ASIO's assistant director-general. In his notes from the call, he said his deputies 'had no reason to believe the allegations were true'. But the call was unsettling enough to prompt ASIO to carry out an internal investigation, during which it found that it did have Houghton on file.

In his report on the discovery, the assistant director-general of ASIO admitted to the director-general, Harvey Barnett, that 'through a deficiency in our indices, we had misled the Joint Task Force about not having a record on Houghton.'[4]

In light of its embarrassment, ASIO carried out further investigations into how its former state chief, Leo Carter, knew Bernie Houghton. Alas, Carter had recently died and so ASIO was unable to solve the case of their chief spy and the bar owner turned crooked banker.*

*

In June 1981, two Joint Task Force investigators tracked down Bernie Houghton to the Princess Hotel in Acapulco, Mexico, where he was slumming it in a twenty-sixth floor suite, overlooking Revolcadero Beach.

According to the Joint Task Force report, the investigators interviewed Houghton over a series of days:

> In retrospect, this interview was, so far as Houghton is concerned, little more than a sham, wherein he made every effort to distance himself from the activities of Nugan Hand, particularly in Australia, and to eulogise Hand as 'a great American'. He persistently used the attractive lure that 'Hand will appear' [implying knowledge of Hand's whereabouts but at the same time denying such knowledge] but of course such a lure was simply part of the sham.[5]

The investigators told Houghton that Neil Evans, Nugan Hand's Chiang Mai manager, had made a number of serious allegations about

---

* In 1982, investigators asked Houghton if he knew an Australian named Leo Carter. He said 'No,' leaving the investigators to speculate his reason for lying.

Houghton in relation to the distribution of drugs. Evans also alleged that Houghton was the top CIA man in Australia. Houghton denied the allegations. Evans' 'baseless' statements, he said, were obviously 'predicated upon some hope of personal gain for himself'.[6]

Despite his denials, investigators gleaned from Houghton that, at the time of his hurried departure from Australia, he was partnering with former CIA officer Thomas Clines in a business deal to sell Philippines-manufactured jeep-type vehicles to Egypt.

The investigators spent two weeks with Houghton, but according to Clive Small, Houghton controlled the situation:

> Houghton told them absolutely nothing, and one suspects that using his 'ultimate-host' personality he had obtained what he wanted from them. He wanted to know what the situation was like in Australia, where he stood, and so on, and he played the game well. It showed the force of his personality and the cunning of it. In a warped sense, I give Houghton credit for being able to play the game.[7]

31

ALL THE WAY TO THE WHITE HOUSE

The job of court-appointed liquidator John O'Brien was to hunt down the bulk of the money that Nugan Hand had secreted across its various companies and divvy it up amongst its creditors, which included international banks and insurance companies. Forty-year-old O'Brien was intrigued that very few of Nugan Hand's depositors came to him asking for help to retrieve their funds, which suggested they were using its services for dubious purposes.

As well as the Contra scheme, O'Brien found ample evidence of another money-laundering method promoted by the bank:

> It worked like this: a client would give Nugan Hand a sum of black money in cash. For a handsome fee of 22 per cent, the bank would then 'lend' the money back to the client. With the stroke of a pen, Nugan Hand would then forgive the debt. In this way, the client's black money was neatly laundered lily-white.[1]

Nugan Hand had sold itself as a merchant bank with a billion-dollar turnover, but O'Brien found no evidence to substantiate that claim: 'It was just a beat-up. But behind the beat-up there was another level operating — a clandestine business.'[2]

In a television news interview at the time, O'Brien didn't mince his words: 'There's no doubt Nugan Hand was involved in laundering of money and tax-evasion schemes and there is no doubt Nugan Hand people had military backgrounds and links at a high level with American intelligence organisations.'³

One hot Sydney summer's day in late 1982, John O'Brien received a telephone call from the US consul in Sydney:

> He said a couple of people wanted to meet me. He said I was not to inform the police. I said, 'Hang on; I have to live here. Tell them, if they want to see me, that's fine. But I'm not going to agree not to tell the police that I'm going to meet them!' Anyway, he came back and said that they still wanted to meet me. So I met them. One fellow sat to my right and the other one in front of me. I could see something under his coat. I don't know what it was. Basically, they told me that they had nothing to do with Nugan Hand and left.⁴

Following the meeting, John O'Brien called Corporate Affairs Commission investigator Geoff Nicholson and said that the same officials wanted to see him that afternoon. O'Brien provided a telephone number, which Nicholson called to set up a rendezvous at a café not far from Wynyard Station in central Sydney, which was also attended by Rick Porter and another colleague, John Willis. As Nicholson recalls, this was another strange meeting:

> These two gentlemen with American accents met us at the café. It was quite a warm day, I recall, and they wore their very heavy overcoats. They proceeded to effectively put words in my mouth by saying something to the effect that they hoped that I was satisfied with the great level of cooperation that the American authorities had given during the investigation.

> I had suspicions that these gentlemen were recording me. It was certainly a choreographed set of lines being put to me, to which I responded, 'No, I am not [expletive deleted] satisfied, and, that as far as I can see, I have had no cooperation, no assistance from anyone from your part of the world.' That terminated the conversation rather quickly and they left. That incident certainly fanned my suspicions at the time.[5]

Rick Porter suspected that the men, ludicrously outfitted in trench coats, were representatives of the CIA:

> The three of us believed they were CIA. They told us they had flown in from Manila, which was then a CIA base. They were over here to find out what we knew. We believed they were in touch with Michael Hand and that they were worried that Hand was going to face some charges out of Australia and if he went to court was going to be forced to answer questions about their relationship. They were protecting their interests. They weren't going to help us in our investigations. Eventually, they did release some thirty pages of CIA documentation to us, which had everything bar the As and Bs blanked out. Everything was blanked out! A few weeks after the meeting the Australian Government wrote a letter to the NSW Attorney-General, who was our boss, and we got a kick in the backside for being disrespectful [laughs].[6]

Garnering information from the American authorities about the Nugan Hand bank was never going to be easy. Back in 1978, while the bank was still in operation, *National Times* investigative journalist Brian Toohey had filed a Freedom of Information request for access to any FBI documents relating to Nugan Hand. In early 1979, the FBI supplied Toohey with forty-six pages. Large sections of all but a few of the pages had been redacted. Another seventy-three pages were withheld, on the grounds that they would jeopardise America's national defense or foreign relations.

Following the collapse of the bank, Rick Porter had made a similar request for the FBI's files:

> They were so heavily sanitised that they were completely and utterly useless. I think it went against their interests. Because the personalities involved were members of their hierarchy in their military forces and because none of the offences had happened in America, it wasn't in the national interest.[7]

John O'Brien had little regard for official obfuscation. He wrote to Prime Minister Malcolm Fraser seeking the federal government's help in approaching the FBI and other American law-enforcement authorities. The Department of Prime Minister and Cabinet, which handled the correspondence, had been watching the unfolding case carefully for any political blowback. According to ASIO records, the deputy secretary of the department telephoned the director-general of ASIO Harvey Barnett to say that his department 'had decided to seek a US Government statement refuting claims that Nugan Hand was in anyway involved in relations with the CIA … which could be used by the Prime Minister in the House.'[8]

It was an extraordinary move. Not only did the prime minister's department appear totally disinterested in the desire of Australian investigators to test the allegations of CIA involvement in the bank, it effectively wrote the agency's denial. In response, according to the ASIO document, the US embassy 'indicated there would be no difficulty in providing the statement' to the Prime Minister of Australia.[9]

Prime Minister Fraser duly stood before the parliament and told the Australian public that the CIA had no interest in Nugan Hand.

But that was not to be the end of the matter. *The National Times* newspaper challenged Fraser's assurances. Under the headline, 'New evidence of Nugan–CIA link contradicts PM,' journalist Brian Toohey wrote that a former CIA official had told him about Patry E Loomis, another ex-agency official, who was allegedly a link between Nugan Hand and the CIA. 'While working for the CIA, Loomis allegedly arranged for huge sums to be passed through the Nugan Hand bank for various intelligence operations around the world. Arms deals and political pay-offs were two examples he gave.'[10]

Toohey's source was on the money about Loomis. Two weeks later, Seymour Hersh of *The New York Times* revealed that in 1976 Loomis had been 'an agent assigned to the Far East who was operating under cover for an aircraft company. One of Loomis' functions was to serve as a liaison officer between CIA headquarters and its overseas stations; he was responsible for establishing personal relationships with senior military and Government officials in the Far East.'[11]

Toohey and Hersh alleged that Loomis was assisting arms trafficker Edwin P Wilson, who was then sending former Green Berets to Libya to teach its soldiers and Arab terrorists how to handle volatile explosives. Wilson, of course, had already been linked to Nugan Hand's gunrunning exercises.

In the wake of Toohey's article, Deputy Secretary of Prime Minister and Cabinet John Enfield met with a senior ASIO officer to discuss the Nugan Hand bank. According to the ASIO officer's notes of the meeting, Enfield had quipped, 'The government had hoped the Nugan Hand affair would die, but it kept bobbing up relentlessly.'[12]

In March 1982, three Joint Task Force investigators travelled to the United States to meet with the FBI and request their assistance. A less-than-impressed FBI officer later described the encounter as a 'rather intensive cross-examination'. When details of the meeting appeared in the press back in Australia, the livid FBI officer complained directly to

FBI director William Webster in writing: 'It is a matter of regret that the N-H investigators choose to do their whipsawing in the public press ... Thus we shall very likely treat future requests for assistance from [redacted] and other N-H investigators with considerably more circumspection than in the past.'[13]

In late March 1982, the American media alleged that the CIA was involved in undermining the Whitlam Government in 1975 and was somehow connected to the Nugan Hand bank. This time the CIA took the unusual step of responding directly to the allegations: 'The agency rarely comments on such allegations, but in this case we emphatically deny these charges. The CIA has not engaged in operations against the Australian Government, has no ties with Nugan Hand and does not involve itself in drug trafficking.'[14]

The CIA may have professed that it had no ties with Nugan Hand, but one of the bank's own employees was willing to say otherwise. In February 1981, Neil Evans, who ran the bank's Chiang Mai office, appeared on *Sixty Minutes* in Australia and television-news broadcasts in the United States. He spoke of a meeting in Hong Kong during which Mike Hand told those gathered that he had arranged a 'contract with the CIA whereby the bank was to become its paymaster, if you like, for disbursement of funds anywhere in the world on behalf of the CIA, and also for the taking in of money on behalf of the CIA'. Hand had allegedly told Evans:

> The CIA would deposit the money with the Nugan Hand bank. Some of the money was coming in from various CIA enterprises, namely drugs in Thailand, marijuana in particular, and the Nugan Hand bank would then be responsible for re-routing that money to an account in America with a New York bank.[15]

Evans also spoke of how the Chiang Mai office was set up to attract drug money, how it was conveniently located next door to the US Drug Enforcement Agency (DEA) office and how he socialised with DEA officers and the CIA chief of station for Thailand, Red Jantzen. It so happened that Jantzen was a friend of Nugan Hand bank president Admiral Buddy Yates and General Ed Black. Jantzen later attended a Nugan Hand conference at which Buddy Yates offered him a job with the bank.*

A week after his television appearance, the Corporate Affairs Commission interviewed Evans during which he claimed that Michael Hand became 'quite definitely excited about the prospect' of a link between Nugan Hand and the CIA. He also claimed that Hand had told him that he and Houghton were actively working for the CIA.[16]

Joint Task Force investigators interviewed Neil Evans. Clive Small admits that investigators were wary of many of his claims, but couldn't dismiss them outright: 'I guess we are left to decide whose version we accept, the person who is admitting the criminality, or the crimes, or the people who are denying that they were involved.'[17]

*

Attorney-General Frank Walker was concerned about the connection between drug trafficking and the CIA. He was also sceptical of the CIA's denials of a relationship with the Nugan Hand bank, believing that the American intelligence community had closed ranks to protect the bank's American executives:

> These were serious crimes Nugan Hand had committed — and it wasn't just in Australia. It was all over the world where

---

* Jantzen decided not to take the job after hearing Nugan speak at a conference.

this bank was operating. Investigation may have led to cutting off some of these drug cartels around the world. I think it is a very pertinent question as to why nothing was done about it. I think the reason nothing was done about it was the nature of the people on the board of the Nugan Hand bank. They were very senior military officials from the United States of America and they certainly weren't going to be investigated by the American Government.[18]

Perhaps the most extraordinary headline concerning the rumblings Down Under appeared in the influential magazine *Foreign Policy*, published in Washington. Entitled 'Dateline Australia: America's foreign Watergate?' the article delivered a 'great river of evidence' about the CIA's involvement with the Nugan Hand bank.[19]

US congressmen and senators were soon making their disquiet known in correspondence to the FBI. Their main concern was that narcotics had entered the United States courtesy of Nugan Hand's relationship with drug traffickers and had ended up in the veins of their constituents.

The FBI obstinately stood its ground until the influential *Wall Street Journal* boldly suggested a cover-up, not only by the FBI but also the CIA and the US Customs Service.

The continuing barrage of sensational stories in the American and Australian press prompted the US consul in Sydney to write to the director of the FBI, William Webster. He complained that the US Government and its agencies' non-cooperation with the NSW Corporate Affairs Commission investigators was attracting adverse publicity in Australia and requested that the situation be rectified.[20]

Documents accessed through Freedom of Information reveal for the first time that the Nugan Hand affair ultimately came to the notice of the White House, which finally stepped in and ordered the president's Intelligence Oversight Board (IOB) to contact the FBI and demand details of its Nugan Hand file.*

The IOB wanted to know how former US intelligence officials — people like William Colby, Walt McDonald, Dale Holmgren, George Farris and others –had become involved with the bank. The IOB directive forced the recalcitrant FBI finally to mount an internal inquiry.

The task of reviewing the mysterious Nugan Hand files was handed to the FBI's Criminal Investigation Division. The officer who inspected the documents wondered what all the fuss was about. They contained little more than correspondence to and from the Australian Royal Commission into Drug Trafficking, dating back to 1978.[21]

In its report to the IOB, the FBI confidently stated that it had 'not conducted substantive investigations of Nugan Hand'.

But the FBI was not off the hook. Both the White House's intervention and further allegations in the *Wall Street Journal* linking the bank to arms trafficker Ed Wilson, who was now the subject of a major FBI manhunt, convinced the FBI chief that his agency needed to be seen to be cooperating fully with Australian law-enforcement and corporate authorities.

Finally in late 1982, FBI investigators in six states began tracking down and interviewing American citizens who had either worked for or had dealings with the bank, especially in the area of gunrunning.

I sought the FBI's Nugan Hand files through the Freedom of Information Act and gained access to seven hundred pages of mostly redacted documents. A cover letter stated that dozens of pages had been withheld for national-security reasons. Transcripts of interviews were almost completely blacked out. Bizarrely, even Michael Hand's

---

* President Gerald Ford had created the IOB following the 1975–76 Church Committee investigation into domestic spying, assassination operations and other abuses by intelligence agencies.

name is redacted from every page.* From the non-redacted sections, it is apparent that the FBI interviewed former CIA officers Ted Shackley and Thomas Clines, who were associated with arms dealer Ed Wilson. The FBI also identified Bernie Houghton as a person of interest, but there is no evidence to suggest that he was interviewed.

The Joint Task Force investigators believed the CIA had to know something about Nugan Hand, so they made an official request for assistance to the CIA, which due to protocol had to be sent via Australia's spy agency, ASIO. It got them nowhere, as Clive Small recalls:

> We received not one response. For some reason that was never explained to us, none of the requests were passed on by ASIO to the CIA. How were our own intelligence agencies able to muck up such a serious matter that was supported by both the state and federal governments? Were they covering up for the CIA? They were the two options we were left with and neither of them was a particularly attractive option and [it all] left a serious doubt in your mind.[22]

In all, a dozen Australian and international inquiries probed the activities of the Nugan Hand bank. But by early 1983, the two main Australian investigations had become so politically charged that the federal and NSW state governments had agreed to set up the Royal Commission of Inquiry into the Activities of the Nugan Hand Group. Headed by Justice Donald Stewart and armed with powers similar to those of a Grand Jury investigation in the United States, the royal commission was able to compel Nugan Hand executives and staff to testify under oath.

Anyone expecting a tenacious investigation that would breach the cone of official silence, however, was to be sorely disappointed.

---

* Hand was officially an Australian citizen when he left Australia. The fact that his name was redacted by the FBI suggests they considered him in 1982 a US citizen and therefore beyond the reach of Australian authorities.

32

THE HORNS OF JERICHO

Driving through Dallas city, Doug Sapper couldn't recall the last time he'd given flowers to his mother. Sixty-five-year-old Delphine had done everything she could to get him out of his rat-infested Kathmandu prison cell. She'd even persuaded a handful of Washington politicians and diplomats to look into her war-hero son's case and had flown over to Nepal to meet with King Birendra to plead for his release. Her belief in his innocence was absolute. 'Why would anyone be smuggling five thousand gold watches into Nepal?' she'd pondered over and over. It didn't make sense.

Sapper didn't want to break her heart and tell her that it was true, let alone for whom he was working. But thanks to Delphine, his four-year sentence was reduced to two and he left prison on his legs instead of in a box.

Sapper arrived at his mother's house with a box of chocolates and a bunch of freshly cut roses. Her reaction wasn't as he'd expected. There were no pleasantries. No 'Thank you, son.' Instead, Delphine shut the door behind him.

'Why is the FBI looking for you?' she whispered.

'Did you tell them where I was?' Sapper said, unperturbed.

'No, I just told them I had no idea.'

'Do you think they believed you?'

'Probably not, but what are they going to do?'

Delphine said they had telephoned her from time to time. They'd even sent an agent out to the house. Sapper shook his head, wearily.

'What office of the FBI was it?'

'I think it was the one in Dallas.'[1]

The following day, 2 July 1983, Sapper drove downtown to Dallas's West End, and parked a half block past the red-brick, six-storey FBI building. From a pay phone across the road, he called the number on a card the agent had left with his mother. As Sapper later recalled:

> The guy said, 'Where the hell are you?' and I said, 'Look out your window,' and I waved at him. He goes, 'Don't you move, I'm coming down.' And I thought, 'Good luck, Sparky', so I left. I called him back later and said, 'Sorry, I couldn't wait. I'm late for lunch.' I thought the guy was going to have a stroke on the phone. He said, 'We've been looking for you.' I said, 'I hate to mention this, but you are the Federal Bureau of Investigation, did you look in the phone book?' He basically said, 'Well, here is how we can do this: I can come arrest you and then you are going to stay here until I say you can go home, or you can come in voluntarily and we can just have a chat and you can leave whenever you want to.' I said, 'Okay, I'll come down there.'[2]

The FBI agent ushered Sapper into an interrogation suite. Sapper looked around and noticed what he guessed was a hidden video camera:

> He was in the counter-intelligence. He had a folder. I didn't see what was in it but he kept looking at it and asking questions and this whole thing was an interview on behalf of some niche of the Australian Government [the Stewart Royal Commission].

He said, 'Was Michael Hand a friend of yours from the Army?' and I said, 'Yes.' He said, 'Did you associate with Michael Hand in Hong Kong?' I said we were in Hong Kong at the same time. Michael and I had dinner. Yadda, yadda, yadda. He asked me, 'What did I know about Nugan Hand?' I didn't tell him that I knew anything other than that it was a bank. I didn't tell him I was tasked with some projects that Michael wanted done. He said, 'What did I know about Frank Nugan?' I said, 'I knew Frank Nugan. I had socialised with him. He was probably crazier than a shit-arse rat. He could give you a Scotch, smoke a cigar and bullshit you into believing it was going to last forever.' He said, 'What happened to Frank Nugan?' I said, 'I don't know, but whatever it was, it was the linchpin that started everything crumbling. Somebody blew the horn outside of the walls of Jericho.'

The FBI agent kept returning to Sapper's knowledge of Nugan Hand's operations, including arms dealing: 'I told him I wasn't privy to that inner circle, especially the arms trading. I said it wouldn't surprise me if you told me that some of the ex-station chiefs of the CIA that went to work for Nugan Hand were involved. But I knew nothing of any of that.'

Sapper didn't mention his own arms dealing adventures, some twenty in number, none of which came off. But he did offer a little unsolicited advice:

> I told this FBI agent, 'You are in counter-intelligence; do you really believe that any weapons deals could be done without passive government approval?' I said, 'It is my belief that you do not do arms trafficking without some official sanction from somebody — the French government, the English [sic] government, the

American government — you can't move weapons around the world without somebody slacking off on the deal.' I said, 'If you go rogue, and you decide you are going to do this weapons deal on your own, you are going to get caught because they are going to shut you down as soon as they find out you are going to do it, and they are going to find out.' He said, 'Well what about the drugs?' I said, 'Listen, there is a ton of drug money in Southeast Asia especially out of the Golden Triangle and that kind of money corrupts everybody — government officials, Thai officials, Burmese officials, you name it. If you don't think that there was a lot of drug money moving around you're asleep.' I saw a lot of money, it was unbelievable, you could take a bath in it. The Thai generals shipped $100 million to Hong Kong. The bottom line is where does a Thai general get that kind of money? The bottom line is it was drug money. This wasn't just one Thai general; this was a cabal of them.

As the interrogation progressed, Sapper sensed that the FBI agent was simply going through the motions and was not really interested in assisting the Stewart Royal Commission:

I finally leaned across the table and said to this guy, 'Let's cut the bullshit and cut to the car chase. You already know the friggin' answers to the questions you are asking or you wouldn't be asking them.' So he kind of laughed and said, 'Well, yes, but we want to see what your reaction to them is.' I really got the impression from the interview, as lengthy as it was, that they weren't exactly going to transcribe everything I said and send it to the Australians. He basically intimated to me that the report they were going to send to the Australians was that I didn't know anything and I didn't have anything to say.

33

WHITEWASH

In 1985, following a three-year investigation, the Stewart Royal Commission into the Nugan Hand group of twenty-nine companies tabled its final report to the Australian and NSW governments. It found that the failed bank had committed many breaches of foreign-exchange regulations, was also heavily involved in tax-evasion schemes and that secrecy was the primary goal of most of the bank's clients.

Justice Stewart said the group created the myth of being an international corporation offering a wide range of financial services, but in fact had neither money nor skills. The Nugan Hand group, he said, was insolvent at all times and, from 1976 onwards, hopelessly insolvent. With only one or two exceptions, there was no one within the group who had the slightest expertise in banking skills, trade negotiations or commerce.

The Stewart Royal Commission's main objective was to examine whether the group contravened any federal or NSW laws, particularly those relating to drugs and arms trafficking. Its findings astonished many of the original investigators.

Regarding arms-dealing claims, it found 'no evidence to support the allegations. Several attempts to initiate arms deals are instanced but on each occasion the attempt came to nothing'. Regarding the drug-trafficking allegations, it found 'no evidence to support assertions that the Nugan Hand group was involved in the importation, distribution or financing of the drug trade.'[1]

While there may have been no evidence that Nugan Hand was involved in the importation and distribution of drugs, there was ample evidence that it was involved in the financial side of the drug trade and had profited from money laundering for as many as forty traffickers and syndicates.

The commission also found no evidence that the Chiang Mai office was established 'to attract deposits from drug producers of the so-called Golden Triangle'. Yet Nugan Hand staffer Neil Evans had testified that the office had been opened for precisely that purpose.

Having helped Michael Hand set up the Chiang Mai office, Doug Sapper was derisive of the Stewart Royal Commission's findings:

> So you have a royal commission and they think they are going to find out about Nugan Hand. Three years later they say, 'We have thoroughly investigated this and we have come to the conclusion, based on all the evidence, that there is no conclusion.' Everybody goes, 'See, I told you those blokes would find out!' Hell, it's just like in a western movie — all horseshit and gun smoke! ... Maybe from the Australian side there was no evidence. But, let's face it; the only money in Chiang Mai is drug money. I introduced them to a lot of the shadier characters in that area because I had some inroads there and contacts. Then of course I facilitated helping Michael move money around![2]

Regarding the bank's involvement with the CIA, the royal commission found this allegation to lack substance, being based on 'the coincidence that the Nugan Hand group employed several former US army personnel, some of whom had had CIA connections at some stage.'[3]

But John Dowd is another who remains sceptical:

> The fact that [Justice Stewart] couldn't find any evidence connecting the bank [to the CIA] isn't a finding that there wasn't any connection. It is simply that there wasn't any evidence and that means the CIA was doing its job. The CIA, as do all security agencies, make sure there are no fingerprints. I believe that there was a connection between the CIA and the Nugan Hand bank. There is no other reasonable inference available when you've got retired military officers running a shonky bank, which isn't a bank by any sense of the word other than that it is part of the US Defense/CIA connection and the CIA is the obvious inference. They were using it for transferring money because it was a convenient means of doing so. Therefore, it was an agency in effect 'of the CIA'. And that is why the fuss was made by the British secret service agent, who came to talk to me about the CIA connections.[4]

Frank Walker acknowledges the commission's efforts but feels it didn't go far enough in probing the CIA connections:

> The CIA neither confirms nor denies most of the time, but at least Justice Stewart got a firm denial rather than anything else, so I suppose we have to be satisfied with that. But I find it most unsatisfactory that there wasn't some public hearing and the CIA agents actually put into the public arena to make their denials — they may have felt differently then.[5]

As a participant in the original inquiries, Clive Small is far more critical of the commission's conclusions:

> The royal commission was so dismissive of an American connection that many people who read it simply felt that it was a cover up, because it was in effect so superficial and so

dismissive. It never attempted to explain or put into context its findings with the findings of the Joint Task Force, which have not been found to be in any way, shape or form inaccurate or unreliable. Simply said, [the royal commission] was a whitewash and that is what many people believe today.[6]

In the United States, businessman and future presidential candidate Ross Perot held suspicions of the CIA's relationship with the Nugan Hand bank.* Perot clashed with Admiral Bobby Inman, director of the CIA from 1981 to 1982, over the Nugan Hand matter.

Inman said that he had personally conducted the CIA's investigation into the bank and determined that while there had been 'CIA operatives on the bank's payroll, all were short-term contract employees of Air America, a CIA-controlled airline disbanded in 1981 … [but] none were career employees, who received more rigorous vetting.'[7]

Inman conveniently overlooked both Walt McDonald, a twenty-five-year veteran of the CIA, who rose to the position of deputy director of economic research, and William Colby, a career CIA agent who ran the agency from 1972 to early 1976.

*

History has shown that the CIA has rarely been open and honest about any of its covert operations or its connections. Indeed, the CIA has been found to have withheld information and lied to US congressmen and senators about its covert activities throughout the 1960s, 70s and 80s, including its operations in Laos, Angola, South Africa, Rhodesia, Honduras, Nicaragua and dozens of other countries.

Numerous former CIA agents have since revealed that banks are

---

* Ross Perot had long been concerned that the CIA had carried out drug smuggling to finance its secret war in Laos in the 1960s.

as fundamental to its covert operations around the world as its other assets. At least half a dozen merchant banks have been outed for dealing with the CIA before and since the Nugan Hand scandal.*

One such bank was Castle Bank & Trust, incorporated in Nassau, in the Bahamas. Run by former CIA agent Paul Helliwell, Castle Bank specialised in money laundering and tax avoidance before it collapsed in the mid-1970s. A few years later, a photograph emerged of Paul Helliwell and Michael Hand meeting together.

For good reason, CIA assets, such as banks, are firewalled from both government interference and internally from other CIA departments. The CIA makes it clear to assets that if they get into trouble then they are on their own — the agency will deny any connection.

The dramatic case of Edwin P Wilson lifted a lid on the CIA's methods when things go wrong. After a six-year FBI investigation, which turned into an international manhunt, Wilson was arrested in June 1982 for supplying explosives, weapons and mercenaries to Libya for Muammar Gaddafi's terrorist program. At his trial, Wilson claimed that he was working on the orders of the CIA. The CIA denied the claim and said it had had no contact with Wilson since he had departed from the agency in 1971.

Wilson was found guilty and sentenced to thirty-two years in prison. But, in 2003, Wilson's conviction was overturned when he and his lawyer, an ex-CIA agent, uncovered documents showing that between 1971 and 1978 there had been at least eighty instances when CIA officers had met with Wilson on a professional basis and had indirectly used Wilson's services. The CIA was found to have lied in a US court of law. In September 2004, Wilson won his release after twenty-two years in prison.

---

* Most recently, in 2014, the former CEO of the First Mariner Bank, Ed Hale, revealed his double life as a CIA agent throughout the 1990s.

The Wilson case clearly demonstrates that the Stewart Royal Commission was naïve to expect the CIA to provide a knowledgeable answer about its operations, let alone an honest one about its relationship with the Nugan Hand bank.

Michael Hand was intent on turning the Nugan Hand bank into a clandestine operation. To achieve that end, he employed former CIA operatives and military men and set out to link up or collaborate with other like-minded companies and individuals, such as Wilson and Tom Clines.

Nugan Hand's Washington DC branch, for example, was run by war hero Brigadier General Erle Cocke and shared an office, secretary and phone number with the general's own company, Cocke & Phillips International.* This convergence wasn't about saving money on telex machines and paper clips: Cocke's expertise was in clandestine banking.

Ten days before his death in 2000 from pancreatic cancer, Cocke gave a deposition to the New York District Court during which he admitted to carrying out clandestine banking activities for a number of US Government intelligence agencies. One of his long-term assignments, dubbed Project Hammer, dealt with the repatriation of billions of dollars from all manner of legitimate and illegitimate activities around the world, including arms trading, so that the funds could be diverted into covert activities, which included military operations in South Africa.

During his court deposition, Cocke was asked who was behind Project Hammer. He responded, 'Obviously the CIA, the FBI, the national security agencies of all types, the Pentagon, in the broadest sense of it, and the Federal Reserve. Nobody got out of the act. Everybody wanted to get in on the act.'[8]

---

* Between 1961 and 1964 Cocke was the first full-time US alternate executive director of the World Bank.

33 Whitewash

So too, it seems, did Nugan Hand. In 1982, Cocke told *The Wall Street Journal* that he had introduced Nugan Hand bank executives to high-level White House contacts.[9]

Telexes uncovered by Australian corporate investigators reveal that Nugan Hand was clearly pursuing moneymaking opportunities in the clandestine area, including weapons deals with rogue states, such as Rhodesia and South Africa, despite international embargoes. Correspondence was also uncovered regarding arms deals with Thai and Indonesian military officials.

Possibly the most contentious issue was the allegation by Nugan Hand's Chiang Mai manager, Neil Evans, that Michael Hand had told him in mid-1977 that the bank had become the paymaster for the CIA. In 1982, former CIA agent Kevin Mulcahy, who had worked for Ed Wilson, backed Evans' claim that the agency had used Nugan Hand for shifting money for various covert operations around the globe.

Geoffrey Nicholson believes the paymaster allegation should have been fully probed:

> The Nugan Hand bank, internationally, had the capacity to be a paymaster, or alternatively, a money laundry, or both. When one looks at the identity of some of the people who occupied executive roles in that organisation and the credibility their backgrounds brought with them, the possibility of at least official blind-eyeing of the activity must be real. Unfortunately, an inquiry into something of that nature would require the assistance of intelligence agencies in this country and overseas. During the period of time of my involvement, I did not have that advantage.[10]

According to Nicholson his investigators found coded messages that may have shed light on the bank's covert activities:

When Michael Hand departed Australia, he left behind certain documents concerning his activities, in code. It was in the nature of an alphanumeric code, a grid pattern, which would require a key to unlock it. The existence of the code, itself, was enough to raise the suspicion that it was a very sophisticated operation. At the time, as I recall it, the attorney-general referred the matter on to the Australian Defence Authority. But we were unable to obtain any meaningful results at the time.[11]

One of those closest to Michael Hand, Doug Sapper, professed firsthand knowledge of the bank's relationship with the CIA:

> Nugan Hand became the conduit bank for the CIA for both moving money in and moving it around for somebody that they wanted in their pocket. Was there money to be moved? Oh, yes, my god. It allowed the CIA to finance things in various areas in the world without getting directly involved. It also allowed them to move what they call 'flight capital' and this is from people who are despotic dictators. Why would the US Government be involved in that? I'll tell you why because when you've got their money, you've got their balls. You own them. When General Black and my good friend Admiral Yates and Bill Colby and all these guys were involved, you've got to assume it isn't because they just bought a Tupperware Franchise. Did I have personal knowledge of this? The answer to that is: yes.[12]

34

UNDER THE GUN

It is remarkable that a single gunshot discharged on an isolated country road in Australia could leave some of the world's most powerful intelligence and law-enforcement agencies scrambling and resound all the way to the White House. Equally remarkable is the fact that tens of thousands of man-hours and millions of dollars were expended on dozens of international investigations, yet more than three decades on the Nugan Hand saga is still shrouded in mystery and controversy.

There are many people, including some of the investigators, who still believe that there was more to Nugan's death than 'a simple suicide'. So will we ever know the truth?

The Lithgow police found no 'suspicious circumstances' and determined that Nugan's death was a straightforward suicide. The coroner and the royal commissioner both concurred. In his final report, Justice Stewart said there was a wealth of evidence to show that 'Mr Nugan had a strong motive to take his own life'. He pointed to his heavy drinking from early morning to late at night and the strain of concealing the group's disastrous financial mess. He suggested that Nugan probably committed suicide because he knew public exposure was imminent. 'He feared the shame and humiliation of the exposure of six years of infamy during which he had interwoven fraud upon fraud, produced grossly false accounts and plundered clients' funds.'[1]

In September 1980, four months after the Nugan inquest, Stephen Hill made an extraordinary declaration to Joint Task Force investigators. He said that the day before Frank Nugan's death he had met with him to discuss the serious problems with the bank's accounts. Hill claimed that Nugan said to him, 'I don't know how I got into this mess. I sometimes think the only way out is to shoot myself.'

Incredibly, Hill had not offered this information to the coroner or the detectives who were investigating Nugan's death. A few days after speaking with the Joint Task Force investigators, Hill explained why to *The Sydney Morning Herald*: 'Nobody asked me and I didn't want to get involved.'[2]

Police prosecutor Sergeant Colin Wedderburn is sceptical about the timing and veracity of the staffer's statement, 'That statement goes to the heart of this whole matter. We were not privy to it. In no way were we privy to that allegation!'[3]

Another former Nugan Hand staffer, who did not wish to be identified, told me that he believed 'Frank feared going to prison. He was a proud man.' Indeed, Frank projected the image of a brilliant, self-made millionaire banker. He had set out to go 'right to the top' and that is what he had achieved. His knowledge was the lifeblood of the Nugan Hand financial empire. It was his idea: the moving of money around the world without actually moving it. Such genius made him the true emperor of his tribe of moneymen. Go to jail? Not on your life. And prison was certainly on the cards. In June 1982, in the Nugan Fruit Group case, Frank's brother Ken pleaded guilty to three charges of misappropriating $11,700 and was later sentenced to six months in prison, of which he served three months. As a co-defendant in the case, Frank Nugan would have likely also served time in jail.

★

For Frank Nugan's friends, however, it was inconceivable that he would take his own life. Frank was the boy who fell from his pony and got straight back onto it. If he had taken a fall in business, why didn't he simply dust himself off and get back into the saddle? Why would he tear down everything he had built and devastate his family?

Two years after Nugan's death, *The Sydney Morning Herald* interviewed his mother-in-law in Tennessee. She said that her daughter was still not sure if her husband's death was suicide or murder, and she had doubts too: 'I'd known him for ten years and he never gave a hint that he was the sort of man who could commit suicide. They were very happy. He was crazy about her and the children.'[4]

Joint Task Force investigator Clive Small also admits to lingering doubts about the finding of suicide:

> I think it is fair to say that Nugan's death wasn't what you'd classify as a normal suicide. There were a lot of matters that arose at the time of his death, the location, and a range of other matters that would raise suspicion. For example, the documents that were found in his possession: he was carrying a list of names of all these drug traffickers who were a major risk to him, and you see the name of the former head of the CIA, who has a reputation for killing people when the need arises. It may well be that he was simply saying, 'I am carrying this on me because these are the people who I see as the biggest threat to my life.' There were also people who were aware that there were other police investigations and Corporate Affairs Commission investigations being undertaken. I guess you can look at them both ways. You can say, 'Yes, there is a lot of suspicion', but what does this suspicion mean? I am still not completely convinced it was suicide. I've got a lot of suspicions, but I just can't push it over the edge.[5]

The gun licence bearing Nugan's name and the testimony of the gun-shop owner who sold him the weapon clearly pointed to suicide. But one could equally concoct an elaborate, alternative scenario, in which evidence and testimonies had been manufactured.

When police turned up to search the Nugan home, they found that it had been recently fortified with bars on every window and door, but its expensive back-to-base alarm system had not been activated. Had a visitor arrived that Saturday, a person Nugan knew, who had then drugged him or taken him at gunpoint by car to Bowenfels and staged his murder to look like suicide? The fact that the police happened upon Nugan within hours of his death was suspicious in the minds of some. So too was the lack of fingerprints on the weapon.

Former Attorney-General Frank Walker suggests there was no shortage of candidates who may have wanted Nugan dead:

I think there were a number of people who had dealings with the bank or had an interest in the bank who were capable of carrying out serious harm to anyone they wanted to in the bank. We had a number of drug traffickers who were the most obvious ones, some of whom already had records for killing people who displeased them. We had certainly a number of police from state or federal agencies with a significant interest in whether or not Nugan might roll over and implicate them. We've also seen a number of people who have been involved in the military and in CIA operations, who would no doubt have had the capability of causing harm to anyone, if they wanted to.[6]

★

Frank Nugan was not the first of Mike Hand's business associates to die young. In January 1975, his former real-estate associate Bud King had died in mysterious circumstances in Sydney. The state of the former CIA pilot's body, the bruise to his temple and the pills in his hand suggest that King may have been murdered and his body clumsily arranged to appear as if he had accidentally or deliberately died from a self-inflicted drug overdose.

For Mike Hand to lose one associate was bad luck. To lose two could be interpreted as a pattern.

Within days of Bud King's death, Mike Hand resigned from the bank and headed to South Africa. Within months of Nugan's death, he went into hiding and planned his disappearance from Australia with the help of a former CIA colleague.

I obtained a copy of Michael Hand's travel records. They confirm that he was overseas when both Bud King and Frank Nugan died. But as Hand's Special Forces colleague Doug Sapper had discovered in Hong Kong, the bank was not above procuring people to carry out murder.

There was also the astonishing statement made by the firm's CEO Frank Nugan to British intelligence officer Peter Wilcox in Hawaii: 'We, Nugan Hand, do the bastards over. Anybody that gets in our way, we can take care of. We put people away.'

*

Police prosecutor Colin Wedderburn believes Derrick Hand was one of the most competent and thorough coroners he had ever assisted, but feels that the inquest did not adequately examine the circumstances that led up to Frank Nugan's death:

> When all the evidence was taken at the inquest, there were only three possibilities that raised themselves. One, it was an accident. That was dealt with and it wasn't an accident. Two, it was murder by some other person shooting him. And three, it was suicide. I don't believe it was anywhere near a straight

suicide — not within a million miles of an ordinary suicide. I believe a fourth possibility is the fact.[7]

The fourth possibility, Wedderburn suggests, comes from within a Bible found on Nugan's body, which was not fully assessed at the time:

In the Bible it was indicated to me that certain words were underlined — the words 'wife', 'children' and 'death'. I drew the inference from that that he was leaving a message that there was someone, person or persons, who were a serious threat to his wife and children. So you draw the inference from that that he was told, 'Commit suicide or they die.'

Bank employees told investigators that following Nugan's death Mike Hand had made threats against their families. Unless they cooperated in the destruction of documents, Hand had warned, their wives and children would be cut up and posted back to them. And George Shaw told investigators that Hand had threatened him and his family almost daily and said that Bernie Houghton had connections who could carry out the threats.

Bernie Houghton visited Frank Nugan unexpectedly at his Sydney office the day before his death. Such a meeting was unusual, in that he had often professed a dislike for Frank because of his brashness and lack of respect. His abhorrence was so great, that he even had an agreement with Mike Hand that he did not have to take instructions from Frank.

Clive Small believes that Houghton would have had a specific and possibly sinister reason for calling on Frank Nugan:

Houghton was a calculating person, who planned everything he did. He would have gone there with a message, 'Frank you are in a lot of trouble.' Not, 'We're in a lot of trouble,' but 'Frank you're in a lot of trouble,' and [his intention] certainly would have been to put pressure on him.[8]

Prior to the inquest, Colin Wedderburn was concerned that Nugan's death was a murder staged to look like a suicide. On viewing the contents of the Bible, he came to another startling conclusion:

> He pulled the trigger, but he did not voluntarily pull it. He pulled it because a threat was being held out to him. If he wanted his wife and children safe, I don't believe he had any other option. That is my fear and belief. I've been doing coronial inquests for thirty-odd years and I've never seen this happen before. I've never had anyone where they were threatened that something would happen to their family if they didn't kill themselves.

Forced suicide was common in ancient times. The Romans and Greeks offered suicide over execution to allow the family of the condemned to keep their property. In more recent times, Hitler forced Field Marshal Erwin Rommel, whom he suspected of being involved in a plot to kill him, to commit suicide rather than face execution, in order to save his family and his honour. In the Republic of Tajikistan, forced suicide is still common enough for it to be recognised in the criminal code and punishable by up to five years' imprisonment.[9]

To protect his wife and children, Nugan may have felt he had no option but to take his own life. Doug Sapper came to a similar conclusion, but with a twist:

> I knew Frank Nugan and I had socialised with him and I had the feeling that Frank Nugan was a narcissist. When he was telling a story you better listen to him, you better show him

deference. He was also a guy that didn't give a shit if he knew the hand was bad or not, he was going to bet it. I don't think he was too concerned the way something was going to turn out as long as he was still on stage and tap dancing and playing Frank Nugan. But once narcissists realise that they can't sell the program any more — that people now realise what they are — they become destructive. First they try to destroy other people — anybody who stands in the way of anything they want to do — and they lash out at them. Now, this could be a case of Frank lashing out, saying, 'You threaten my family or you threaten me, I'm going to kill myself and I'm going to arrange it so it is the linchpin, it is the keystone in the arch. I pull it out: crumble, crumble, crumble. All you sons of bitches are going to have to scramble.[10]

Sapper may well be right. As evidenced by the sequence of events illuminated in previous chapters, Frank Nugan was haplessly playing bad hand after bad hand. On the financial side, he was robbing Peter to pay Paul on a daily basis. The official liquidator estimated that the bank was more than AU$50 million in the red. One only has to read the massive Corporate Affairs Commission investigation reports to appreciate that the bulk of its transactions were fraudulent in some respect. Nugan's heavy-handedness in dealing with his family company's problems — the use of standover men and the buying, threatening and blackmailing of politicians — exposed a pathological narcissism.

But it was the re-ignition of the Narcotics Bureau interest in the bank in October 1979, and his incoherent, self-serving speech to his legal staff demanding that they rid the bank of its illegal activities, which marked a turning point. By then, the bank was a far bigger ship than Frank Nugan could turn around from his Sydney office. The diminution of his influence on the direction of Nugan Hand was clearly apparent that same week during the conference in Kings Cross. Regardless of the backslapping and compliments, the complaints against Frank from within the local and international executive were mounting and far from trivial. For Michael Hand to demand that Walt McDonald, a twenty-five-year veteran of the CIA, chaperone him on all overseas business trips suggested that Nugan was a liability. Indeed, Nugan would have had to be blind not to notice that Hand's and Houghton's growing cabal of former military and intelligence operatives had usurped his authority.

We don't know what led to the physical altercation between Nugan and Hand at the conference, but it marked the end of their relationship, which had begun twelve years earlier, barely one hundred metres away, at the Bourbon & Beefsteak. Three months later, Frank was dead and the bank came tumbling down.

Doug Sapper's belief that Frank Nugan's action was a way of 'lashing out' against his enemies fits new evidence presented here for the first time. A family connection, who attended Griffith High with Frank Nugan, sent me the school's 1956 yearbook, which features a disturbing but illuminating essay by fourteen-year-old Frank Nugan, in which he prophetically imagined how his life would end.

Entitled 'Inattention', the essay depicts Frank as a novice pilot facing a life-and-death situation hauntingly akin to the circumstances he would face twenty-three years later:

> 'When this happens you increase speed and wing your way out of it, home, but if you are holed, you turn your plane down at full throttle and race for the horizon,' the lecturer's monotonous voice went on. You are the small lad in the back row. While everyone else is learning, you're intent on carving your name in the desk.
>
> War is declared two days later but you don't worry. You'll

never need the stuff the lecturers talk about. No, how little they know about it.

Ten weeks later!

Yes, you're the boy in the long silver jet. You've got lost. You're all alone now. No one to get you home now, is there? Yes, those are the enemy over there.

What are you going to do, fight, run or land? What did the lecturer say? You want to know. You're afraid, not only of the enemy, but of yourself. Your radio works, why don't you call your lecturer? You are afraid to do that, too. Then you must fight and die.

How do you fight them? Did the lecturer say how to? You can't remember whether he did or not.

You remember he said, 'Increase speed and go for the horizon.' Was that to fight or not?

Your fear is gone. There is only a faint tinkling going through your body. You must crash your plane and kill yourself!

Yes, that's your mother getting a telegram to say that you were killed in action.

Only you know how you died and the secret will never be told.

You should have paid attention, shouldn't you?'

Frank Nugan, 2A[11]

35

THE HUNT FOR MICHAEL HAND

During the 1970s and 80s, scores of financial institutions crashed and burned, but few so ingloriously as Nugan Hand. Most of the investigations into its operations concluded that it was poorly managed and many of its activities unlawful. The Joint Task Force, alone, investigated more than two thousand people and organisations linked to Nugan Hand. In February 1982, the Joint Task Force chairman advised Australian Prime Minister Malcolm Fraser that criminal prosecutions would soon commence against several individuals for drug, conspiracy, perjury and passport offences. Incredibly, only two people ever faced court. Nugan's secretary, Patricia Swan, and lawyer, Michael Maloney, were both charged with conspiring with Michael Hand in the willful destruction of the firm's financial records. Some staffers at the heart of Nugan Hand's corrupt activities received immunity from prosecution in return for their testimonies.

Several of the bank's staff, including most of the international executives, proved to be untrustworthy witnesses but got away scot-free. Bernie Houghton sat at the top of the list. After a yearlong sojourn by the beach in Acapulco, Houghton returned to Sydney and the Bourbon & Beefsteak in Kings Cross, which he managed until his death in 2000. The only impact the Nugan Hand scandal had on his reputation was to enhance his mystique. Indeed, two years after his death, the adoring Kings Cross community erected a bust of Houghton in a small park that flanked his famous bar.

Doug Sapper believed that the wily Texan was a protected species: 'Bernie seemed to be one of those people who was Teflon. Nothing stuck. How do you explain that? How do you explain that he got away with stuff other people would have spent time in a Sydney jail for? Somebody protected him.'[1]

Some of the other executives attempted to capitalise on the nefarious skills acquired while working for Nugan Hand. In 1986, George Courtney-Smith, who had represented the bank in Hong Kong, was jailed for eight years for importing cannabis resin into Australia. Frank Ward, who worked at the Sydney office, went into arms trading. In 1989, he was sentenced to thirty-two months in prison for an infamous tax-avoidance scheme dubbed 'Bottom-of-the-Harbour'. General Edwin Black went to work for the Hawaii-based merchant bank Bishop, Baldwin, Rewald, Dillingham and Wong, which also had ties to the CIA. The CIA admitted some connection to the BBRDW bank in 1983 during a court case involving one of its directors, Ronald Reward, a former CIA officer. In almost identical circumstances to Nugan Hand, the BBRDW bank collapsed when investigators found Reward in a hotel room with wrist cuts sustained in an apparent suicide attempt. The firm's records then disappeared.[2]

★

Several people associated with Nugan Hand met with far stickier ends. Law clerk Brian Alexander, the go-between for the bank and the Mr Asia syndicate, disappeared two years after Nugan's death. The police found his car abandoned at the notorious suicide location, The Gap. The talk in Sydney's underworld was that Alexander was taken out to sea on a cabin cruiser and dropped overboard with an antique oven tied to his legs. According to 'Diamond Jim' Shepherd, the bagman for the Mr Asia drug syndicate, the vessel was a police boat.'[3]

Tom Clines, the former CIA officer who had helped Bernie Houghton leave Australia, was implicated in the Iran-Contra affair and sent to prison for tax evasion. Bernie Houghton's business partner, Bob Gehring — who had told investigators how Michael Hand had fled from Australia — was found dead in a hotel bathtub while on a visit home to the United States in 2003. He was 57. His wife told me that she never believed it to be a natural death.

William Colby, the former director of the CIA and legal advisor to Nugan Hand, went missing in 1996. Eight days later, searchers found his body drifting in waters near the shores of Rock Island, Maryland. The police said he had gone out paddling his canoe at nightfall and drowned. Predictably, Colby's death sparked a host of conspiracy theories.

★

As for Michael Hand, he had vanished into the ether, allegedly with as much as fifty millions of dollars of depositors' funds. New South Wales Attorney-General Frank Walker regarded Hand's disappearance as an admission of guilt:

> He was due to reappear before the Corporate Affairs Commission to answer questions. He knew he would find it very difficult, given other evidence that had been given in the commission. I think he made up his mind that this was to the time to leave. The fact that he has never been seen since proves exactly that. I don't think we will ever find Hand; I think he has been

very nicely buried, metaphorically, somewhere in America and I think he has got a false name and a new life there, somewhere.[4]

Colin Wedderburn was one of the last law officers to see Hand before his disappearance:

I would love to be back at Lithgow Court asking Michael Hand some questions because, at that time, we had no idea what his real background was and we had no idea he had connections with the CIA. But he walked out of that court after Frank Nugan's inquest and no one has ever seen him since. He is not a ghost. Surely someone must know where he went?[5]

In 1983, the FBI repeatedly quizzed Doug Sapper about Hand's whereabouts:

The FBI agent kept saying, 'Do you know where Michael Hand is?' and I said, 'No.' He said, 'Are you sure?' I said, 'Yes. I'd like to know where he is. I'd like to have lunch with him, give him a hug and everything.' I said to him, 'If I were running this investigation and you really wanted to know where Michael Hand is you might place a call to Langley, Virginia.' Langley is the headquarters of the Central Intelligence Agency. Some people call it the 'puzzle palace', the 'repository of the monkey handlers', whatever. I said, 'Why don't you get your FBI liaison in Washington to go over there and press the flesh, because they know where he is.' But I don't think they were looking for Michael Hand, because they may have already known where he was. But they weren't going to tell the Australian Government where he was.[6]

It now appears that the CIA knew precisely where Michael Hand was. Among the hundreds of pages I received from ASIO, I came upon an intriguing telex sent from a security liaison officer in Washington to 'Scorpion' in Melbourne. Scorpion was the code name for ASIO's director-general, Harvey Barnett. Dated 7 December 1982, the cable reveals that an undisclosed 'source' had told Joint Task Force investigators that Michael Hand was a US military advisor to Honduras' elite Fifth 'Puma' Battalion during the Honduras–Nicaragua dispute in Central America. At the time, 150 current and former US Special Forces members were running a CIA paramilitary training camp at Durzana, in eastern Honduras.

The Top Secret operation, later exposed by *The Washington Post* and confirmed by the Reagan government, involved preparing the Honduran forces to conduct paramilitary operations inside Nicaragua against the Sandinista revolutionary forces. The Sandinistas had toppled the Nicaraguan Government in July 1979.

Some of the CIA-employed military advisors were helping anti-Sandinista exiles obtain weapons, which eventually culminated in the Iran-Contra scandal, involving Oliver North, Richard Secord and Bernie Houghton's friend Tom Clines. The operation involved recruiting drug traffickers to the cause and using drug money to buy weapons.

So Michael Hand was back working for the CIA, carrying out similar duties to those he had performed for the agency during its secret war in Laos. For Hand to slot back into such a role suggests that he had never ceased his association with the CIA. The most extraordinary aspect of this scenario, however, is that Hand was still technically an Australian citizen and the subject of a New South Wales arrest warrant.[**]

---

[*] Investigators later discovered that the immigration official who had approved Hand's citizenship application in 1977 had also approved that of American Mafia lawyer Harry Wainwright, who was at the time on the run from the FBI. On hearing of Hand's Australian status, the US government made numerous requests for him to return his US passport. Hand simply refused.

After receiving this information, Joint Task Force investigators sought ASIO's help to track down Hand in Honduras. But they were to be sorely disappointed. ASIO's Washington representative said that he was unable to assist, as ASIO had no direct liaison in the Honduras–Nicaragua region and there was no Australian embassy in Honduras.[7]

There is no evidence in the declassified ASIO files to suggest that Australia's spy agency ever asked the CIA to help track down Michael Hand.

*

What became of Michael Hand after this alleged sighting? In 1987, following the release of Jonathan Kwitny's exposé on the Nugan Hand scandal — *The Crimes of Patriots* — Hand's photograph was plastered across the pages of *The Wall Street Journal* and other US newspapers. If he hadn't done so already, it seems logical that Hand would have changed his name and possibly his appearance. Indeed, in 1979, a year before Frank Nugan's death, Hand wrote to Stephen Hill at the Sydney office regarding Hill's concern that the bank may collapse. Hand suggested that they all had the same alternatives, one of which was to commit suicide, while another was to 'Quit, go to France, have a new face/passport.'[8]

In 1991, following a tip-off, investigative journalist Ross Coulthart traced Michael Hand's Australian-born wife, Helene, to France. Allegedly, she was attending the Institute of American Studies in Aix-en-Provence. *The West Australian* newspaper received a similar tip-off but was not able to interview or photograph Mrs Hand. Coulthart then traced the Hands to a post office box in Bellevue, Washington. Before he could arrange to intercept the couple, another Australian newspaper revealed the location and the trail went decidedly cold. Since then, dozens of professional and amateur sleuths have

35 The hunt for Michael Hand

attempted to track down Michael Hand without success. For a failed a merchant banker, he was proving to be a clever fugitive.

★

In the digital age, it is said that everybody leaves a trace of his or her presence online. As a professional researcher, I have located and subsequently interviewed dozens of people who had never owned a computer and were not even aware that they had an online presence. Recently, for instance, while researching for a documentary on the early years of ASIO, I set out to find a Russian-born woman named Lydia Mokras, who had immigrated to Australia in the late 1940s. In the early 1950s, she became the lover of ASIO agent Michael Bialoguski, who befriended and ultimately brought about the defection of Soviet official Vladimir Petrov in 1954. Tracing the woman, whom ASIO believed to be a KGB agent, was complicated by the fact that she had since changed her name numerous times. But a single page in her thousand-page ASIO file revealed the name of a young boy, who for a time she had been taken into her care. Fifty years on, I was able to trace the boy, now a retired businessman, to within a kilometre of my home. The businessman put me in contact with the now elderly woman, who was happy to reveal her pivotal role in an espionage story that greatly impacted on Australia's political history.

Michael Hand was always going to be far more difficult to locate. He was an outlaw who did not wish to be found.

Of the thousands of websites that mentioned the Nugan Hand bank, none offered any clue to Hand's current whereabouts. An online search for Michael Hand delivered hundreds of images of other men of all ages, shapes, colours and sizes; I found two people who bore a slight resemblance, but they proved not to be the fugitive merchant banker.

I looked for international connections. Various acquaintances had told me of sightings of Hand in Nepal, South Africa and South America. I also trawled numerous Vietnam War veterans' websites. Only one site mentioned Michael Hand and that was in unflattering terms.

In 2012, when I interviewed Doug Sapper at his home in Tulsa, Oklahoma, he told me of his attempts to find Michael Hand:

> Michael has not talked any sense and refuses to let anybody that knows where he is, tell me. Even Buddy Yates, who I used to communicate with regularly, was appalled at the fact that Michael wouldn't have anything to do with any of us. Back in 2002, I ran into a guy at a Special Forces reunion who was on Michael's team and I asked him, 'What do you hear from Michael?' and he said, 'I've been told not to tell you anything.' I said, 'Well, that's kind of chicken shit,' and he said, 'Well, he just doesn't want to have anything to do with you.' The bottom line is the agency has given him a new identity and I couldn't find him. I'm pretty good at finding people, so I'm assuming that he was under an assumed name.

In my last telephone conversation with Doug Sapper before his death in December 2013, he urged me to keep looking for his old army buddy. After years of searching, I felt it was the story of the proverbial needle in a haystack, where the haystack no longer exists. That said, as I neared the end of the first draft of this book, I compiled a list of broad assumptions in the hope that one might point me in a fresh direction:

– Michael Hand is still alive.

– He has changed his name.

– Once the heat had gone out of the Nugan Hand story, he would have come out of the shadows and attempted to gain normalcy.

– He would be living in a city or town where nobody knows his true identity or his background.

– The funds from his Nugan Hand days would have long since been exhausted.

– To maintain a comfortable quality of life he would have needed to work.

– He would have most likely returned to an occupation in which he was proficient.

– He had three major careers: the military, real estate and merchant banking.

It seemed improbable that a man in his mid-seventies would still be working for the military or the CIA. But there was every possibility that he was involved in the business world.

Across America, however, there are as many as thirty million registered companies. Finding Hand was going to be a monumental task. If he had changed his name, it would be nigh on impossible. My best hope lay in the possibility that he had maintained his first name and his middle name, Jon.

I began trawling through corporate and government records, state by state. I started with Arizona, where Hand had allegedly lived with

James Oswald Spencer following his escape from Sydney. I discovered evidence that his wife, who had changed her surname, had moved to Arizona sometime in late 1982. Police records revealed that she was fined for speeding in 1989. But Arizona's corporate records drew a blank. I then tried Washington, New York and New Jersey records – states where Hand had once lived. Again I came up with nothing. I then tried the corporate records of Idaho. They delivered up a manufacturing firm located in Idaho Falls founded by a man named Michael Jon Fuller.

I trawled the company's registration documents and was struck by the similarity of Fuller's handwriting and his signature. They matched those in Hand's Australian immigration records from 1967. A search of Idaho's Department of State records revealed that Fuller's date of birth was identical to Michael Hand's birthday. Needless to say, it was a Eureka moment.

A number of websites noted that Mike Fuller had served his country, from Southeast Asia to Africa, with Special Forces and other US Government agencies. The locations mirrored Hand's military duty in Vietnam and Laos and his arms trafficking to South Africa, Rhodesia and Angola.

A recent photograph of Mike Fuller taken at a tradeshow provided further verification. Here was a thickset man in his mid-seventies with a full beard, grey hair, pearly white teeth and piercing blue eyes. When superimposed over a photograph of Michael Hand's face taken four decades earlier, the eyes, nose, ears and teeth aligned perfectly.

I then placed a call to his company and asked to speak with Mike Fuller on a private matter. A gravel-voiced woman answered the phone. She barked that the only means of communication with anyone in the company was via email address. It appeared that Mike Fuller had constructed a firewall around himself. More than thirty-five years had passed since his disappearance from Sydney, but he was still careful about dealing with the outside world.

I still needed hard evidence to prove that Hand/Fuller was alive. I approached three private investigation companies in Idaho Falls. When I mentioned the name of the person of interest, they all declined the assignment. I then looked further afield and contacted Boise private investigator Neal Custer. The former U.S. Marine Corps Sergeant and criminal investigator for the Idaho Attorney-General's Office had no qualms about the target.

On Wednesday 24 June 2015 Custer's surveillance team drove over 400 kilometres from Boise to Idaho Falls. At 7 am, the following morning, they staked out Fuller's residence. At 7.30 am they spotted Fuller departing the area driving a Chevy Malibu. Half an hour later, he arrived at TOPS Knives headquarters in Ukon, Idaho. The corrugated-iron building, set in a flat, semi-rural location beside a rail line, offered the security team little in the way of cover. To prevent being spotted, they were forced to set up three hundred metres from the building. Around lunchtime, and through a shimmering heat haze, they captured Fuller exiting the building. He was wearing shorts, a casual shirt and a neck brace. His rolling gait suggested that he suffered from arthritis or something equally debilitating. At the railway line, which divides the town, he slowed, half-turned his body to ensure that it was safe to cross, before continuing on slowly to a local diner. A week later, Neal Custer drove to Idaho Falls and captured close up hidden-camera footage inside and outside the diner. Fuller was relaxed and blissfully unaware that his identity had been cracked.

The man whom Neal Custer and his team had filmed was but a shadow of Hand's former 'suave de bony' self. But one thing was certain – he was not a ghost.

36

AS CRIME GOES BY

As a leopard can't change its spots, Michael Hand had not changed his nature. He hadn't run for public office, become the head of IBM or the Pope in Rome. Instead, he remained within the world of his formative years: the world of warriors and their weapons. Hiding behind his new persona, Mike Fuller, he was manufacturing knives for US Special Forces, special-operations groups and hunters. Many of his weapons were designed to work in the unforgiving conditions of combat and hark back to that Technicolor moment in the battle of Dong Xoai when, out of ammunition, Hand used his Ka-Bar knife to rip up through the sternum of a Viet Cong attacker before removing the man's head from his body with his bare hands.

It appears that Hand had spent the previous seventeen years alchemizing that critical, existential moment in his life when a blade honed and sharpened to a micrometre represented the line between life and eternity. He was now producing tens of thousands of such weapons a year, many of which were destined for commercial sales agents and military outfits around the world, including Australia.

I tracked down registration documents relating to another company that Fuller had set up in the early 1990s with four business partners. The firm's speciality was paramilitary training for special-operations groups, SWAT teams and law-enforcement agencies around the world. His business partners were all former military men, one of whom boasted involvement in operations that remain 'data classified'. The Stewart Royal Commission's dismissive assessment of Michael Hand's arms trading, plus its declaration that the appointment of former military and CIA officers to the Nugan Hand bank was 'coincidental', rang ever more hollow.

Uncovering Hand's new identity was a breakthrough that had evaded investigators and journalists for three and a half decades. But would it finally bring Hand to justice? I felt that the only way to test the waters was to go public with what I had uncovered. A feature-length documentary on the Nugan Hand story that I had developed with Australia's public broadcaster, the ABC, would have been the perfect vehicle. But government funding cuts to the broadcaster had derailed the project in the final days of fundraising. Another public broadcaster immediately picked it up, but its budget was also cut, and the project stalled again. The only option was to give the story to a current affairs program. I screened the surveillance footage to journalist Ross Coulthart, who had been trying to trace Hand's whereabouts for decades. He was now working for Sixty Minutes Australia and was keen to cover the story. A month later, Ross and his film crew flew from Sydney to Idaho. With the help of private investigator Neal Custer, they followed Mike Fuller from his home to his factory and staked it out. Later in the day, they followed Fuller to a shopping mall. As he emerged from the mall, the Sixty Minutes team swooped with multiple cameras rolling. Wearing dark sunglasses and a neck brace, Fuller appeared shocked at the sight of multiple cameras rushing towards him. He froze momentarily, paralyzed like a deer caught in the headlights. He realised the game was up.

Coulthart closed in on his quarry: 'Michael Jon Hand — Ross Coulthart, Sixty Minutes Australia. We've been looking for you for a long time, Sir. We'd really like to talk with you, Mike. There are a lot of people who are owed a lot of money — fifty million dollars. A lot of good people lost their livelihood because of you, Mike...'

Despite Coulthart's persistent questioning, Fuller said nothing. He didn't deny that he was Michael Hand. He simply got into his car and drove off. He later ignored a written request for an interview.

I assumed that by the time the story hit the news in the United States, the former Nugan Hand banker would have conjured a way out of his predicament. With his shadowy connections and rat-cunning, I wouldn't have been surprised if he had vanished into the ether, yet again.

Two weeks after the Sixty Minutes confrontation, Hand/Fuller 'retired' from his business, assigned registration of his company to two of his employees and moved out of his home.

When the Sixty Minutes expose' went to air in Australia, U.S. news agencies, including Newsweek, jumped on the story. Pulitzer Prize-winning journalist Ray Bonner penned a story for ProPublica and the Daily Beast entitled: *Decades After Disappearing From Australia, A CIA-Linked Fugitive is Found in Idaho.'*

The following night, Idaho television station KTVB-7 News lead with story *'Australian Fugitive Found in Idaho Falls'*. The next day, a crew from another local television station turned up at Fuller's home, but he was nowhere to be found.

Fuller's clients and customers across the United States were gob-smacked to hear that he had a shady corporate past involving drugs and money laundering. In response, TOPS knives put out a statement confirming that Mike Fuller had once been involved in finance, but claimed that the stories about him 'are inaccurate.'

In Australia, the story made the front page of the Sydney Morning Herald and featured Hand's fake passport photograph. Radio interviews allowed me to give further background to the story. In political and corporate circles, in the city that had hosted the notorious bank and facilitated its criminal activities, the discovery of Michael Hand's new identity and whereabouts became the water-cooler conversation of the week.

In February 2016, the Shadow Attorney General in the New South Wales State Parliament, Paul Lynch, questioned the Deputy Premier and Minister for Justice and Police, Troy Grant:

'What steps have NSW Police taken and will you take to ensure Michael Jon Hand (also known as Michael Jon Fuller) is brought before New South Wales courts?'

Grant responded:

'The NSW Police Force has advised me that this matter has been reported to the Australian Federal Police, which is the appropriate agency to determine any ongoing investigative activity arising from the Stewart Royal Commission.'

By then I had handed the AFP documents relating to Hand's new identity and current whereabouts. I had also provided a précis of his criminal deeds, including money laundering for drug traffickers, promoting tax evasion schemes, gunrunning, corrupt dealings with public officials, corporate malpractice, including 370 foreign exchange breaches, fraud, the destruction of company records, conspiracy to pervert the course of justice, conspiracy to commit murder, the provision of false evidence to the Royal Commission into Drug Trafficking while on oath, the fabrication of a passport, the making of a false declaration to customs officials and the booking of an airline ticket in a false name.

The AFP made clear to me from the outset that the possibility of Michael Hand's extradition would rely on the discovery of an outstanding warrant for his arrest. That suggested that they we're not going to open a rancid can of worms again if they could help it.

In September 2017, I received a letter from the Fraud & Anti-Corruption Centre of the Australian Federal Police. In short, it noted that the AFP had 'consulted with a number of Commonwealth agencies and investigative partners, both domestic and international' and concluded that 'there were no outstanding Commonwealth offences that would warrant an AFP investigation.' It also stated: 'While there was a warrant for the arrest of Mr Hand from April 1980, due to the statute of limitations of five years, corporate offences under the New South Wales Companies Act would render further investigation redundant.'

People who reported on the Nugan Hand saga or played a part in the original investigations were never under any illusion that Hand would be brought back to Australia.

In 1991, Australian investigative journalist Brian Toohey suggested there was little chance of Hand facing justice:

> In the end, the (Australian) federal Attorney-General's department would have to try and extradite Hand from America. I don't think there is any strong will to get him, nor is there any obvious attempt of help from the United States. They clearly know Hand is back in America and haven't offered to tell us ... I think there is a fear here of getting offside with the American intelligence networks.[9]

Former NSW Attorney General, Frank Walker, who went on to become a member of the federal parliament and later a judge, also believed that even if an arrest warrant existed, intelligence priorities would certainly have precedence over criminal matters:

> In fights with the security industry, the result is usually Lions 10 – Christians 0. And I think that is what happened in the Nugan Bank saga. In terms of government policy, I found, not only as a state minister but later on as a federal minister,

that the interest of the security service is often put first and the national interest is often seen in terms of keeping the good relationship between ASIO, the CIA, MI5 and other agencies around the world. Having that good relationship is seen to produce intelligence that is more important to Australia than bringing some criminals to justice. That is a judgment that people in high places make. I don't agree with it, but that is the judgment they seem to make.[10]

The 8th of November 2020 marked an end to the final chapter in the Nugan Hand saga when Michael Jon Hand died. He was 78. Following his public outing in September 2015, his last years were possibly far from sanguine. Those who knew him — his neighbours, customers and employees — were now privy to an unflattering portrait of his background. He may have escaped any legal consequences, but he will be remembered as one of the most notorious merchant bankers of the Cold War.

Former New South Wales politician, John Dowd, who went on to become a Supreme Court judge, considered the Nugan Hand saga both a defining moment in the history of crime in Australia and a turning point in the relationship between Australian and American law-enforcement authorities:

> Australia changed during the R&R period when drugs were available to the American servicemen during their rest and recreation here. Nugan Hand became a vehicle to help the drug industry move money quietly. This was an enormous change in direction for Australia. Once you deal with the transport of money for drugs purposes, once you are dealing with corrupt governments and the CIA, then Australia is in a new league. At the time, I don't think people quite realised what was involved,

because the CIA were the good guys and we were mates with America and all of that. This was a change of direction from which we could never go back. The penny-ante organised crime was nothing compared with this.

Merchants of Menace Podcast Series is available on most podcast apps and at www.merchantsofmenace.net

Follow future developments at: www.merchantsofmenace.net

ACKNOWLEDGEMENTS

For their assistance to this project, I am indebted to many people.

I owe special thanks to Rick Porter and Clive Small, who recalled in vivid detail the highs and lows of the corporate and police investigations into Nugan Hand. They were always keen to point out that their respective inquiries were team efforts.

Thanks also to John Dowd, Bill McDonnell, Colin Wedderburn, Phil Bailey, Arina, Paul Owens and Harry Bancroft who recalled their own, often dramatic, roles in the unfolding story. Sadly, three major contributors have since passed away — Frank Walker, the former NSW Attorney-General, Geoffrey Nicholson QC, who headed the corporate investigation and Doug Sapper, who entrusted me with details of his nefarious activities for the bank, supplied photographs and shared his unique gift for the uninhibited metaphor. Thanks are due to my film colleagues Anna Grieve and Harry Bardwell who kindly read the penultimate draft of this book and along with Glenn Burge have pushed our documentary project about the Nugan Hand saga at home and abroad.

Special thanks to Scott Forbes for his editor's eye and splendid advice, Calvin Gardiner who filmed the major interviews, John Agapitos who processed the digital files, Maureen Clarkson for transcription typing Screen Australia, Rex Hogarth for the Griffith High School yearbook, Neal Custer and his team from Custer Agency Inc. for their impressive research and investigative work and the ABC, Screen Australia and ScreenWest for assisting the development of my film project.

My gratitude also goes to the City of Sydney History Publication Sponsorship Program for its generous financial support to assist the publication of this most extraordinary chapter in Sydney's history.

When a monolithic project invades one's life for the best part of five years, it inevitably overturns normality. My dear wife Sarah watched on without complaint as this book became all consuming. She has supported all my efforts and proof read each infinitive-splitting draft. For her indefatigable encouragement and love, I am eternally grateful.

Peter Butt, September 2015

ENDNOTES

In large measure, this work has drawn on information contained in many thousands of pages of official documents and investigation reports, some of which had not until recently been available for scrutiny. In the case of FBI and Department of State documents, individual records were supplied void of file numbers.

Where the work of another author has been quoted, permission has been sought from the publisher. When no response has been forthcoming, we have assumed no objection to its usage. In some cases, where the original publisher has ceased operating, we have attempted to trace the author. In the case of John Owen's *Sleight of Hand*, we were unable to find either the publisher or the author.

The photographs in this book have been kindly sourced mostly from private individuals, including Arina, Bill McDonnell, Ross Coulthart and Doug Sapper. The original sources of some of the images have proven untraceable.

Should any copyright holder of any material featured in this book come forward, they shall be duly acknowledged in future editions.

Prologue: Wealthy, Handsome Guys
1. *Seventh Interim Report of the Corporate Affairs Commission*, vol. 2, p. 704
2. ibid., p. 703

Chapter 1: Watch out for Crocodiles
1. Author's interview with Doug Sapper, December 2011
2. ibid.
3. ibid.
4. ibid.
5. Mike Hand is interviewed about the fight at Dong Xoai, where he won the DSC for his gallant action; US Department of Defense, US National Archives, 110482
6. Author's interview with Doug Sapper, December 2011
7. Vietnam Service Awards, 1967, Record Group 472, US National Archives, p. 10 (http://www.fold3.com/document/269629162/)
8. Author's interview with Doug Sapper, December 2011
9. ibid.
10. ibid.
11. ibid.
12. National Archives of Australia, NAA: A2562, 1969/1768
13. Author's interview with Clive Small, June 2011
14. Author's interview with Doug Sapper, December 2011
15. ibid.

Chapter 2: Jurisprudence is Crap
1. Essay by Ken Nugan, Griffith High School Yearbook, 1956
2. Author's interview with school friend (name withheld), November 2014
3. *Seventh Interim Report of the Corporate Affairs Commission into the Affairs of Nugan Hand Limited and Other Companies*, vol. 1, p. 10

Chapter 3: The Spaniard
1. Author's interview with school friend (name withheld), March 2012
2. National Archives of Australia, NAA: SP11/5, NUGAN, ALFREDO
3. ibid.

Chapter 4: Take-off
1. Author's interview with (name withheld), September 2015
2. *Report of the Commonwealth–New South Wales Joint Task Force on Drug Trafficking*, p. 295
3. A Private Pair, *Asia Week*, 3 Feb 1978, p. 40
4. Author's interview with Nugan Hand staffer (name withheld), May 2011
5. Author's interview with Rick Porter, June 2011

Chapter 5: The Man Who Fell to Earth
1. Author's interview with former Ocean Shores employee (name withheld), January 2013
2. Federal Bureau of Narcotics, Nugan Hand file, unnumbered
3. Author's interview with Arina, 2012
4. NSW Police Internal Investigation, file no. 73/20622
5. Chauncey Holt, *Self-portrait of a Scoundrel*, Trine Day, 2013
6. Lee Robins, Darlene Davis and Donald Goodwin, 'Drug Use by US Army Enlisted Men in Vietnam: A follow up on the return home', *American Journal of Epidemiology*, 1974, vol 99, pp. 235-249
7. Lee N Robins, 'Lessons from the Vietnam Heroin Experience', *Harvard Mental Health Letter*, December 1994
8. William Lloyd-George, 'The CIA's "Secret War"', *The Diplomat*, 25 February 2011
9. 'R&R', *Four Corners*, ABC Television, July 1967
10. Hand, Michael [American migrant; immigration file], NAA: C321, N1968/34014
11. Chauncey Holt, *Self-portrait of a Scoundrel*, Trine Day, 2013
12. Author's interview with Professor Jo Duflou, January 2012
13. Northern Suburbs Crematorium records, Kermit Walker King
14. US Department of State, STATE 242930, p. 1
15. Author's interview with former Ocean Shores employee (name withheld), January 2013

Chapter 6: The Contra
1. Author's interview with Rick Porter, June 2011
2. Author's interview with Geoffrey Nicholson, July 2012
3. *Seventh Interim Report of the Corporate Affairs Commission into the Affairs of Nugan Hand Limited and Other Companies*, vol. 1, p. 14
4. *Report of the Joint Task Force on Drug Trafficking*, p. 534
5. ibid., p. 72
6. Author's interview with Clive Small, June 2011
7. Author's interview with Geoffrey Nicholson, July 2012
8. *Report of the Joint Task Force on Drug Trafficking*, p. 73
9. ibid., p. 84

Chapter 7: Turkey Farming
1. *Seventh Interim Report of the Corporate Affairs Commission*, vol. 2, p. 649
2. ibid., vol. 2, p. 651
3. ibid., vol. 2, p. 658
4. John Stockwell, *In Search of Enemies*, (Futura, 1979), p. 185
5. ibid., p. 186
6. ibid., p. 186
7. ibid., p. 162
8. *Report of the Joint Task Force on Drug Trafficking*, p. 812
9. ibid., p. 812
10. Angola 1975–1976, GlobalSecurity.org, (http://www.globalsecurity.org/intell/ops/angola.htm)
11. Author's interview with Rick Porter, June 2011
12. Keith Schneider, 'North's Aides Linked to Australia Study', *The New York Times*, 8 March 1987

Chapter 8: The Return
1. Author's interview with Arina, 2011
2. Author's interview with Nugan Hand staffer (name withheld), June 2011
3. *Further Report of the Royal Commission into Drug Trafficking*, May 1980, p. 85
4. Author's interview with Clive Small, June 2011

Chapter 9: What Happened at the Circus
1. Author's interview with Doug Sapper, December 2011
2. ibid.
3. ibid.
4. Anthony Paul, *The Correspondent*, vol. 3, no. 1, 1978, p. 17
5. *The Florence Times*, 8 May 1975, p. 5.
6. *Eugene Register-Guard*, 4 May 1975, p. 5A.

7   Author's interview with Doug Sapper, December 2011
8   *The Indiana Gazette*, 9 May 1975, p. 35
9   *The Tripod*, 7 October 1975, p. 4
10 Author's interview with Doug Sapper, December 2011
11 ibid.
12 ibid.
13 ibid.
14 ibid.
15 ibid.
16 ibid.

Chapter 10: The Hub of Good and Evil
1   *Seventh Interim Report of the Corporate Affairs Commission*, p. 524
2   Author's interview with Rick Porter, June 2011
3   Author's interview with Doug Sapper, December 2011
4   Author's interview with Doug Sapper, December 2011
5   *Report of the Joint Task Force on Drug Trafficking*, p. 82
6   ibid.
7   ibid.
8   ibid.
9   ibid.
10 ibid.
11 John Owen, *Sleight of Hand* Colporteur Press, 1983, p. 45
12 *Report of the Joint Task Force on Drug Trafficking*, p. 320
13 Author's interview with Doug Sapper, December 2011
14 Author's interview with John Dowd, June 2011
15 *Report of the Joint Task Force on Drug Trafficking*, p. 321
16 ibid., p. 322
17 Author's interview with Clive Small, June 2011
18 Interview with Neil Evans, *Sixty Minutes*, Channel 9, 15 February 1981
19 Author's interview with Clive Small, June 2011

Chapter 11: Paymaster
1   John Owen, *Sleight of Hand* Colporteur Press, 1983, p. 62
2   Interview with Neil Evans, *Sixty Minutes*, Channel 9, 15 February 1981
3   *Report of the Joint Task Force on Drug Trafficking*, p. 300
4   Interview with Neil Evans, *Sixty Minutes*, Channel 9, 15 February 1981

Chapter 12: Ricochet
1   Author's interview with Clive Small, June 2011
2   ibid.
3   Author's interview with Frank Walker, June 2011
4   *The Sydney Morning Herald*, 24 April 1988, p. 9
5   Author's interview with Peter Davies, 2012
6   Author's interview with John Dowd, June 2011
7   ibid.
8   Author's interview with Frank Walker, June 2011
9   John Owen, *Sleight of Hand* (Colporteur Press, 1983), p. 131

Chapter 13: Infiltration
1   Author's interview with Phil Bailey, June 2012
2   ibid.
3   Federal Bureau of Narcotics, Nugan Hand file, unnumbered
4   Transcript of proceedings/Royal Commission of Inquiry into the Activities of the Nugan Hand Group, pp. 14,119–43
5   *Report of the Joint Task Force on Drug Trafficking*, p. 333
6   ibid., p. 355
7   Author's interview with Clive Small, June 2011
8   Transcript of proceedings/Royal Commission of Inquiry into the Activities of the Nugan Hand Group, pp. 14,119–43
9   ibid.
10 Author's interview with Phil Bailey, June 2012
11 ibid.
12 *Report of the Joint Task Force on Drug Trafficking*, p. 324
13 Author's interview with Phil Bailey, June 2012
14 ibid.
15 Author's interview with John Dowd, June 2011
16 Author's interview with Phil Bailey, June 2012
17 Author's interview with John Dowd, June 2011
18 Peter Wilcox interview, *Federal Bureau of Narcotics*, Nugan Hand file
19 Author's interview with Phil Bailey, June 2012
20 Transcript of proceedings/Royal Commission of Inquiry into the Activities of the Nugan Hand Group, pp. 14,344
21 *Royal Commission into Nugan Hand, Interim Report No. 1*, p. 491
22 Phil Bailey, Official Statement, 27 Aug 1979
23 Transcript of proceedings/Royal Commission of Inquiry into the Activities of the Nugan Hand Group, p. 14,395
24 ibid., p. 14391
25 Author's interview with Phil Bailey, June 2012

Chapter 14: The Phantom
1   *Seventh Interim Report of the Corporate Affairs Commission*, p. 261
2   ibid., p. 263
3   John Owen, *Sleight of Hand* (Colporteur Press, 1983), p. 121

4   ibid., pp. 171–2
5   *Royal Commission into Nugan Hand, Interim Report No. 1*, p. 56
6   Author's interview with Nugan Hand employee who asked not to be named
7   *Royal Commission into Nugan Hand, Interim Report No. 1*, p. 55
8   Transcript of proceedings/*Royal Commission of Inquiry into the Activities of the Nugan Hand Group*, p. 18,926
9   ibid.
10 ibid.
11 Apocryphal
12 Les Collings, Nugan Hand Hong Kong correspondence, 6 June 1978
13 Author's interview with Frank Walker, June 2011
14 ibid.
15 *Seventh Interim Report of the Corporate Affairs Commission*, p. 266
16 Author's interview with John Dowd, June 2011
17 Author's interview with Harold Bancroft, January, 2012
18 Author's interview with Frank Walker, June 2011

Chapter 15: The Business of Murder

1   Author's interview with Doug Sapper, December 2011
2   James Sanders, *South Africa and the International Media, 1972-1979*, Frank Cass Publishers, 2000, p. 59.
3   'He's Hung up on ASIA', *The Hour*, 1 June 1978, p. 35
4   Author's interview with Doug Sapper, September 2011

Chapter 16: Killing the Goose

1   Federal Bureau of Narcotics files, Nugan Hand investigation
2   *Royal Commission into Nugan Hand, Interim Report No. 1*, p. 73
3   Author's interview with Clive Small, June 2011
4   FBI documents and correspondence
5   John Owen, *Sleight of Hand* (Colporteur Press, 1983), p. 114

Chapter 17: Coup d'État

1   Ron Scherer, 'Shah's Fabled Riches: Millions? Billions?', *The Christian Science Monitor*, 23 April 1980
2   *Seventh Interim Report of the Corporate Affairs Commission*, pp. 596–604
3   ibid.
4   'A Short Account of 1953 Coup', (Iran Chamber Society, http://www.iranchamber.com/history/coup53/coup53p1.php)
5   David S Robarge, review of Stephen Kinzer's '*All the Shah's Men: An American Coup and the Roots of Middle East Terror*, Central Intelligence Agency Library, (https://www.cia.gov/library/center-for-the-study-of-intelligence/csi-publications/csi-studies/studies/vol48no2/article10.html)
6   *Seventh Interim Report of the Corporate Affairs Commission*, pp. 596–604
7   ibid.
8   ibid.
9   Andrew Watson, 'Nugan bank "stung" Shah', *The Sunday Telegraph*, 29 Mar 1981, p. 3

Chapter 18: In the Lord's Hands

1   *Royal Commission into Nugan Hand, Interim Report No. 1*, p. 50
2   Author's interview with Paul Owens, July 2012
3   ibid.
4   *Sydney Morning Herald*, 28 November 1985, p. 4
5   Jonathan Kwitny, *The Crimes of Patriots* (WW Norton & Co, 1987), p. 21

Chapter 19: The Fortune of War

1   *Report of the Joint Task Force on Drug Trafficking*, p. 326
2   *Seventh Interim Report of the Corporate Affairs Commission*, p. 659
3   ibid., pp. 660–2
4   ibid.
5   ibid.
6   Author's interview with Rick Porter, June 2011
7   FBI Files on Nugan Hand
8   John Owen, *Sleight of Hand* (Colporteur Press, 1983), p. 132
9   ibid., p. 189

Chapter 20: Bernie of Arabia

1   Author's interview with John Green (name changed), September 2015
2   Author's interview with Doug Sapper, December 2011
3   Jonathan Kwitny, *Mother Jones*, Aug–Sept 1987, p. 19
4   Author's interview with Rick Porter, June 2011
5   Author's correspondence with Edward P. Wilson
6   ibid.
7   *Kiss the Boys Goodbye*, Monika Jensen-Stevenson, William Stevenson, Dutton Books, 1990, p. 282
8   *Report of the Joint Task Force on Drug Trafficking*, p. 823
9   ibid.

Chapter 21: The Architect of Fact

Endnotes

1. James Shepherd, *Mr Asia, Last Man Standing*, (Pan Macmillan, 2010), p. 152
2. Shaw testimony during JTF inquiry, recorded Sydney.
3. *Seventh Interim Report of the Corporate Affairs Commission*, pp. 633–42
4. Author's interview with Clive Small, June 2011
5. Author's interview with Rick Porter, June 2011
6. *Royal Commission into Nugan Hand, Interim Report No. 1*, pp. 51–2

Chapter 22: The Last Supper

1. *Seventh Interim Report of the Corporate Affairs Commission*, pp. 674–706
2. ibid.
3. ibid.
4. ibid.
5. ibid.
6. ibid.
7. ibid.
8. *Royal Commission into Nugan Hand, Interim Report No. 1*, p. 57
9. ibid.

Chapter 22: The Last Supper

1. *Seventh Interim Report of the Corporate Affairs Commission*, pp. 674–706
2. ibid.
3. ibid.
4. ibid.
5. ibid.
6. ibid.
7. ibid.
8. *Royal Commission into Nugan Hand, Interim Report No. 1*, p. 57
9. ibid.

Chapter 23: Eternity

1. Author's interview with Paul Owens, July 2012
2. ibid.
3. Jonathan Kwitny, *The Crimes of Patriots* (WW Norton & Co, 1987), p. 288
4. *Royal Commission into Nugan Hand, Interim Report No. 1*, p. 59
5. Jonathan Kwitny, *The Crimes of Patriots* (WW Norton & Co, 1987), p. 324
6. Author's interview with Paul Owens, July 2012
7. *Royal Commission into Nugan Hand, Interim Report No. 1*, p. 10
8. Author's interview with Rick Porter, June 2011
9. Jonathan Kwitny, *The Crimes of Patriots* (WW Norton & Co, 1987), p. 319
10. *Royal Commission into Nugan Hand, Interim Report No. 1*, p. 59
11. ibid., p. 521
12. Jonathan Kwitny, *The Crimes of Patriots* (WW Norton & Co, 1987), p. 91
13. ibid.
14. Author's interview with Bill McDonnell, June 2011
15. ibid.
16. ibid.
17. ibid.
18. Police statements of Bill McDonnell, Ian Strathdee and Brian Alexander, lodged Lithgow Court.
19. ibid.
20. Author's interview with Nugan Hand staffer (name withheld), June 2011

Chapter 24: The Twilight Zone

1. Author's interview with John Dowd, June 2011
2. Author's interview with Frank Walker, June 2011
3. ibid.
4. Patricia Swan testimony regarding the destruction of Nugan Hand documents, Sydney Court of Petty Session, October 1981
5. ibid.
6. Shaw's evidence to the Corporate Affairs Commission
7. Author's interview with Geoffrey Nicholson, July 2012
8. Author's interview with Rick Porter, June 2011
9. *Report of the Joint Task Force on Drug Trafficking*, p. 466
10. Author's interview with Frank Walker, June 2011
11. Jonathan Kwitny, *The Crimes of Patriots* (WW Norton & Co, 1987), p. 327
12. *Report of the Joint Task Force on Drug Trafficking*, pp. 386–7
13. *The Sydney Morning Herald*, 1 April 1980, p. 14
14. *Report of the Joint Task Force on Drug Trafficking*, pp. 387–8
15. ibid.

Chapter 25: The Gap

1. Author's interview with Paul Owens, July, 2012
2. ibid.

Chapter 26: Where the Buck Stops

1. *Report of the Joint Task Force on Drug Trafficking*, p. 823
2. ibid., p. 414
3. US Department of State correspondence re Nugan Hand, unnumbered
4. Author's interview with Rick Porter, June 2011
5. Author's interview with Frank Walker, June 2011
6. Author's interview with John Dowd, June 2011

7 Author's interview with Frank Walker, June 2011
8 Author's interview with John Green (name changed), September 2015
9 Author's interview with Rex McGowan, September 2015

Chapter 27: Inquest

1 Author's interview with Col Wedderburn, June 2011
2 ibid.
3 ibid.
4 ibid.
5 ibid.
6 Author's interview with Bill McDonnell, June 2011
7 Author's interview with Col Wedderburn, June 2011
8 Transcript of Nugan Inquest, Lithgow Court, May 1980
9 Derrick Hand and Janet Fife-Yeomans, *The Coroner*, (ABC Books, 2004), p. 11
10 Author's interview with Col Wedderburn, June 2011
11 *The Sydney Morning Herald*, 24 April 1980, p. 5
12 Derrick Hand and Janet Fife-Yeomans, *The Coroner*, (ABC Books, 2004), p. 11
13 Nugan Inquest records, Lithgow Court, May 1980
14 Transcript of Nugan Inquest, Lithgow Court, May 1980
15 Author's interview with Col Wedderburn, June 2011
16 Author's interview with Bill McDonnell, June 2011
17 Transcript of Nugan Inquest, Lithgow Court, May 1980

Chapter 28: The Magician

1 Author's interview with Clive Small, June 2011
2 Paul Black, Channel 7, June 1980
3 *The Sydney Morning Herald*, 6 July 1980, p. 9
4 Report of the Joint Task Force on Drug Trafficking, p. 500
5 Author's interview with (name withheld), June 2011
6 Author's interview with Clive Small, June 2011
7 Report of the Joint Task Force on Drug Trafficking, p. 469
8 ibid., p. 469
9 ibid., p. 429
10 Author's interview with Doug Sapper, December 2011
11 ibid.
12 ibid.
13 Report of the Joint Task Force on Drug Trafficking, p. 830
14 Jonathan Kwitny, *The Crimes of Patriots* (WW Norton & Co, 1987), p. 339

Chapter 29: Resurrection

1 Author's interview with Bill McDonnell, June 2011
2 Author's interview with Geoffrey Nicholson, July 2012
3 Author's interview with Frank Walker, June 2011
4 *The Sydney Morning Herald*, 3 February 1981, p. 3
5 TCN Nine News, 1 Feb 1981
6 Author's interview with Frank Walker, June 2011
7 *The Daily News* [Western Australia], 6 February 1981, p. 1
8 Coroner's Report — Francis John Nugan, 7 February 1981
9 Author's interview with Rick Porter, June 2011
10 Author's interview with Frank Walker, June 2011

Chapter 30: Listed ASIO

1 Nugan Hand Bank, ASIO, NAA A6122, 44/2/881, vol. 2, p. 121
2 Report of the Joint Task Force on Drug Trafficking, p. 406
3 Author's interview with Clive Small, June 2011
4 Nugan Hand Bank, ASIO, NAA A6122, 44/2/881, vol. 2, p. 123
5 Report of the Joint Task Force on Drug Trafficking, p. 428
6 Bruce Stannard, *Nugan Hand from the Inside*, The Bulletin, 5 June 1984, pp. 22–5
7 Author's interview with Clive Small, June 2011

Chapter 31: All the Way to the White House

1 Author's interview with John O'Brien, June 2015
2 ibid.
3 *National Nine News* report, 16 April 1982
4 Author's interview with John O'Brien, June 2015
5 Author's interview with Geoffrey Nicholson, July 2012
6 Author's interview with Rick Porter, June 2011
7 ibid.
8 Nugan Hand ASIO, NAA A6122, vol. 1, p. 2581
9 ibid.
10 Brian Toohey, *National Times*, 31 May 1981, p. 1
11 Seymour M Hersh, 'The Qaddafi Connection', *The New York Times*, 14 June 1981
12 Nugan Hand Bank ASIO, NAA A6122, 44/2/881, vol. 2, p. 108
13 FBI document accessed by the author under FOI

14. Jonathan Kwitny, *The Crimes of Patriots* (WW Norton & Co, 1987), p. 354
15. Neil Evans, *Sixty Minutes* interview (Channel 9), 15 Feb 1981
16. *Seventh Interim Report of the Corporate Affairs Commission*, pp. 665-666
17. Author's interview with Clive Small, June 2011
18. Author's interview with Frank Walker, June 2011
19. *Foreign Policy*, winter 1982–83 edition
20. FBI document accessed by the author under FOI
21. ibid.
22. Author's interview with Clive Small, June 2011

Chapter 32: The Horns of Jericho

1. All quotes in this chapter from author's interview with Doug Sapper, December 2011

Chapter 33: White Wash

1. Royal Commission of Inquiry into the Activities of the Nugan Hand Group, NAA: A9488, F1983/631 Part1
2. Author's interview with Doug Sapper, December 2011
3. Royal Commission of Inquiry into the Activities of the Nugan Hand Group, NAA: A9488, F1983/631 Part1
4. Author's interview with John Dowd, June 2011
5. Author's interview with Frank Walker, June 2011
6. Author's interview with Clive Small, June 2011
7. Brian Duffy, US News and World Report, *Lakeside Ledger*, Florida, 16 June 1992, p. 10A
8. David Guyatt, *Project Hammer*, Nexus Magazine, volume 9, no. 1, December–January 2002
9. 'US Servicemen Big Losers in Nugan Hand Saga', *The Wall Street Journal*, 25 August 1982, pp. 1–2
10. Author's interview with Geoffrey Nicholson, July 2012
11. ibid.
12. Author's interview with Doug Sapper, December 2011

Chapter 34: Under the Gun

1. 'Royal Commission Report Nugan Hand "Not into Drugs, Arms".' *The Canberra Times*, 28 November 1985, p. 8
2. 'Nugan Spoke About Suicide,' *The Sydney Morning Herald*, 14 September 1980, p. 7
3. Author's interview with Col Wedderburn, May 2015
4. 'No Attempt to Find Hand', *The Sydney Morning Herald*, 8 February 1982, p. 2
5. Author's interview with Clive Small, June 2011
6. Author's interview with Frank Walker, June 2011
7. Author's interview with Col Wedderburn, June 2011
8. Author's interview with Clive Small, June 2011
9. 'Developing Legislation on Violence against Women and Girls', UNIFEM, May 2011, p. 499
10. Author's interview with Doug Sapper, December 2011
11. Griffith High School yearbook, 1956

Chapter 35: The Hunt for Michael Hand

1. Author's interview with Doug Sapper, December 2011
2. Rodney Stitch, *Explosive Secrets of Covert CIA Companies*, (Silverpeak Enterprises, 2008), p. 19
3. James Shepherd, *Mr Asia, Last Man Standing*, (Pan Macmillan, 2010), p. 153
4. Author's interview with Frank Walker, June 2011
5. Author's interview with Col Wedderburn, June 2011
6. Author's interview with Doug Sapper, December 2011
7. National Archives of Australia, NAA, A6119, 5540
8. *Royal Commission into Nugan Hand, Interim Report No. 1*, p. 510

Chapter 36: As Crime Goes By

1. Brian Toohey, ABC interview, 1991, accession number 149167
2. Author's interview with Frank Walker, June 2011
3. Author's interview with John Dowd, June 2011

INDEX

A

Air America, 16, 27, 35, 236
Alexander, Brian, ix, 98, 99, 106, 149-52, 161-62, 172, 200, 252
Allen, Gary, ix, 90-93, 96-97
Angola, 46-51, 146, 236, 260
Apocalypse Now, 54
Australian Security Intelligence Organisation (ASIO), 7, 215-17, 222-23, 228, 254-57, 264
Arina, x, 18, 34-35, 52, 267
Arms dealing, vii, 5, 44-51, 136-41, 146-47, 185, 231-32, 233, 237, 239, 255, 265
Aston, John, ix, 83, 98-99, 106, 125, 149-52, 161, 179-80

B

Bailey, Phil, ix, 85-86, 90-100
Bancroft, Harold, 210, 211*n*
Bangkok, Thailand, 17, 55, 60, 62, 70-71, 75, 84, 90-91, 103, 127, 136-37, 141, 173
Barnett, Harvey, 217, 222, 254
Bates, Brian, 98, 152
Bates, Harvey, 98
Beazley, Donald E, ix, 155-56, 158-59, 164-65
Bishop, Baldwin, Rewald, Dillingham & Wong, 252
Black, General Edwin F, ix, 45-47, 55, 73, 93, 95, 107-08, 130-31, 138-40, 158, 160, 219, 225, 240, 252
Boone, Pat, 18
Bourbon & Beefsteak Bar & Restaurant, 2, 17-20, 24, 27, 54, 92, 117-18, 133, 164, 202, 249, 251
Brindle, Wayne, 152, 161, 200
Brown, Neville, 167-69, 195, 197
Business Standard and Business News, 108

C

Cambodia, 57-61, 118
Carter, Leo, 216-17
Carter, Owen, 168, 171, 195-96
Castle Bank & Trust, 237
Catch 22 (Heller), 16
Cayman Islands, 31, 55, 129, 132, 190
Central Intelligence Agency (CIA), vii-xiii, 4-8, 15-16, 18, 35-36, 46-50, 55, 58, 73, 76-77, 89, 94-95, 123, 125, 129-30, 145-47, 155-59, 163-64, 173, 185, 189, 197, 202, 204, 208-09, 218, 221-28, 231, 234-40, 243-45, 249, 252-56, 260, 262-65
Chiang Mai, 69-74, 77, 91, 95, 124, 137, 217, 224-25, 234, 239
Chinatown, vii

Choo, Jack, 150, 152
Church, Frank, 50
Clark, Terence John, 149, 152, 161
Clines, Thomas, 48, 145-46, 185, 202, 218, 228, 238, 235, 255
Cocke & Phillips International, 238
Cocke Jr, Earle, ix, 238-39
Colby, William, x, 4, 47-50, 159, 164-65, 172, 197, 227, 236, 240, 253
Collings, Clive, x, 30-31, 39, 43, 53, 56-57, 84, 95, 108, 136
Commonwealth of Australia – New South Wales Joint Task Force on Drug Trafficking, 41, 43, 49, 55, 72-76, 87, 95, 132, 147, 151, 177, 184, 202-06, 209, 216-17, 223, 225, 228, 236, 242-43, 251, 255, 275-78
Connaught Centre (Hong Kong), 56, 93, 118
Continental Air Services, 15, 18
Coppola, Francis Ford, 54
Coulthart, Ross, 256
Countis, George 'Duke', x, 24-26, 40-41, 54, 124
Crimes of Patriots (Kwitny), 256
Cross, Les, 167-68
Custom's House, Sydney, 161

D

Dallas, Texas, 229-30
Darling, John, 166-67, 196
Deak & Co, 91
Derley, Ken, 81
Drug trafficking, vi-xiii, 4, 5, 7, 19, 33-37, 40, 43, 51, 54, 67-98, 107, 124, 139-41, 149-52, 157, 161, 172-73, 179-80, 188-89, 200-04, 214, 218, 224-27, 232-34, 236, 243, 251, 255
Dowd, John, x, 72, 82, 83, 94, 108-10, 120, 125, 141, 173, 189, 234, 264, 267
Dong Xoai, Battle of, 12-15, 261
Doyle, John, 69

E

Edelsten, Graham, 105, 176
Evans, Neil, x, 71-77, 137-38, 217-18, 224-25, 234, 239

F

Fear and Loathing in America (Thompson), 71
Federal Bureau of Investigation (FBI), 7, 41, 126, 140-41, 209, 221-32, 237-38, 254, 255*n*, 266, 273
Federal Bureau of Narcotics, (Australia) 34-37, 85-86, 90-101, 126, 151-53, 161, 180, 226, 248
Ford, Gerald, 48, 50, 59, 227

Index

Foreign Correspondents' Club (Hong Kong), 117, 121
Foreign Policy magazine, 226
Fort Benning, Georgia, 9
Fort Bragg, North Carolina, 11, 15, 208
Fraser, Malcolm, 251
Fratianno, James 'The Weasel', x, 40, 54
Freeman, George, 81

G

Gaddafi, Muammar, 237
Gehring, Robert, 178, 184, 186, 203-07, 253
Gilligan's Island, 208
Golden Triangle, 70-71, 74, 89, 91, 232, 234
Goulding, Peter, 147
Griffith, New South Wales, 21, 78-79, 82, 107-10, 169, 249
Green Berets, see US Special Forces
Gunsmoke television series, 167

H

Hand, Derrick, 191, 198, 245
Hand, Helene, x, 19, 32, 81, 95, 207, 256
Hand, Michael, vii, x, 2-4, 6-8, 16, 27-40, 52, 53, 55-57, 62-65, 67, 68, 75-77, 81, 93, 95, 104-05, 108, 113, 116-18, 121-23, 124-27, 129-31, 136-42, 143, 147, 148, 154, 155-60, 163-65, 169, 172, 174-81, 183, 184, 186, 187-91, 216, 217, 221, 228, 231, 245, 249, 251
   arms dealing, 44-51, 136-41, 146
   arrest warrants, 188, 206
   background, 9-10
   CIA activities, 15-16, 76-77, 224-25, 237-40
   disappearance, 5, 7, 203-09, 245, 253-54
   drugs and traffickers, 54, 69-74, 86-90, 95, 124, 151, 234
   Interpol alert, 206
   military background
      Distinguished Service Cross (DSC), 15, 17
      Laos, 15-16, 146,
      Special Forces training, 9
      Vietnam, 11-15
   Nugan inquest, 197-99
   Ocean Shores, 18
   Southern Africa, 44-51, 146
   Sydney arrival, 17-20
   threats to staff, 175, 179, 246
   whereabouts, 254-65
Hand, Oscar, 10, 207
Hans, Wilhelmus, 44-48, 50
Harpoon Harry's, 117
Hawaii, Nugan Hand branch, 31, 44, 46, 55, 94, 96, 107, 140, 163, 245, 252
Helliwell, Paul, 237
Heroin, 35-36, 43, 54, 70, 73, 8-91, 97, 99, 136, 150-51, 173, 265
Hersh, Seymour, 223
Hill, Stephen, x, 30-31, 53, 127, 150, 165, 174, 242, 256
Hitler, Adolf, 247
Hodgekiss, William, 195-96, 200-01
Holden, William, 18
Holmgren, Dale, x, 55, 155, 227
Holt, Chauncey, 35
Hong Kong, 2, 30, 38, 39, 41-43, 51, 53-56, 62-69, 75-76, 87, 89-93, 95, 97, 108, 112-21, 123, 126, 127, 137, 149, 158, 160, 180, 186, 188, 207-08, 231-32, 245
Honduras, 236, 255-56
Houghton, Bernie, x, 6, 17-18, 24, 32, 40, 48, 49, 54, 55, 92, 95, 117, 120, 137, 142-48, 156-58, 175, 177-78, 181, 184-86, 189, 202-05, 207-08, 215-18, 225, 228, 246, 249, 251-53
Hungerford & Associates (auditors), 80, 82

I

Inman, Admiral Bobby, 236
Intelligence Oversight Board (IOB), 227
Iran, 128-32
Iran Contra Affair, 146, 253, 255

J

Jantzen, Red, 225
John F Kennedy Center for Special Warfare, 15
Judge Judy Show, 266

K

Kelly, Dennis, 86, 97-98
Kelly, Keith, xi, 80-81, 106
Kenny, Russ, 34
Khmer Rouge, 58-62
Kilkenny, Rae, 110
Kings Cross, Sydney, 1-2, 6, 17, 18-19, 23, 24, 36, 39, 95, 119, 143, 155, 249, 251
   GI's on R&R, 17-19, 27, 36, 58, 62, 117
King, Kermit 'Bud', x, xi, xiii, 6, 16-18, 20, 27, 33-36, 52, 90, 244-45
Kissinger, Henry, 47, 162
Krahe, Fred, xi, 80-81, 106
Ku-ring-gai Municipal Council, 106, 109-10
Kwitny, Jonathan, 163, 166, 256

L

Labor Party (NSW), 82, 108-09, 125, 140, 141
Laos, xi, xiii, 15-19, 35-36, 48, 58, 70-71, 89, 146, 185, 236, 255, 260
Lee, Alexander, 106
Lee, Yolanda, 105-06
Liberal Party (NSW), 72, 78, 82, 102, 109, 110, 125, 141, 211
Lincoln-Smith, Paul, 165-66
Ling Siew Eng, 150-51
Lithgow, New South Wales, 167-69, 192, 194, 196, 201, 210, 241, 254
Loomis, Patry E, 223
Lowe, Andrew, xi, 85-90, 92, 97-99, 124

M

Mackay, Donald, 78-79, 82, 84
McCoy, Alfred, 36*n*
McDonald, Bruce, 102, 109
McDonald, Walt, xi, 155, 157, 158, 160, 165, 227, 236, 249
McDonnell, Bill, xi, 168-72, 194, 196, 199-200, 210-14
McGowan, Rex, 190

Mafia, 40, 41, 54, 78, 107, 189, 255
Maloney, Michael, xi, 176, 177, 251
Manor, Leroy, 66, 155
Marcos, Ferdinand, 155
Marcos family, 157
Marijuana, 36, 41, 54, 73, 76, 124, 224
Miller, Michael, 179
Moylan, Michael, 40
Mr Asia drug syndicate, 149, 151, 152, 161, 172, 179-80, 201, 252
Mr Asia, Last Man Standing (Shepherd), 149
Mulcahy, Kevin, 239
Murdoch Lewis Propriety Ltd, 45, 140

N

National Times, 216, 221, 223
Needham, John, 29-30
Nepal, 121-23, 229, 257
New South Wales Corporate Affairs Commission, 32, 38, 39, 42, 44, 50, 67, 83-84, 102, 108, 131-32, 139, 145, 176, 187-88, 204, 209, 211, 220, 225, 239, 243, 248, 253
Nicaragua, 236, 255
Nicholson QC, Geoffrey, xi, 38, 42, 176, 187, 211, 220, 239
Nicholson, Jack, vii
Nixon, Richard, 58
Neugarten, Alfred and Annaliese, 25-26
New York Times, 51, 223
North, Oliver, 255
Nugan, Frank, vii-viii, 3-8, 21-34, 38-45, 52-55, 65, 68, 74, 77, 80, 83-84, 87, 92, 96-113, 117, 131, 133, 139, 142, 150, 152-66, 169-74, 178, 179, 231
  arrest, 106
  background, 25-26
  blackmail attempt of attorney-general, 111-12
  contra system, 42-43, 54, 67-69, 150, 219
  death, 4, 167-10, 241-50
  drinking, 53, 54, 92, 96, 103-06, 133, 134, 166, 241
  drug trafficker dealings, 87
  early business dealings, 27-29
  education, 21-22
  exhumation, 211-214
  Federal Bureau of Narcotics investigation, 86, 92, 98-100, 152-53
  fraud allegations, 80, 82, 106, 112, 125, 158, 173
  funeral, 182-83
  going straight, 153
  inquest, 192-201
  items found on body, 4, 173, 197
  legal background, 22-23
  personal character and behaviour, 21, 22, 65, 103, 105, 126, 243, 249
  political dealings, 120, 141
  religion, 133-35, 159, 162, 163, 200
Nugan Fruit Group, 21, 80-84, 98, 101, 106, 108-12, 125, 140-41, 160, 165, 242
Nugan Hand bank:
  aiding procurement of a hit man, 119-21
  CIA paymaster, 76, 224, 239
  codes, use of, 45, 125, 151, 163, 203, 239-40
  conference in Sydney, 2, 154-59
  destruction of documents 176, 177, 180
  establishment in Sydney, 29
  gunrunning, see arms sales
  infiltration, see Federal Bureau of Narcotics
  money laundering, 29, 43, 51, 88, 93, 130, 131, 219, 220, 234, 263, 265
  propaganda and advertising, 126-27
  provisional liquidation, 190
  recruitment of military and CIA officers, 50, 93, 118, 137, 143, 155
  South African intelligence job, 114-16
Nugan Hand International, 3, 108, 113, 164
  branches
  Bangkok, 55, 75, 84, 91, 103, 127, 136-37, 141
  Chiang Mai, 69, 71, 72-74, 77, 91, 95, 137, 217, 224-25, 234
  Frankfurt, 130-31
  Hawaii, 31, 44, 46, 55, 107, 138, 245, 252
  Hong Kong, 2, 30, 38, 39, 41-43, 51, 53-56, 62-69, 75-76, 87, 89-93, 95, 97, 108, 112-21, 123, 126, 127, 137, 149, 158, 160, 180, 186, 188, 207-08, 231-32, 245
  Manila, 55, 69, 72, 163
  Saudi Arabia offices, 117, 143, 147, 148, 185, 186, 189
  Singapore, 51, 69, 131,138, 150-51, 164, 179, 187, 188
  Taipei, 155
  Washington DC, 238
Nugan, Ken, xii, 22, 80-81, 83, 106-07, 110-11, 169-75, 183, 200, 242
Nugan, Charlotte Lee, xii, 28, 32, 53, 135, 162-64, 169, 174, 200, 212-13

O

O'Brien, John, xii, 219, 200, 219-20, 222
Ocean Shores, 18,
Office of Naval Intelligence (ONI), 48, 49
Ogden, John, 101-02, 175, 176
Ontario Securities Commission, 23
Operation Eagle Pull, 59
Operation Rolling Thunder, 11
Opium, 35-36, 70-71, 89n
Oettle, Dr Godfrey, 214
Owen, John, xii, 75, 84, 91, 103, 127, 136-37, 141
Owens, Paul, xii, 133, 135, 162-63, 182

P

Panga Airways Ltd, 97
Parkin, Reginald, 180
Pauker, Dr Guy, xii, 162-63
Paul, Anthony, 59
Pentagon, 95n, 142, 162, 202, 238
Perot, H. Ross, 236
Petrov, Vladimir, 257
Pink Panther, 206
Polanski, Roman, vii
Politics of Heroin in Southeast Asia (McCoy), 36n

Index

Porter, Rick, xii, 32, 51, 68, 139, 145, 151, 163, 176, 187, 220-22
Project 404, 15
Prouty, Fletcher, 162
Pulger-Frame, Ron, xii, 21, 91-93, 96-97

Q

Quintero, Rafael, 185

R

Rand Corporation, 162-63
Reagan, Ronald, 225, 255
Reserve Bank of Australia, 41, 54, 188
Rewald, Ronald, 252
Rhodesia, 45-47, 49-50, 114, 179, 236, 239, 260, 265
Riley, Murray Stewart, xii, 40, 42, 43, 54, 69, 73, 81, 124, 202
Rommel, Erwin, 247
Roosevelt, Franklin D, 10
Royal Commission of Inquiry into the Activities of the Nugan Hand Group, see Stewart Royal Commission
Rudakewych, Lee, 60

S

Sa, Khun, 89
Saigon, Vietnam, 12, 14, 17-18, 143
Sapper, Delphine, 229-30
Sapper III, Douglas A, vii, viii, xii, 2, 6, 9-11, 13-16, 18-20, 56-71, 113-24, 144, 160, 207-08, 229-34, 240, 240, 245, 247-49, 252, 254, 258
Schuller, Karl, 129-31
Secord, Richard, 145-46, 185, 255
Sergi, Antonio, 79, 82-83
Shackley, Theodore, 146, 228
Shah of Iran, 66, 128-32, 136
Shaw, George, xii, 3, 39, 42-43, 45, 51, 87-88, 92, 99, 134, 149-51, 176, 178-81, 246
Shepherd, James 'Diamond Jim', 149, 252
Sixty Minutes, 224
Sleight of Hand (Owen), 75
South Africa, 44-47, 50-52, 114-15, 138, 140, 198, 236, 238-39, 145, 257, 260, 265
South African Bureau of State Security, 47
Soviet Union, 47-48, 50, 130, 257
Small, Clive, xii, 18, 41, 55, 72-73, 78, 88, 125, 151, 177, 203, 206, 216, 218, 225, 228, 235, 243, 246
South Bowenfels, 167-68, 244
Spencer, James Oswald, xii, 208-09, 259
Spencer, Richard, 99, 151, 152, 161, 180, 200
Star Trek, 208
Stewart, Justice Donald, 228
Stewart Royal Commission, 5, 97, 100, 111, 161, 163, 228, 230, 232, 233, 234, 235, 236, 238, 262
Stocker, Paul, xiii, 16-17, 33-34, 37n, 90
Stockwell, John, 46-49
Swan, Patricia, xiii, 29, 103, 108, 174, 175, 177, 251
Sydney, Australia, 1-8, 17-24, 28-43, 46, 51-53, 68, 79, 80, 81, 85, 87, 89, 105-09, 117-19, 124, 125, 133, 151, 164, 169, 178, 182, 202, 215, 216, 220, 244, 246
    Botanic Gardens, 89
    Chinatown, 85-87
    Customs House, 34
    Kings Cross, see Kings Cross, Sydney
    Macquarie Street, 1, 29, 52, 92, 94, 154, 177, 180
    Mrs Macquarie's Chair, 165
    NSW Parliament House, xii, 78, 82, 83, 94, 109, 119, 173, 187
    Pyrmont, 178, 203, 205
    St Andrews Cathedral, 133
    Sydney Opera House, 1, 29, 189
    Texas Tavern, Kings Cross 117, 143
    Ultimo, 178
Sydney Morning Herald, 242, 243
Task Force 157, 48-49
Thompson, Hunter S, 71
This Day Tonight (ABC), 107
Toohey, Brian, 221, 223, 264
Triads, Hong Kong, 68-69
Trimbole, Robert, 82-83

U

University of California, Berkeley, 22
University of Sydney, 22, 28
US Drug Enforcement Agency (DEA), 72-73, 77
US Department of State, 7
US National Security Council, 47, 162
US Special Forces, 6, 10-12, 15, 56, 70, 121, 207-08, 245, 255, 258

V

Vasey, Admiral Lloyd, 95
Viet Cong (VC), 12-14
Vietnam War, 11-16, 17-18, 58, 71, 143

W

Wainwright, Harry, xiii, 40-43, 54, 180, 202, 255n
Wall, Dr Thomas, 101
Wall Street Journal, 60, 166, 226, 227, 239, 256
Walker, Frank, xiii, 4, 80, 82, 83, 107-12, 120, 125, 140, 173-74, 78, 187-89, 211-14, 225, 235, 244, 253, 264, 267
Washington DC, 15, 47, 49, 50, 155, 229, 238, 255
Washington State, 256, 260
Webster, William, 224, 226
Wedderburn, Colin, xiii, 192-95, 197, 199, 242, 246-47, 253
West Australian, 256
White House, 226, 227
Whitlam Government, 224
Wilcox, Peter, xiii, 94-96, 245
Wilson, Bob, 164, 173, 197
Wilson, Douglas and Isabel, 152, 161
Wilson, Edwin P, xiii, 28-49, 137-38, 146-47, 185, 202, 223, 227, 228, 237, 238, 239
Winter, Alan Glen, 206
Woodward, Justice Philip, 53
Woodward Royal Commission, 53, 78, 80, 82, 107, 180

Y

Yates, Rear Admiral Earl 'Buddy', xiii, 3, 45-46, 55, 66, 93, 95, 108, 117, 121, 126, 130-31, 137-41, 155, 157, 174, 177, 225, 240, 258

www.ingramcontent.com/pod-product-compliance
Lightning Source LLC
Chambersburg PA
CBHW051039160426
43193CB00010B/998